DJANGO

DJANGO

The small dog with the big heart

Peter Comley

Jonathan Ball Publishers

JOHANNESBURG & CAPE TOWN

Originally published in South Africa in trade paperback in 2013 by
JONATHAN BALL PUBLISHERS (PTY) LTD

A division of Media24 Limited
PO Box 33977
Jeppestown
2043

ISBN 978-1-86842-598-3
eBook ISBN 978-1-86842-599-0

Twitter: http://www.twitter.com/JonathanBallPub
Facebook: http://www.facebook.com/pages/Jonathan-Ball-
Publishers/298034457992
Blog: http://jonathanball.bookslive.co.za/

Cover by publicide, Cape Town
Photo section by MR Design, Cape Town
Maps by Jan Booysen, Pretoria
Design and typesetting by Triple M Design, Johannesburg
Printed and bound by Interpak, Pietermaritzburg
Set in Rotis Serif Std Regular, 11/15pt

CONTENTS

In loving memory of Salome
1954–2010

Late is never better.

1

A COWBOY IS BORN

Maun – 'The Place of Reeds'. It should have been called 'The Place of Goats', I mused, or perhaps 'The Destiny of Donkeys'. In the shade of a mopane tree outside the Duck Inn a goat was dancing on the bonnet of a hire car, striving to reach the ever-receding leaves. Little dents were appearing. The driver was sitting at a table next to me, smiling ruefully at the scene while he sipped on his beer. He made no effort to chase the animal away when it moved to the roof and teetered on its hind legs, its sharp hooves beating a tattoo as it continued its tireless quest for the leathery foliage. Perhaps the vehicle had let him down in the bush and he was exacting revenge on its owners.

In the 1980s, Maun was a virtually inaccessible dustbowl 300 gruelling kilometres from the nearest paved road. A small but exceedingly energetic frontier town, its human population was outnumbered by the goats, cattle and donkeys that roamed the rutted tracks. The livestock needed more grass than the Kalahari could produce and so, when the wind blew, the sand billowed off the naked land and blotted the world from view. Dust stung the eyes, blocked the nose and, if you opened your mouth to protest, clogged the teeth.

And I lived here by choice – not only that, but I had enticed my future wife, together with her favourite cat, away from their city comforts to join me.

Maun lay just south of the Okavango Delta – one of the world's wildlife treasure chests – and, as such, was an ideal springboard for the slumbering tourist giant that was just beginning to stir. The runway had recently been tarred and, in season, there was a regular drone of small Cessnas taking off and landing as they conveyed their clients to the few lodges that were scattered through the Delta.

Dusty 4x4s brought rugged, sunburnt and decidedly dustier tourists to town and deposited them at campsites and rough budget lodges, where they crowded the showers and the bars. They partied either because they had just survived the wilderness, taking home memories of snarling hyenas, mating lions and trumpeting elephants, or they were about to disappear into that wilderness in search of their own adventures. Maun was a lively place.

Unfortunately, with life comes death, and death must play its parallel role in any tale about this wild piece of African bush. The puppy you give your child for Christmas could become part of a python's New Year banquet just a week later; the sparkling eyes of the graceful impala you've been quietly observing – together with the stalking predator – could glaze over in death moments later.

A dog – a humandog if you like – came into our lives as the result of the death of Marmalade, Salome's rotund ginger tom. Marmalade put me in mind of Garfield, the overweight comic-strip hero, except that our feline was considerably chunkier. That I played an unwitting role in his departure from this world has haunted me since the night he suffered a stroke. I argue in my defence that he was old and indolent, his idea of exercise being to stand, stretch and take two arthritic paces to his bowl of milk. He did, however, try to wake me, not Salome, to let me know that he was in distress and as I struggled irritably to avoid surfacing from a deep sleep, I clearly remember kicking him off the bed and onto the floor.

Some time later, Salome woke me in a panic.

'There's something terribly wrong with Marmalade! He seems paralysed from the waist down!'

And there he was, prone on the floor, scrabbling with his front limbs and growling deeply; each accusatory mewl percolating from some inner depth: 'Why did you forsake me in my time of need? Murderer!'

So it was in the middle of the night that I drowsily chauffeured Salome and her limp pet through the thick, sandy tracks of Maun to a sleepy government vet who, after a quick examination, declared that Marmalade was beyond help.

Salome was distraught. She could not bear to witness his suffering but neither could she mouth the fatal words. I sounded calmer than I felt.

'I think it's time to put him out of his misery.'

She nodded consent and fled the room, unable to watch her beloved Marmalade rendered into a state from which he would never awake.

'Hold the cat down, then, while I put him to sleep,' the vet instructed.

The very last place that I wanted to be was in that vet's living room as he charged a syringe with the lethal fluid that would take the life from a fellow traveller on this planet, and one who had been my wife's close companion for nearly two decades. I felt like an executioner as I held his wriggling limbs until they stilled.

Not only am I a murderer; I am also a con man. For many years I have been a professional wilderness guide, charging people good money to explore with me the remotest spots in Africa when, in fact, I would happily part with my own meagre resources for the privilege. This engenders a certain amount of guilt – but not enough, it must be said, for me to change my calling. Regrettably, this very lifestyle, with its regular exposure to animal death in varied forms, did not equip me to console Salome in her grief, and for days nothing I could do or say would cheer her up in the slightest. I tried all the platitudes: 'These things happen,' 'It was time for him to go,' and 'He had a good life.' Each attempt successively induced a longer, more miserable, but surprisingly tearless, face.

'Let's find another pet,' I suggested eventually, my mind secretly filled with the image of an endearing German Shepherd puppy.

'No. It's too soon to replace Marmalade,' she protested. 'I just couldn't bear it.'

She moped around the house listlessly until our neighbour, Bobby John Bulger, a sinewy, phlegmatic American wildlife scientist who had spent the better part of a decade living with baboons (hence his name, from the Afrikaans word *bobbejaan* for baboon), came up with an ingenious idea to lift flagging spirits – a video and popcorn evening.

'That sounds like fun!' Salome responded with much more enthusiasm than she had shown for anything since Marmalade's passing – watching a good movie is her idea of pure escapism. Besides, this would be a novelty for us in the Maun of 1988. 'Bobby John, you do the popcorn, I'll go to town and pick up a movie of choice for each of us and we can make a whole night of it. Peter, you can sort out the machine, and don't forget some fuel for the generator, OK?'

At last, she was being her assertive self again.

We did not own a video machine, or a television for that matter, largely because we had no steady source of electricity. Two obsolete Rolls-Royce generators, which in their heyday had powered searchlights during the London Blitz in World War II, had found their way to Maun. They only served a four-kilometre radius and since we lived 10 kilometres from Maun we were spared the power surges that reduced the innards of most electrical appliances unfortunate enough to be in use at the time to a tangle of charred wires and molten plastic. This meant the townsfolk of Maun had good cause to be grateful that these museum pieces did not work very often, yet they grumbled incessantly about the lack of reliable electricity.

We resorted to a primitive, but considerably more reliable, combination of light sources: candles, paraffin lanterns, gas lamps and a 12-volt fluorescent bulb that ran off the car battery. My favourite joke at the time was to ask, 'What did Maun use for lighting before candles?' The retort I used in answer to all blank stares was, of course, 'Electricity.'

None of the above, I must say, was conducive to an indulgent evening of video watching, so I trundled off as commanded to scrounge a generator, TV and video machine from three different sets of friends. I even remembered to pick up some fuel.

Salome had chosen three films: *Gone with the Wind* for herself for maximum viewing time – but also, I suspected, an excuse to have an overdue sob; a forgettable crime movie for me, and a spaghetti western called *Django Shoots First* for Bobby John. He had requested a Clint Eastwood film, but as none was available, Salome considered this would be the next best option.

Our neighbour duly arrived, carrying what looked like the nose cone of Challenger 1 filled to the brim with steaming hot popcorn and soon our home smelt like a genuine movie theatre. Since the evening was Bobby John's idea it seemed right to start with his film so, munching handfuls of popcorn, we watched *Django Shoots First*. If you have ever endured this sloppy cowboy film you probably will not have forgotten it, and if you have not yet seen it, I urge you to seek it out and watch it, preferably over a large bowl of popcorn. It must surely rank as one of the worst films ever made – it was shamelessly overacted, the background purr of traffic was distracting and the film sets were disturbingly unconvincing.

The great thing about it, however, was the disarming simplicity of the story line. Django, the blue-eyed hero, trotted into a troubled Western town and single-handedly took on three warring armies – mostly without emerging from his bathtub or dropping either his cigar or the revolver, which he hid under the soapsuds, and from which he fired at least 60 rounds without reloading. When the baddies did manage to shoot him 15 times through the chest, it barely slowed him down. He saved the town and inevitably broke the girl's heart when he rode off into the sunset in search of new bathtubs. Django was, in my opinion, the toughest hero ever to grace a screen.

That we ran out of petrol for the generator ten minutes into *Gone with the Wind* and had to retire to bed did little to dampen my spirits. If I am to be honest, it may have secretly lifted them a touch as I went to sleep with sweet dreams of riding into battle with Django at my side.

*   *   *

October, in the southern African tropics, is commonly known as 'suicide month'. During the weeks preceding the first rainfall of the season, the heat is oppressive, often soaring into the mid-forties and seldom dropping, even at night, below 30 degrees Celsius. The ions in the atmosphere are so negatively charged that they are blamed for inducing the Bushmen, as with the Aborigines, to 'go walkabout', when for no apparent reason they will drop whatever they are doing and head off for a little wander around the countryside. In Maun the locals do something similar. They abandon work and head for the pub.

This year was more desperate than most. For nearly a decade the rains had been poor and the Thamalakane River, which usually flows purposefully out of the Okavango and through Maun before reaching for the Makgadikgadi Salt Pans, had dried for the first time in living memory. Where there should have been a wide river ferrying boat-loads of tourists into the Delta, there was instead a trickle of water surrounded by bleak, bare desert – the dried-up riverbed where goats, cattle, donkeys and a smattering of hardy horses, competing desperately for survival, had long since devoured the last vestiges of grass. Debilitating winds that seared exposed flesh carried with them a fine powdery grey dust which transformed everyone – no matter their skin pigmentation – into a similar ashen duskiness.

No one that I know has committed suicide in October, but perhaps that is because my 'walkabout' acquaintances are prepared to sit out the extreme heat in the bars of institutions such as the Okavango River Lodge. A gathering of them was there now, cooling themselves with Castle Lagers. As I walked in I greeted them all but, to their astonishment, declined a beer. I went in search of Penny, owner of the Lodge, who had recently told me she was seeking homes for four six-week-old pups. I thought I should have a look at them to see if I could take one home to Salome, whether she wanted it or not – the movie night had not helped to lift her spirits nearly as well as it had worked for me.

I found Penny pottering, somewhat futilely, in a garden that always seemed to need more attention than it received. As the river had dried, so had her source of water for her plants – and the municipal supply was as expensive as it was unreliable. If ever she managed to grow anything, the village goats and donkeys would find a way through the fence to devour her greenery.

A petite, affable blonde with a broad, toothy smile and an oddly attractive receding chin, Penny had tried hard to introduce some culture to the khaki-clad, beer-swilling Maun crowd. Once a month, at great expense, she would import foreign delicacies from Johannesburg and attempt to instil an appreciation for a more genteel style of living by throwing a theme evening. A sushi night found everyone sitting on the floor, the men in khaki shorts and shirts, the women also in shades of brown, barring a few ladies like Salome who would happily unpack their mothballed evening finery for the event. The gentle art of delicately sipping herbal tea from miniature porcelain teacups, sampling sake from sherry glasses and eating raw fish wrapped in seaweed was anathema to the rough and ready bush people, who would continue to swig beer from cans, order hamburgers from the bar and inevitably knock over prized Japanese crockery, bringing tears to Penny's eyes. Undaunted, the next month she would throw a 'Nuevo Cuisine' evening that was doomed to end up the same way.

The lodge, in contrast to its more refined touristy counterparts, was one of those places that appeared perpetually run down from the day it was built, and the dwellings all shared a common fragrance, as if they had recently been used to stable donkeys – which perhaps explained the exaggerated sag of the beds. In fact, the furnishings in all the rooms would have caused a Spartan to recoil in alarm. Thin foam mattresses, most of which had taken on the U-shape of the springs, were complemented by mismatching sheets and cheap grey blankets that never fully covered the two single beds pushed together as one. The rest of the furnishings consisted of small wobbly pine tables and plastic chairs with legs that bent precariously under the strain of their own weight. If you were lucky enough to occupy the luxury chalet, a polyester shower curtain and a frayed bedside rug added glamour. The curtains were two sizes too small for the windows, leaving the occupants feeling decidedly exposed, especially at night, so they would often undress in the dark.

Penny smiled: 'Go up to my room at the back of the lodge and choose any one of the puppies.'

Sweating freely, I climbed a gravelly slope and opened the unstable door to her modest manager's quarters. When first I squinted into the gloomy interior I could distinguish little. Penny had obviously grown tired of wondering who might be ogling her and had painted the windowpanes black – an unusual step, I thought, when she could have just added another curtain to each and retained the option of daylight. Eventually, once my eyes had adjusted to the darkness, I could make out the shapes of three tiny, extraordinarily unattractive whelps – all female – that were mirror images of each other. With off-white wiry coats devoid of distinctive markings, and eyes that bulged disconcertingly from unnaturally pink sockets, they looked rather like the result of some failed Frankenstein's experiment. These short-haired, pink-eyed runts ran over and frantically started licking my fingers.

Their appearance startled me because their mother was a purebred Lhasa Apso. If you are not familiar with this breed, it looks like a floor mop. I have a book that shows 367 breeds of dogs and the illustration of the Lhasa Apso is the only one that requires arrows to point out the animal's front and rear. Curiously, these diminutive symmetrical furballs somehow manage to see and hear through the enormous mops of hair that engulf their heads and, because they do bark at sound and movement, have earned themselves the Tibetan name of 'hairy barking dog'. In fact they are bred as workers whose task, dating back to antiquity, has been to act as vocal sentinels within the palace of the Dalai Lama. The dog book, rather unnecessarily, adds that Tibetans breed this species for temperament rather than looks. Their popularity rests in part on their unusual combination of intelligence, aloofness and alertness and in part on a restful character that suggests they are much more advanced than the average canine – and for this reason they became the coveted companions of religious leaders. Indeed, some of these hairy barking dogs had such an air of higher spiritual being that they were considered to be the reincarnation of former Lamas, and as such, were bred exclusively in Tibet and kept secret from the rest of the world until smuggled to the west as late as 1921.

This trio of persistent rodents, however, did not remind me in any way of the re-embodiment of the spiritual leaders of Buddhism. If anything, they were the reincarnation of a group of high-kicking gals from a 1920s cabaret show, judging by the way that they jumped up at me in unison. I knew better than to take one of them back to Salome.

I looked around for the fourth pup. The furnishings, even in Penny's home, were sparse – a single iron bed in the centre of the floor and an old wardrobe shoved against the wall were about the extent of it. There was an entrance to a bathroom with the door missing and I peeked inside to discover that, apart from a bowl of dog food, messy paw prints and some puddles, there was nothing else. Being careful not to tread on the pups, still leaping up at my ankles and whimpering, 'Me! Take me, please take me,' I looked under the bed, but the chipped green concrete floor revealed nothing save for a little brown blob that I did not want to investigate too closely. The wardrobe did not look promising either, until I noticed that it was raised slightly by means of half bricks at each corner. I bent down to look underneath and in doing so offered my bearded face to the pups, which they slobbered over delightedly.

Under the cupboard and in the furthest corner was the missing member of the litter. I could not see much, so I reached in to pull him out. He growled at me, which I thought admirable. Then he sank needle-like teeth into my finger, which I did not find quite so winning. Nursing my savaged digit, I extracted him from his security cave and there, wriggling in the palm of my hand, was the diminutive dog that was destined to spend the rest of his life with us.

I was hugely relieved to discover that he was neither pink-eyed nor short-haired like his sisters, nor would he ever be mistaken for a mop. Much stockier and longer legged than his kin, his disorderly coarse coat was of medium length, but on the crown of his head he had an unruly, soft flick of a curl, which edged his high-set expressive ears. He had also inherited the golden-brown and white skewbald markings of his putative father, a well-known Jack Russell-about-town, and clearly possessed his sire's air of independence and self-confidence. His square face was inset with intelligent, deep brown eyes, while a pointed muzzle surrounded by a soft moustache suggested maturity beyond his weeks. His tail had a natural curl, and he proudly held it high to display his alert and inquisitive nature. He was as handsome and endearing as his poor sisters were ugly and unappealing.

I never set him down again; I simply shook loose three desperate, whining guinea pigs from my ankles and marched out of the room, clutching him like a trophy as I went in search of Penny to thank her. I am not sure how she had managed it, but her face by this time was covered in so much earth that I suspect she had used her perky snub nose to turn over the garden soil. She cheerily waved me on my way and I drove home proudly to proffer Salome that which I had found to replace her prized cat.

She took one look at the tiny offering and burst into tears.

'How can you expect that thing to replace my Marmalade? It will never, ever be able to take his place. Nothing will. Besides, I do not want a dog. Just take it back!'

The metal door to our home slammed hard as she left the little pup and me forlornly outside.

For two days Salome would not even look at the new arrival, which rather suited the little fellow as he was reserved and did not take to too much fussing. It was left to me to feed and exercise him and, most distinctly, to clean up any accidents, usually following the barked instruction, 'Your dog has messed on the bedroom floor. When you've cleaned it up, you can take that filthy thing back to Penny.'

Then she caught him squatting on her lounge carpet. She rubbed his nose in the mess, spanked him on the bottom and set him outside with a firm reprimand: 'Bad dog!' He never erred again. At a tender six weeks of age he displayed the rare and welcome ability to understand what was acceptable behaviour and what clearly caused displeasure, and the instruction never had to be repeated. From that time onwards he would go out into the garden and very discreetly find a spot that was not offensive as a toilet.

I attract dog poo. I manage to seek it out in the most unlikely places, step in it and then succeed in liberally smearing it wherever I walk – usually over the thick-pile carpet of a home-conscious hostess. I never stood in our pup's poo, ever. In fact, we would struggle to find his toilet if we suspected that he might be off-colour and needed a check-up. It would take considerable sleuthing to find the bush under which he had hidden 'that which he did not want his nose ever to be rubbed in again'. Throughout a life that involved countless hours of travelling in confined vehicles and numerous nights closeted in hotel and lodge rooms, he never had a single accident of nature again.

If he needed to go outside but found the door closed, he would ask for it to be opened – not by scratching at the hindrance or by barking, as is the wont of the common dog, but by staring at you silently until he caught your attention. Then he would look in the direction of the exit and telepathically communicate the message that he needed you to assist in the small matter of opening the door. He would wait quietly for you to open it, but if you were too dim to understand this simple request or too preoccupied to notice him standing there, he would poke his nose into your ankle until you paid heed and then walk to the doorway to await your response.

Without ever being obsequious, he would understand what we expected of him and if it did not conflict with his own innate good sense, he would simply do what was required. This behaviour did not go unnoticed by Salome and she started to spend more time with the pup. After three days she sheepishly admitted, 'I do kind of like this little fellow. He is sort of special.' By the end of the week they were inseparable.

One thing had not happened, however: a name had not been found for him. We came up with many ideas, and turned them all down.

'Every idiot calls their dog "Spot",' Salome objected.

'But he has a spot right here.' I pointed at the fawn saddle on his back.

Salome remained unconvinced and when she proposed we call him 'Beethoven' it was my turn to reject her suggestion – he was too tough looking to be a composer. 'Attila-the-Hund' seemed more appropriate, but she flatly refused to accept a name with negative connotations. While we debated, our new family member remained untitled.

Salome quoted from a book that she was reading, 'It is said that the incoming soul has to whisper the name telepathically into the ears of the parents and that it reflects the path the soul has chosen to walk during its current incarnation.'

'I hope this pup whispers before long or he will be called "Just Dog",'

I responded, knowing that a suitable name, which showed insight into his character, was important to her.

He did soon tell us what he wished to be called, but his message did not come in the form of a gentle whisper.

The first Sunday after the puppy's acceptance we went to have lunch at Okavango River Lodge, where the community had gathered for another weekend of revelry. We joined some friends at a table and, with the pup asleep on my lap (which was rare as he was definitely not a lapdog), the subject of names came up. Despite many suggestions, it ended as inconclusively as before.

Then, as we ordered another round of drinks, I noticed with alarm that an American Pit Bull by the name of Buford had arrived. Buford's owner, André, was typical of the men that Maun attracted – adventurous, hard living and fun loving, but at the same time bright, in a wily and ambitious way. Apart from dabbling in hunting, guiding, construction and book writing, he had also bought and sold a lodge in a short period of time.

As smart as André was, Buford was not. An American Pit Bull, despite its name, is not bovine; rather it descends from the two breeds of bull baiters and pit fighters that were thrown into arenas to inflict snarling, gnashing, bone-crunching deaths on their opponents, while scores of frenetic onlookers cheered from the safety of the grandstand. My dog book describes Pit Bulls as being 'lethal to other dogs, with the jaw power and tenacity to inflict horrific wounds'. It also states, 'This breed is so mentally challenged that it is estimated 300 dogs of the same breed share a single brain cell.' No, of course the book does not really say that, but based on Buford's behaviour, it is an oversight.

André's hound was a living legend in Maun. He used to ride on the back of his owner's pick-up, leap off at the sight of any animal, wild or not, and give chase. He was particularly unselective about his victims, which rather confirmed my theory about his intelligence. Impala, donkeys and giraffe were great fun to pursue, but then he launched himself at a spotted hyena – a beast that not only outweighed him, but also possessed considerably more formidable jaw power. He came back so badly mauled that you would have imagined it to be his last such sortie, but, quite undeterred, on his next trip he picked on an entire pride of lions and only André's quick intervention plus skilled veterinary care saved him then from a ravaged death. I had once watched in close-quarters horror as Buford tackled a group of goats that had wandered inside the fence at Okavango River Lodge. In a blur, he had charged into the middle of the herd and, with three economical bites, crushed the skulls of a trio of hapless victims before victoriously sauntering away.

I admit I was not merely in awe of Buford's enormous power, I was positively terrified of it, and when I saw him spot the little creature nestled in my lap and charge toward us, I nervously paid full attention. Our new dog, and with him a significant part of my manhood, was about to disappear in one hideous chomp as the savage Pit Bull arrived at my chair, the hair on the back of his neck rising in anticipation of another notch on his collar. But this diminutive pup had other ideas. He sprang up, gathered himself to his full height of six inches and, with hair bristling, let out a growl of such ferocity that Buford was rooted to the spot by his pint-sized gall.

Stupefied and utterly relieved, I watched as the grizzled aggressor deflated visibly, gave an uncertain wag of his tail and beat an ignominious retreat.

The pup had ridden into town and stood up to the dreaded killer.

His name had to be Django!

2

A DAY AT THE DUCK

Django was not destined to live a secluded, boring life in the lap of luxury, but it was a close call. A week after we named him we received a visit from an unspeakably arrogant woman whose sharp features and stilted puppet-like gait drew me irresistibly to the conclusion that her mother had slept with a garden gnome. She demanded in a clipped East African accent that we hand over the dog, immediately and without question, to an 89-year-old aunt of Bernadette Lindstrom – the owner of Maun's famed pub, the Duck Inn. The old dear had seemingly tottered up to Penny's room a few days before me, with sufficient presence of mind and eyesight to choose Django to take back to her sprawling estate on the Kenyan coast. She had forgotten to mention this to Penny; in fact she had forgotten the entire experience for a full three weeks.

After Buford, the fight I did not want to pick in Maun was with Bernadette, a slim, ruggedly attractive woman of Swiss origin who owned not only the Duck Inn but also a black belt in karate. Her notorious watering hole was the rowdiest in what was widely considered the liveliest frontier town in Africa, but moreover she had a well-earned reputation of being able to deal effectively with unruly drunks. Whereas other less robust publicans might rush for the phone to call the police in the event of a disturbance, she simply waded fearlessly into the fray and physically evicted louts who invariably outweighed her by several stone.

'You can't take a dog back once it's got a name,' Salome snapped at our unwelcome visitor, as if there were a law against this. 'His name is Django.'

My spouse is a genuine redhead and, true to type, she most decidedly does not possess a tranquil disposition.

Garden Gnome, who I started to recall was Auntie's personal caretaker, retorted, 'I have been sent to fetch the pup now and that is what I fully intend to do. Aunt Gerri Attrick is leaving on this afternoon's flight and we will be taking this mongrel with us. I have no idea why she wants it, but I insist that you hand it over without a fuss.'

Django growled – I am not making it up, I swear he did – not as violently as when he saw off Buford, but a menacing, low and guttural sound as if he knew what was being demanded and wanted no part of it.

'Please go away,' I said.

Here again I must be honest; I did not put it quite that way. There was not much of a please in it and perhaps the words were less gracious than stated.

'How despicably rude you are,' she rejoined peevishly, her long nose quivering.

I too found myself trembling in a mixture of outrage and no small fear that Bernadette would come storming over to our home and throw me about a bit. Yet I could not reconcile myself to the idea of such a differing lifestyle for Django. With us, he could lead a life of unbridled adventure, while as a lapdog, dressed in booties and coat, the most daring thing that might happen to him would be to go 'walkies' around a manicured garden in the wake of a creaking octogenarian.

'Which part of "this is our dog" did you fail to understand?' I asked in what I intended to be measured tones, but which seemed to come out rather too high-pitched to be manly. 'I suggest you leave now before you miss your plane, as that would disappoint all of us.'

'We'll see about that!' The Gnome collected her skirts and clunked her way off the property.

I settled into a fathomless funk, akin to Salome's when Marmalade had died. The idea of losing Django was as unthinkable as was the prospect of confronting Bernadette.

'You'll have to go and speak to her about this if you want to keep your pup,' Salome pronounced.

'What if she throws me through a Duck Inn window?'

'Your dog, your choice.'

With a leaden heart I climbed into my oversized American Ford F250 safari truck with Django protectively close and thundered – F250s cannot do anything else but thunder – into town to confront Bernadette over the smallest issue that was ever likely to trigger a conflict.

As distracted as I was by my pending mission, I couldn't help noticing that the landscape, which should have been drab at that time of year, was vibrant with colour. Maun, it seemed, was holding a carnival of litter. Bright red Coke cans, golden beer tins and the starry sparkle of clear plastic wrappers were sprinkled in abstract designs over the terrain, while the heated winds had festooned the leafless trees with multi-coloured shopping bags. I could not help but feel that the rest of the world wasted much artistic potential by hiding its garbage in landfills. My appreciation was clearly shared by the goats munching on discarded beer cans in the parking lot of the Duck Inn as I pulled up next to Bernadette's canary-yellow Land Rover.

*   *   *

As reluctant as I was to leave the sanctity of my car, as excited was Django. Even at such a tender age, he found the vibe at the Duck Inn unsurpassable; there were so many jovial people and so many chances to watch a scuffle. He always loved that. The austere bar-cum-restaurant was empty of people but bore signs of numerous vigorous parties. Solid tables, selected for durability rather than aesthetics, were blemished with burn marks from carelessly stubbed out cigarettes and the deep scars of bush knives – the results of spirited competitions between hunters and guides as they challenged each other to justify their choice of blades. Chairs were chipped from drunken clumsiness or regular brawls and the single overhead fan wobbled uncertainly on squeaky bearings, the victim of numerous objects – salt and pepper pots, ashtrays, beer cans and the like – that had been flung into it.

Bernadette was in her compact but chaotic kitchen, scurrying around preparing for the lunchtime rush. It was always a mystery to me how the place passed even the most rudimentary hygiene requirements that Maun's officials demanded of such establishments in an isolated frontier town in the mid-1980s. For a start, everything, including the wooden steak boards, was washed in cold water, as there was no hot water facility – with the result that remnants of previous meals often added substance to a subsequent one. The shiny white floor and wall tiles insisted upon by health departments around the world had not yet entered the law books here; neither had gleaming stainless steel working surfaces. In their place was a bare cement floor covered in stains from years of spilt food, and old wooden tables deeply scored from long use as chopping boards, while the staff dodged overflowing garbage bins which were stored inside the kitchen to avoid the attention of goats and village dogs.

Django had followed me into the kitchen.

'I expected you. Aunt Gerri has just phoned,' Bernadette said without emotion.

'This is my-little-dog, he's already-been-named and stayed-with-us-for-more-than-two-weeks,' burst from my mouth in a frantic gabble as I pointed at Django.

She stared at me, perplexed. 'Your mouth moved and sound came out but I didn't understand a word. Try again, perhaps more slowly this time.'

With an effort I gathered myself and spoke more clearly. She smiled at my pup and waved a dismissive hand.

'I don't care. She's too frigging old to take on a puppy now and I told her that when she phoned.'

Sweeping past us into the restaurant, she went to check the tables and to make sure that the fridges were stocked with enough beers for the expected run on the bar. Joy flooded over me. We had been reprieved, and to celebrate I ordered a beer while Django settled happily for the bowl of milk and a plate of raw mince offered by Bernadette.

From midday, the restaurant filled up quickly with a mix of locals and travellers. The regulars who would flock to the Duck during the day were mostly people who worked hard and then played harder. Many of them were highly qualified and successful in their own sphere and all were attracted to Maun because of the freedom from regimen that it offered. The eight-to-five routines of city dwellers simply did not apply to the denizens of Maun and if they felt the need to party on a weekday, they would not think twice about it.

A sallow-faced, wiry former professional hunter by the name of Willie Phillips was the first to arrive and take up an inside table near the window. I left the bar to join him, Django in tow. Willie loved dogs – his Staffordshire Bull Terriers went everywhere with him, even when hunting, but Bernadette had banned them from the Duck Inn recently as they had caused too many fights with the local hounds. They now waited patiently for their owner in his vehicle in the car park.

Firm friends at a glance, Django stood quietly staring up at Willie until he had finished greeting me and turned his attention to the newest member of our family. The grizzled old man and the reserved young hound addressed each other in an understated way, in the manner of those who are comfortable with themselves and therefore feel no need to make an impression.

'This is going to be a great dog,' Willie predicted. Django agreed with a wag of his tail.

The ex-hunter, a seasoned carnivore who disdained vegetables, ordered a rump steak and I called for another beer.

'I'm going to walk across the Okavango from Mombo to Maun in April for my annual charity fund-raiser,' Willie announced. 'It should be one of the best. I already have permission from the Wildlife Department to transit the Moremi Game Reserve.'

* * *

Willie was a living legend. Born to an English father and a Motswana mother, he was raised in Francistown, which was then the largest town in Botswana but still had a population of less than 100 000 nearly 50 years later. Thanks to his mixed parentage he straddled both the white and black communities with ease, and having started his career as a crocodile hunter, he later used his rifle in pursuit of big game, until he tired of the killing and took on the role of an active environmentalist.

The sponsored expeditions that he led through the bush traversed amazing wilderness areas and raised welcome money for various children's charities. Although every hike was different, none of them was short on adventure and this particular route, which would cover over 180 kilometres of the game-rich, fabled Okavango Delta, promised to be the liveliest yet.

Willie was a man of few words and almost every sentence of his contained a charged curse word or two, which I have reluctantly omitted. (Much the same applied to Bernadette.)

'Why don't you and Salome come along?' he asked.

He posed the question casually, as if inviting us for Sunday tea.

'Yes, we will,' I accepted enthusiastically and without hesitation. It was an honour to be invited and I knew what Salome's answer would be.

'We'll fly in and walk out. You'll have to get a backpack, a mosquito net if you don't have one, and a blanket. We'll talk more about this later. There's lots of time to sort out the details. You sure you're in?'

'We're in,' I affirmed, 'but Django will have to come with us.'

'Of course he must. He's the reason I invited you,' Willie chuckled as he reached under the table to ruffle the pup's head and he nodded sagely. 'He will be old enough by then and it will be good to have a reliable dog on this trip.'

When Willie's steak was served I felt my decision to stick to beer had been vindicated.

'This cow must have walked across the whole bloody Kalahari,' he commented dryly as the wooden handle of his knife parted company with the blade. Pulling his Bowie hunting knife from the scruffy briefcase that went everywhere with him, he severed a finger-sized sliver, fished about in his knapsack again and pulled out a wrapped condom, which he carefully opened and, dangling it high above the table, inserted the shard of steak before calling the waitress and coolly demanding that she give it to Bernadette.

Without changing expression the young lady delicately took the condom between two fingers and, clutching it at face height, walked through the restaurant past astonished tourists and into the office. For the second time that day I feared that Bernadette would resort to violence, but she came to the table with a wide grin on her bronzed face and, with a characteristic tilt of her head, slapped Willie good-humouredly on the back, apologised for the steak and immediately arranged for a replacement.

Willie finished his more acceptable meal and left to continue with his arrangements for the walk. Django and I departed the pub with him to run errands for Salome – and instantly regretted being out in the blazing sun. Django was fiercely independent and hated to be picked up right from his early days but the hot sand scalded his feet and left him with a dilemma. He could ask to be picked up or he could take care of himself. He chose the latter and through a carefully planned strategy he darted from the shade of one vehicle to the next until he was close enough to the tree line to make a charge for it. He arrived in the safety of the shade panting furiously.

The tourists were filing out of the Duck Inn and traipsing across the car park towards the airport building, a mere 100 metres away. It was boarding time for the thrice-weekly flight to Johannesburg and an Air Botswana official had just walked across to the restaurant to announce that it was check-in time. Maun must be the only place in the world where an airline official would leave his office and walk through energy-sapping heat to an outlying restaurant to make sure that his passengers would not miss their flight. If they were having too much fun or too many beers to pay attention, he would return for a final call and even help with the bags. He was an asset to be treasured.

I saw a vehicle pull up and disgorge Aunt Gerri and her caretaker. The old duck struggled painfully into the airport building while Garden Gnome strode purposefully past us, pointedly ignoring our existence.

Minutes later she returned with Bernadette in tow, summonsed to bid farewell to her aunt.

Strident words drifted over the car park: '... never in my life ... such disgraceful behaviour towards an old lady....'

'Have a lovely flight,' I waved cheerily in her wake, checking surreptitiously that Django was still safely in his shady patch.

Garden Gnome stopped in her tracks, and, turning around, gave me a stare that could freeze nitrogen at a thousand paces. I shivered as I climbed into my Ford and set off to do the shopping.

*　　*　　*

Chores finally done, which in Maun took longer than in most towns, we returned to the Duck, where I sidled up to my old spot at the bar while Django proudly claimed the stool next to me so he could watch the goings-on. He was still too small to leap onto the stool himself so after one unsuccessful try he stared at me and then at the stool until I helped him up. There was a crowd of end-of-season locals settling in for a party and I was happy to linger and celebrate with them. The tourists had either caught the plane to Johannesburg or fled.

Even by Maun's wacky standards, the afternoon that unfolded was bizarre. First an argument developed as to which man in the crowd was the most well-endowed. The group included a smattering of pilots, hunters, guides and town planners, accompanied by a number of women who never appeared to do anything other than party. In no time, Bernadette was called in to measure the leading contenders one by one on a restaurant table, and she declared the winner to be a man who seldom wore shoes and who furthered the theory of large feet. One participant who was woefully out of his depth was doused with Tabasco and retired, embarrassed, to a corner, his sizzling entry immersed in a glass of ice. Ribald applause followed the announcement of the winner and Django leapt from his chair to congratulate the victor with a gentle nudge of his nose to an ankle. He never pawed or licked like other dogs.

I was still registering relief that I had evaded both the measuring tape and the risk of chilli sauce, when a prim English couple appeared at the door and tried to attract someone's – anyone's – attention over the deafening background noise.

They peered in some dismay at the raucous crowd inside, who were dressed almost to a person, men and women alike, in faded khakis, invariably bearing dust and sweat stains.

'I say,' began the man, whose pristine polyester khaki outfit had pre-sumably been sold to him by a persuasive salesperson from a Banana Republic outlet. His glossy pointed footwear had not yet been worn in, judging by the way he trippled around uncomfortably, and his long multi-pocketed trousers displayed an obviously factory-pressed pleat. Epaulettes proudly adorned his non-wrinkle shirt, which boasted equal-ly impressive pleats and prominent breast pockets that bulged with passports, airline tickets and spectacles. On his head rested an oversized broad-brimmed hat, complete with artificial leopard-skin band.

'I say', he called louder. 'Can anyone render assistance?'

A tsunami of disbelief rolled through the bar, starting at the door and engulfing the interior until all its occupants sat in silence, their collective gaze fixated on the gatecrashers.

His wife (she really could not have been anything else because of her identical hat and matching sleek pleated skirt) was the first to take advantage of the silence. 'Oh dear, we're so dreadfully sorry to inter-rupt, but could someone please direct us to the Aerkavango office? We don't seem to be able to find them and we have a flight booked to go into the Okavango.'

'Come on in, love,' one of the crowd of men called. 'Come on in and we'll tell you where to go.'

The two straight-laced folk – of the type that probably came from a quiet, conservative English hamlet – entered the Duck Inn expecting to be given a courteous welcome, perhaps even offered a beer which they would politely decline, and be sent on their way with directions and a handshake. Instead, within moments of their entrance, they were liberally decorated from the crowns of their irksome headgear to the toecaps of their painful boots in a brightly coloured mixture of condi-ments from the tables by a wildly whooping mob. It was the man with the big feet, flushed with recent victory, who started it. He splashed a full bottle of tomato sauce down the fronts of the wretched two-some before the others upended the Mild and Mellow mustard over their hats. The town's helicopter pilot led a mad dash to the kitchen in search of further ingredients and, in less time than you could say 'mind the gap', the spotless khaki uniforms were transformed into something resembling a child's birthday cake mixture. Then, caught up with the sense of occasion, someone threw an open pepper pot into the overhead fan, causing its contents to spray over everyone, which had us all sneezing violently.

The hapless couple spluttered and sneezed and spat out sundry sauces as they tried to make sense of what had just happened to them.

'Your clothes were too new and clean to go into the Okavango,' someone offered by way of explanation. 'The lions would have nailed you for sure. You'll be fine now.'

One of the ringleaders led them outside, a trail of food in their wake, and pointed to an adjacent door. 'Aerkavango is just in there. I'm sure you'll find a sober pilot somewhere. Enjoy your visit!'

The revellers happily returned to the task of partying, the incident soon forgotten, whilst the detritus that littered the pub replicated the chaotic state of the kitchen earlier that day.

In this heat the 'walkabout' phenomenon saw many a party start at mid-morning and continue late into the night, with a wave of new party animals following the one before. Sometimes the gathering swirled from venue to venue but did not really end for days at a time – rather it flared and fizzled like one of those fireworks that you suspect has come to its end until it suddenly bursts energetically into life again.

* * *

That evening, many beers later, one of the Duck's most entertaining regulars swaggered in. The night was due to take a livelier turn.

Simon was a marketing genius but a below-average guide, who had once invited his parents on safari, stipulating that his father should write a glowing report to the press afterwards. This the doting father did, with enthusiastic descriptions of all that they had done and seen in the bush. Unfortunately, the son's naming of the various birds and animals they saw was severely flawed and his lack of true knowledge was cruelly exposed when the article boasted about the many saddle-backed ducks they had seen. Sadly, such a bird does not exist. Undeterred, Simon memorised a series of Latin tree names and would fire these off in random order when pointing out botanical species on his game drives. This ruse and his quick-fire marketing speak seemed to fool enough gullible tourists for him to run a busy if unprofitable organisation.

Simon also had the short man's drive to pick a fight with anyone larger than himself (and that was just about everybody) in the belief that one day he would score a lucky punch. As if weighing up his chances, he threw me a haughty glance, then cast his eyes down at the stool where my ally Django sat exuding an air of self-confidence, and decided to annoy someone else. His eventual target, Mike, was a powerful man with a long fuse but a reputation for finishing fights. Spoiling for a brawl, Simon decided to goad him to find his breaking point.

After fielding insults for longer than the most even-tempered could tolerate, Mike started to become angry. Bernadette had noticed and rushed to save Simon from a certain beating when Mike, fuse finally ignited, unleashed a right hook. Simon ducked, but the approaching Bernadette did not. It caught her flush on the jaw, lifted her off her feet and knocked her out cold. This was an unexpected turn. Django was the first to reach her but could only nudge her face with his nose. Simon fled from a barroom of vengeful men while Mike could not stop apologising to Bernadette as she slowly came round. Perhaps he too was worried about being thrown through windows.

Instead of returning to his stool, Django went to inspect the kitchen. He was hungry and, amidst all the distractions, I had neglected to feed him. Salome had made it clear that while he was still a pup he needed many small meals and I hoped that he would not mention my neglect to her. He came back with a fried chicken wing. I do not know how he always managed to charm someone to feed him, as he never stole food.

I took him to the outside veranda where he could eat in peace and I could clear my head of beer fumes. There I found Salome, who had decided that I needed to be fetched, in earnest conversation with Bernadette's latest employee – a strikingly handsome man, I had to admit. He should have been queuing for a Hollywood job rather than dishing up hamburgers in Maun.

He claimed to be a chiropodist from Francistown, who just happened to prefer to wait on tourists in a dump like Maun for a paltry wage rather than manipulate people's feet in a comfortable city for vastly more money. Django edged away from him whenever he came near. Although generally polite to a fault, he would display an uncanny ability to size up disingenuous human beings and would make his judgement plainly known through his actions.

'He'sh a fraud,' I slurred slightly to Salome as soon as the chiropodist left to fetch more hamburgers.

'Are you saying that because you're jealous that such a dish is chatting to me or is this drunken talk?'

'Neither,' I swayed just a touch. 'Anyone can see through him. He'sh a conman and a fraud.'

'Oh, don't talk such nonsense. I think he's cute.'

'He'sh nothing but a fraud and a crook, you mark my words.'

And, indeed he was. He was neither a chiropodist, nor did he come from Francistown. Interpol was particularly interested in him, partly because he sold farms that he did not own to gullible people around the world. He provided his buyers with rich soil samples, a map with a big X which marked a prime site, often straddling a major river in the Okavango, and title deeds. Apart from the properties not belonging to him, the rich volcanic soil samples did not come from anywhere in Botswana, the maps were falsified and even the farms themselves did not exist. People poured off scheduled flights proudly clutching a shoebox full of sand, a map and a sheaf of title deeds and, one after the other, left Maun utterly dejected; in some cases, destitute.

Salome hated to apologise. Much later, she did so in her own way. 'You were right after all,' she admitted. 'How did you know he was a conman?'

'Intuition,' I replied, but I suspect she was right the first time – drunken jealousy.

When Salome finally enticed me from the bar my legs seemed to have acquired a certain independence of movement, both from each other and from what I wanted of them, and my voice was thickly slurry, but so full of the happy news about our pup's escape from Aunt Gerri that I shared it with her at least three times on the way home. Django enjoyed each retelling as enthusiastically as if it were the first time, whereas I doubt my wife had listened to a single word.

3

THE DERELICT BARN

And so with Aunt Gerri gone, Django was officially established in our barn. Situated on the banks of the Thamalakane River, it was a curiously large edifice because its original purpose was to treat and store elephant hides. Its walls were made of chicken wire that had once seen a splash of cement – to reduce, but not quite eliminate, transparency – and this makeshift structure was strung between widely spaced mopane tree poles. The uprights had long since rotted away at their base, adding to local conjecture that the roof would soon collapse and inflict grave physical harm upon us. The remaining thatch was so thin that alluring patches of sunlight sprinkled across the interior of the barn and the tropical rain fell inside with much the same ferocity as it did on the outside. Consequently, our collection of buckets became truly impressive as we tried to catch the rainwater before our furniture floated out of the door, and during any severe downpour we stayed alert, slopping around our lounge in raincoats as we emptied bucket after bucket into the bath.

You may be wondering why we tolerated such a derelict abode. Available housing in Maun – of any standard – was rarer than sobriety at the Duck and we were grateful to find somewhere to call home. We even became attached to its eccentricities and lingered longer than our landlady had anticipated. She was waiting only for us to tire of the place and depart, as she was determined to level it before it fell down and wisely refused to spend money on it. We did not want to pour our own cash into someone else's property either, so we tolerated the disadvantages instead.

Our bathtub was designed to wash the hide of the largest animal to tramp our planet and was quite unlike any we had ever encountered before, or since, for that matter. Deep enough to drown in while sitting upright, which in itself is a little unusual, it was also almost long enough in which to do laps and, as a result, required significantly more water than an average tub.

Normally, soaking neck deep in a steaming bath of the earth's most precious resource merely demands the suppression of conscience. Our impediments, however, ran rather deeper. The first problem was that the taps provided only cold water. Either we had a bracing soak, which in midwinter was a form of unnatural torture, or we heated pot after pot of water on the gas stove. It was quite astonishing just how many pots were required to provide a tepid mix for a tub of that size. Heating the water, however, was certainly the lesser of the two problems we faced when drawing a bath. Far more challenging was sourcing any water at all. We were not on mains supply, the property did not have a borehole and the Thamalakane no longer flowed, thus we had to pump directly from a permanent pool in front of the plot.

This pool was the happy consequence of an eccentric act by a fellow named Naus who, in the 1930s, was tasked with the challenge of clearing the build-up of reeds and papyrus that was choking the life from the vast inland delta. That papyrus and reeds occur all over the Okavango, as a natural consequence of the shifting watercourses and the innate shallowness of this water wilderness, did not deflect Naus's enthusiasm to alter radically this unique wonderland. The only problem he faced was how. One evening he was playing with a water pistol when he noticed how much further it would shoot if a nozzle was fitted to the end of the barrel. In a moment of epiphany, he knew how to rid the Okavango of papyrus. All he needed to do was to create a series of 'water pistols' by building numerous dams all over the delta, each with a constricting hole in the middle of the wall which would cause the water to squirt out with the force needed to carry the reeds off for tens, if not hundreds, of kilometres. To start his project he built three such dams upstream from Maun, and the retaining wall of one doubled as a bridge near where we lived.

The flow of water did indeed speed up as it passed through the restriction and this gouged out a deep permanent pool below the bridge before the current slowed down again about 30 metres downstream, leaving the offending papyrus and reeds largely unscathed. Naus may have failed to clear the reeds – the drying of the river in subsequent years took care of that little problem – but his pool afforded five hippos, a few large crocodiles and us a supply of life-giving liquid. When the river stopped flowing, the hippos established permanent residence because there was nowhere else to go, and the pond slowly turned a dark, dirty colour with arresting bits of partly digested vegetation floating in it.

The process of enticing water from the hippo pool and into our bath presented interesting challenges. First, we needed to visit the only hardware store in town, to buy a tinny-looking petrol-driven water pump and assorted bits of piping, non-return valves, clamps and a host of unidentifiable gadgets which the store claimed were essential. These mystifying parts had to be carted down to the water's edge to be connected to the pipe leading to the water tank – all this while wading waist-deep in crocodile- and hippo-infested waters. The pump then had to be primed, a task which proved to be much more difficult than described in the instruction manual in both impenetrable Mandarin and unintelligible English. Somehow, the newly joined pipes always leaked air into the system, signalling a long and arduous battle. Once victory on this small front was achieved, we had to fire up the engine, another process that was far more complicated than the manual indicated. '*Setting choke to full way pulling cord smooth hard once engine to start*' meant 20 minutes of energetic tugging before the engine took. The unbridled joy, the setting of the heart to wing on hearing water squirting merrily into the tank, was almost too much to bear. With yelps of delight we would run muddy water – which still harboured solid bits of chewed vegetation – into every pot and kettle we possessed, including a plastic tub for Django, and finally filled our bath to the brim. How we wallowed, gleefully, with the hippo poo.

On many a morning, however, when we eagerly turned the tap on for yet another indulgent soaking, all we would hear was the hollow gurgling of empty pipes. Upon inspection, we would discover that the 10 000-litre water tank had leaked our precious liquid into the sands overnight. Then someone sneaked in under cover of darkness and stole the pump. After that, we had to take the replacement home at the end of every day and regularly submit ourselves to the entire procedure of reconnecting and priming it. Within a week the aluminium thread had stripped and the new pump was impossible to prime. We left it outside for some wanton thief, but none showed interest in the scrap.

The hippo pool was right in front of Bobby John's house, which we had to pass in order to reach the pump. Django enjoyed that because there was a chance to meet up with his first grown-up friend and misguided mentor – Nari, Bobby John's black Labrador. Nari adopted the pup and taught him some fun games, which included chasing the neighbours' chickens and hiding bones. One morning as we passed by, Nari saw the cocky rooster whose pre-dawn crowing drove me to thoughts of violence, leading his hens into Bobby John's garden, and immediately gave chase. Django sped through the open gate to support his buddy and feathers flew from startled fowl as they tried to escape the small but very mobile and noisily ferocious bundle of fur and the chubby Labrador who, as a result of a crocodile attack, was no longer nimble. For the sake of good neighbourliness we called Django, who returned immediately with a bunch of feathers in his mouth, which, as luck would have it, belonged to the crowing cock. Salome firmly explained that this was not acceptable behaviour – and that was the last time Django ever chased any kind of bird. Never once did he get a hiding for bad conduct. All he needed was to understand what was not tolerable and he simply did not repeat it, and so we had to be careful never to scold him unnecessarily, in case we put a stop to perfectly acceptable behaviour.

* * *

Another intriguing curiosity about our two-roomed barn was the deep crack in the centre of the concrete floor. This fissure was wide enough to swallow a beer can lengthways and longer than a man lying prostrate after imbibing too many of those beers. It appeared to open into a large cavern under the floor and Salome, with her usual practicality, had covered the eyesore with a rug and a coffee table. One day a researcher friend was quietly reading in the lounge when a spitting cobra emerged from under the carpet and made its way across his outstretched feet before slithering out through the front door with the confident air of a permanent resident. On careful inspection, we found that our lounge was home to a nest of spitting cobras, which explained the occasional sightings around the house.

It also explained the one we discovered in our home after an evening out. I had not bothered to connect the car battery to the lamp as we were impatient to get to sleep, and as a result, we entered the dark barn using a flashlight with batteries so drained that its beam struggled to reach the ground. Django had trotted just ahead of us into the shadows, but, with a low, urgent growl, he stopped suddenly, quivering.

'What's upsetting him?' Salome questioned immediately. She was always fine-tuned to his signals.

'Light a candle and we might be able to see more than we can with this torch. I thought I asked you to buy new batteries?'

'There were none in town. Here's a light.' She handed me a candle.

Django had not budged and was still growling softly.

I held the flickering light as far from me as my arms could stretch and there, coiled on the rug, was a spitting cobra – head raised, but no hood displayed. A spitting cobra does not need to display its hood to make me feel vulnerable or for me to find many reasons to treat it with reverence. It sprays two streams of venom at its victim's eyes from any position, including supine, either with its mouth wide open or so barely ajar that it appears closed. The poison, if it hits the target, causes excruciating pain and can lead to blindness if you do not find someone to pee in your eye immediately.

Urine, it seems, may not be the only thing that will save your sight,

31

but as it is mentioned in every snake book, it must be the liquid of choice – though milk or even plain water might work just as well. If you happen to be in the bush and have a nasty encounter with one of these snakes, please bear in mind that you could ask someone – preferably the man with the big feet, if he is around – to help.

'It's just a spitting cobra. Let's go to bed. It will move off by itself,' I proposed.

'Are you quite mad? I'm not going to bed with that thing in here. Get rid of it. Now!'

'It's a spitter. We don't have any light to find it if it climbs into the cupboard,' I objected hopefully.

The 'cupboard' needs some explanation. It consisted of roof-high shelving made from rough pine, deep enough to store outspread elephant hides, tusks and whatever bits of other slaughtered beasts the taxidermists thought they could turn a buck on. Salome had cleverly hidden its cavernous scale with long reed mats as curtains. I doubt that there was a single person on this planet who could claim a larger storage unit.

Salome, when we first met, was the editor of a range of specialised computer magazines and she lived a high-flying city existence in Johannesburg, the most sophisticated metropolis on the African continent. Her life included peripheral luxuries like electric lights, clean water on tap, sunken baths and a modern home that did not harbour spitting cobras. She also had disposable income that allowed her to accumulate shoes. I would be surprised if there was another woman anywhere who owned more shoes than she did – with the possible exception of Imelda Marcos, whose fetish caused the overthrow of a government. I reminded myself of the deep bond that had enticed her to move into my elemental life, as I prepared to do battle with a snake that could blind me before I even knew that it felt provoked.

I wanted some glasses to protect my eyes from its certain expectorating defence and knew that we owned a pair of clear, non-focal spectacles that we kept as a prop for fancy-dress parties.

'Where are those clear glasses?' I asked.

'No idea. Use these.' She passed me her tinted sunglasses.

'I can hardly see anything with this candle. Now you want me to use sunglasses to fight a cobra?'

She shrugged. There was not really an option.

I edged my way towards my section of the 'cupboard' where I kept my clothes and carefully felt for a pair of jeans and boots, as I needed protection in case the snake tried to strike at my legs. Then I grabbed the only weapon I had – a knobkerrie that I had bought years before from a young Xhosa man from the Transkei, who prided himself on carving the finest clubs. It was heavy and somehow comforting as I grabbed it firmly in my right hand. With my left I put on the sunglasses, leaving me virtually sightless, then picked up the only object that I could see, which was the candle.

Gingerly, I approached the spot where the cobra had remained motionless throughout my preparations. I was blundering in the darkness and making my way in its general direction when Salome cried out, 'There it goes ... to your left ... it's gone into the cupboard.'

I took the glasses off and found I was standing more or less where the snake had been. Now there was no sign of it. Django edged towards the right-hand section of the cupboard and growled.

'Oh, great,' I groaned, 'the snake has found the shoes. No chance of getting it out of there. Let's go to bed and see if it's still there in the morning.'

'No. Django and I are not sleeping with a cobra.'

With the added advantage of four candles and a gas lamp, which Salome had managed to assemble in the interim, I started on the pile of shoes. The extra light helped me to see passably, despite the dark glasses. With great care, I flicked one shoe at a time from the mound and called out clearly each time to accentuate just how many there were: one, two ... 62 ... 97 ... 126 ... until finally there was only one pair left. These were gumboots, not shoes – designer Wellington boots – and in one of them resided a very poisonous snake, which I had now cornered.

'If I flip the wellies onto the pile of shoes behind me and the snake manages to escape, it will be highly agitated. Let's rather leave it alone? It doesn't mean us any harm.'

'I said no!' came the implacable answer.

I flicked the first boot out, and to my huge relief nothing came slithering into view. Tentatively I lifted the next one. It felt empty, but I could not be sure: I had never picked up a designer gumboot before, and its weight was not something with which I was familiar. I shook it. Nothing happened. With a false sense of reassurance, I sent it flying far out behind me onto the previous 187 pieces of footwear. The cobra was clearly not in it because suddenly, in the far back corner of the cupboard, 'that with which we could not sleep' reared up.

I admit I am an anthropomorphic bunny-cuddler and I like to hug trees as well. I avow that the snake gazed at me with accusation in its eyes that said, 'I mean you no harm. If you kill me you will never forgive yourself.'

But I slew the wretched serpent with my Xhosa weapon of war. I felt no better than when I had held down Marmalade.

Django, the hero who had saved our sight if not our lives, sniffed the dead body and trotted off to bed; he joined in all these activities with a curious mixture of enthusiasm and detachment. He never reached that state of uncontrollable excitement that so many of his kind do and there was always a certain reserve, a dignity about him that was oddly out of place in our rather impetuous family.

Salome insisted that the hole under the coffee table had to be filled in the very next day.

*   *   *

The plot upon which our old barn was disintegrating was a large piece of land, even by Maun standards. Our landlady and her husband had used it for their dairy cows before they moved their growing herd out of town. A diamond-mesh fence enclosed the property entirely and served to keep the goats at bay. Salome, despite all the hardships of obtaining water, maintained a well-tended, albeit small garden with thrice recycled and, by now, sluggish grey-black water from the house. Despite my comment that she was wasting her energy, since we were not going to live there for ever, and there would be no one else to maintain it when we moved out, she did it for the simple reason that it gave her pleasure to have a splash of colour in the dry barrenness that engulfed Maun. But it was not only Salome who found joy in her small garden.

That November, with Maun still a sandy desert of stifling heat, the neighbouring goat owners, desperate to find food for their livestock, would espy Salome's small piece of paradise, surreptitiously cut the fence and thrust their animals into our territory. The hard-working gardener would suddenly become aware that a herd of ravenous goats was demolishing her precious flower bed. She would charge after them threatening slow and uncomfortable deaths, but always lost the race to the hole in the fence and would stare at the freshly cut wire in exasperation. The breach would be repaired and then a day or two later the whole scenario would be replayed.

Django, who was three months old by this time, always joined Salome in her wild banshee charges but stayed discreetly behind her and had never really thrown his inconsiderable weight behind his ally. However his first adult teeth were making their presence known. One morning it all became too much for him. The goats woke him from a deep slumber at the open kitchen door: he sprang up and, with hackles raised, launched himself at the hapless animals. As he was too small to reach much higher than their ankles, those were what he attacked, evidently inflicting painful wounds. The sight of a trio of goats hobbling through the fence, each one on three legs, clearly gave him the satisfaction of a job well done. With his head held proudly he trotted back to us, three notches chalked, and this before his fourth month. We never had our fence cut again.

By the time he reached six months, Django had filled out in his chest and become stocky and surprisingly powerful, considering his youth and small stature. During the preceding months we had watched him go through various growth stages. He had lost his milk teeth and replaced them with a sturdy permanent set. To relieve himself he no longer needed to squat, nor did he fall over when he raised his leg. In the same way that young elephants struggle to gain control over their trunks, so Django battled to command his ears. The 'see-saw' stage, where one ear went up while the other refused to follow suit, was the first attempt, followed by the 'pagoda' stage, where both his ears stuck out parallel to the ground and made him look like a computer-generated alien. But he finally got the hang of it and could expressively raise his ears at will in a sign language that we were learning to understand.

Though he still had some way to go before reaching full maturity, he was by now a confident bush pup and, in our judgement, ready for his first big adventure – the walk across the Okavango.

4

A STROLL IN THE OKAVANGO

W illie's 'what to bring' list was short on frills:

Backpack (mainly for food)

Mosquito net (to sleep under; a tent would be too heavy, he said, and anyway you wouldn't be able to see what was about to eat you)

Lightweight sleeping bag or a single blanket (the latter was his personal choice, because you could be caught up in your sleeping bag when something came to eat you, whereas you could always just roll out of a blanket)

Water bottle (compulsory) and

A change of underwear (optional and only if you were the fussy or nervous sort).

Salome glanced at the list with incredulity. She promptly added a thin, high-density mattress for herself; extra changes of clothes; a torch; candles and matches; a comprehensive reference library; binoculars; a camera with extra lenses and film; raincoats; inflatable cushions; towels; a roll-up dual-purpose wash basin/water bucket; a sewing kit; a first-aid kit; toiletries and sunscreen; a toilet spade and toilet paper; dog food and lightweight pots, pans, plates, cups and cutlery. The heap

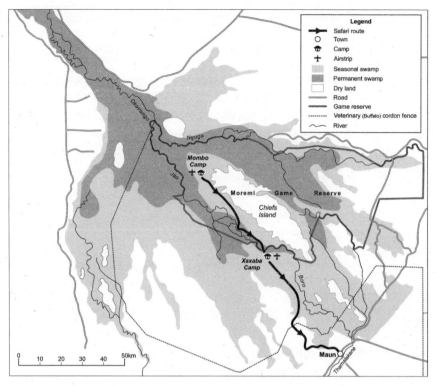

A WALK THROUGH THE OKAVANGO DELTA

took up half the barn floor. Even she conceded that we would never fit it all into the packs, let alone carry it for two weeks along with our share of the food. So most of it stayed, but Salome steadfastly refused to leave her mattress or Django's water bottle behind.

The drive to Maun, a mere eight kilometres from our home, offered us an almost infinite choice of routes. Every track looked much like the other – deep ruts of powdery soft Kalahari sand – and each came about because its predecessor had become impassable. In time, that detour would reach the end of its days and a new track would start. I doubt that we ever managed to explore all the options in the three years that we lived in the barn. To attempt the journey without four-wheel drive was unthinkable and to choose the wrong fork could be a bad mistake. On the way to the airport to join the expedition I opted for a lesser used track and it was, I can confirm, a bad mistake. It took half the local village population a full hour to extricate our vehicle from the sand, which made us late for the start of our adventure.

We parked outside the airport. That we had to leave our open-sided vehicle unattended for two weeks while we were away was not a problem, as there was no danger of theft. Bushie, the autocratic head of the town's CID, saw to that. On the odd occasion that a dishcloth or a handful of sugar went missing, he would sort out the transgressor in a way that ensured recidivism was unlikely. He had a hefty boot – but apparently not too weighty, if the rumours were accurate, to reach groin height. Repeated petitions by injured felons eventually saw him transferred elsewhere and Maun relapsed into crime. However, as we walked to the airport that morning, Bushie still ruled supreme and our property was safe.

What was clearly unsafe was ourselves, judging by the state of the two pilots, who were retching in the shade of the wing of one of the Cessna 206 planes that were waiting to take us to Mombo. These aviators, who disconcertingly looked to be about 14 years old and whose complexions had assumed an eye-catching shade of lime green, appeared to have recently sat through an uncensored version of *The Exorcist*.

'They were at the Duck last night,' chuckled Willie.

'All night long, by the look of them. Can they still fly?'

'They'll be fine once we pass the air pockets.'

'I hope there are enough sick bags on board.'

'They won't need them. They have been chucking for the past half hour. There can't be anything left in those stomachs of theirs.'

Excluding Django, there were seven of us on the walk and as a Cessna 206 could only take five passengers, we needed two aircraft. Willie was our undisputed leader, and he looked the part in his faded khakis, broad-brimmed bush hat and, on his feet, weathered *velskoen* made of kudu hide. Next to him stood an attractive English rose named Victoria. She wore a vague, dimpled smile that gave the impression that she was never entirely sure why she was wherever she was, and her fair complexion was most unsuited to the harsh African sun. Victoria was no stranger to us as she had been working at one of the lodges for the past six months and we greeted her warmly, but I had the feeling that she never quite placed us.

Fussing over a small bag, which turned out to be their toiletries and would need, inconveniently, to be carried separately from their backpacks, were two American girls to whom Victoria introduced us a bit uncertainly, as if she had rather forgotten who they were. The taller girl, Dianne, hailed from New York State, and looked disturbingly young and innocent to be confronting a challenge like this. She looked as if she would struggle to walk further than around a shopping mall in Rochester, NY. Her friend, Sarah, was even younger and appeared as callow as our pilots. She was as soft as a blueberry muffin and as charmingly rounded. Originally from a farm in Iowa, she kept glancing around nervously, as if trying to figure out where all those endless cornfields of her childhood had gone; she and Victoria would get on well.

A blond, lanky Peace Corps volunteer from Montana by the name of Eric looked the only one of these four likely to finish the hike. He was the park warden at the Central Kalahari Game Reserve and we had befriended him on our regular trips through the Kalahari. We knew how much he was looking forward to the wetlands of the Okavango as a break from the arid region in which he had languished for the past two years.

Eric had spent much of that time adorning the Central Kalahari with little green signposts. Before his arrival, it was a true challenge not to become hopelessly lost in the Kalahari. Now removed entirely from the intrepid traveller was the sense of surprise and achievement when he reached a planned destination. This Eric had achieved by erecting shiny new signs at frustratingly regular intervals. The fact that he deemed all this signage to be necessary, even on a straight road with no turn-offs, caused one to ponder just how easily people must lose their way in Montana.

I had no doubt that Salome, a strong hiker and keen mountaineer, would cope easily and that Django would outlast me. As a guide, I walked regularly in the bush and had no worries about the trial ahead – until I saw the mound of food on the tarmac that we were going to take.

'Let's divvy this up and get going,' I suggested.

Willie chuckled. He did that a lot.

That's yours. Our packs are already loaded and in the planes.'

I stared in utter disbelief at the mountain of food that Salome and I were expected to carry; it was no smaller than the pile she had originally spread over our barn floor. Either we were carrying all the provisions or we were preparing for a feast of Roman proportions. I could discern a variety of soups; powered milk; dried fruit; energy bars; rusks; maize meal; rice; endless packets of soya mince; oats; mixed spices; salt; pepper; tea; coffee; sugar; a few tins each of tuna, pilchards and corned beef; two bottles of tomato sauce and a large jar of mayonnaise. My pack, once we had stuffed all this in, bulged to bursting point and while I expected it to be heavy, I was startled at just how much weight it could hold when I attempted to swing it onto my back. Instead of landing elegantly in position, its misdirected momentum swung me off my feet and I landed gracelessly with a soft 'whoomp' on the tarmac.

Eric, smirking openly, helped me up and then held the rucksack so that I could fit the straps over my shoulders. I tottered backwards a bit before he steadied me and I found I had to lean forward to counter the weight on my back. I had no idea how I would be able to lug this load through the bush.

Then Willie handed me a rifle.

'This is my back-up .375. I'm taking my .468 which is like a cannon, so we should have plenty of firepower.'

'To start a war?' I asked in disbelief.

'You never know. If things go wrong in the bush you need to be prepared.'

I hoisted the rifle onto my shoulder. It, too, felt depressingly heavy and we had a long, long way to walk. I glumly felt as if I had signed up for a boot camp. Open revolt was on my mind until Willie showed me his similar load.

The women all had lighter backpacks and Django had nothing to carry but his collar, which was okay – he was only six months old, after all.

What bothered me on a much greater scale was that I had not used a firearm for ages and, in all likelihood, would pose more of a threat to friend than foe. I could see the epitaph on a cross in some deserted wilderness: *Here lie Eric and Sarah, killed by friendly fire.* My dislike of guns had started when I was conscripted into the South African army at the age of 17, issued with an R1 semi-automatic weapon and trained to kill people I didn't know and had no reason to dislike, by people I did know and had every reason to dislike. I kept finding excuses to hand in my weapon to Stores and then devoted all my ingenuity to avoid drawing another.

Before we became airborne I found a window seat in the plane for Django and carefully sought a soft place against which to lean the rifle. At this stage, I must add, there was no danger of accidentally discharging the weapon because the large handful of bullets that Willie had given me sat safely in the pockets of my shorts – the greater danger lay in them dragging my pants down.

*   *   *

The flight to Mombo took over an hour. As I peered over Django's head to watch the wilderness stretching out below us, the enormity of the task that we had so casually taken on became plain. Below us lay endless waterways, streams, savannah and islands of trees; the Okavango is vast. In their popular coffee table book (which Salome reluctantly left behind) Peter Johnson and Anthony Bannister state that it is 30 000 square kilometres of pristine wilderness. With a charitable three square kilometres set aside for every human soul, it was no wonder that Willie had packed so much food. We would not bump into too many Burger Kings along the way.

I glanced at the altimeter. It was reading 4 500 feet, which meant we were flying approximately 1 500 feet above the sparkling delta and its inhabitants. From this vantage point it was easy to see scattered elephant herds where we planned to traipse about. Interspersed among these giants were large gatherings of buffalo and groups of various antelopes – impala, lechwe, waterbuck, wildebeest and kudu. Although we could not see any predators from the air at that time of the day, they were certainly out there too, attracted in droves to this herbivorous smorgasbord. Lion, leopard, spotted hyena, wild dog and cheetah would be competing day and night, often to the death, for prime cuts of venison on the very plains we had to cross. Hippos and monster crocodiles were clearly visible in the rivers and along the sandbanks of the waterways where we would have to find our drinking water. In the skies vultures circled, searching for the latest fatality, ready to claim their share. Perhaps two rifles were not such a bad idea after all.

The flight path then took us away from the waterways and over some disappointingly arid country. The rains had been poor yet again, and now, in April, most of the natural waterholes that in some years survived the entire dry season had already dried. Our plane was taking the direct route between Maun and Mombo. I hoped that Willie would follow the waterways rather than traipsing us through that dry land. It looked extremely parched down there and we only carried a small water bottle each to slake our thirst between water sources.

*   *   *

The Okavango Delta is an anomaly. In the middle of the Kalahari, one of the earth's famed deserts, it lies like a vast oasis of such grandeur that it would have Bedouins palpitating with excitement. We are not talking here of a puddle of water with a few desultory palm trees, but of a vast inland delta filled with innumerable islands, uncountable palms and water enough for every camel ever born. From the air it is a verdant paradise of shimmering blue waterways and copious life of inconceivable variety. Yet, not far from the myriad streams, you are aware of the infinite grey-brown and inhospitable land that stretches away to a distant, featureless horizon.

It is because of a series of natural coincidences that the sparkling waterways of the Okavango Delta exist. Nearly half a million tons of salts are swept annually from the Angolan highlands, propelled by the 18 billion cubic litres of water that the Kavango River carries along its 1 600 kilometre course. The flood is then trapped between two fault lines and evaporated by the fierce sun or drawn up by the innumerable plants, leaving the minerals behind.

These salts should have reduced the Okavango to a lifeless waste-land, making the Dead Sea look positively lively by comparison, yet the Delta's waterways are beguilingly sweet. This wonder is achieved through the employment of hundreds of thousands of sophisticated pumps, which extract the salts from the water and then deposit them in concentrated piles in the centre of the islands. Yet there is no clatter of machinery while these siphoning machines do their work silently and without fuss, each hoisting up to 1 000 litres of liquid daily. Nature's miracle workers – trees – are extremely complex and vulnerable organisms in which life abides in only three delicate layers of cells that are to be found just beneath the bark. They form a wet sleeve around the inert heartwood and, micron by micron, they raise moisture from the ground via the roots and lift it to the leaves from where much of it escapes into the atmosphere, adding a tiny bit of humidity to the air.

Were it not for an ingenious system that rids the Delta of these ever-accumulating minerals, they would overwhelm the trees that created them within 150 years, leading ultimately to the destruction of the Okavango basin. With exquisite timing that spans much the same period, the major rivers and channels – which over the years have been raised above the general ground level by a peat build-up along their banks – burst through their elevated sides and alter direction, leaving behind vast areas to dry out. The salts are gradually leached into the soil by the rains while the peat slowly dehydrates and becomes buried under new vegetation. In time, lightning strikes will start a peat fire that will smoulder underground for decades at a stretch, consuming the salts. All the while, in some other part of the Delta, the process starts afresh.

We were now flying over a section that was clearly in the drying stage. Below us lay endless kilometres of bush that looked just like the rest of the Okavango – tree islands separated by floodplains – except that there was no water, just waving grass. The peat was just waiting for a bolt of lightning. I offered a little prayer that it did not catch alight while we were innocently thrashing about down there.

* * *

When we landed at Mombo airstrip we found a vehicle there for us. Its driver navigated to the nearby lodge through a labyrinth of sandy tracks. There were no guests in camp that night, and we had the run of the place. The guides generously took us on a game drive that lingered into the dark, and we learnt why Mombo is such a popular tourist destination. Every bush seemed to harbour something of unusual interest and as there was nobody else around we did not have to share our leopard, lion and hyena sightings.

Django spent much of the game drive snapping at passing branches, but as soon as we spotted something he would pay it his full attention – quietly, reservedly and with obvious interest. Without our having to caution him, he restrained himself from leaping from the vehicle in pursuit of the springhares that we saw bobbing about, although, judging by the eager wag of his tail as he leaned so far forward that he nearly fell out, he was sorely tempted.

We set off early the next day on our trek from Mombo to Maun, with little more than Willie's experience and the sun and stars to take us across this vast wilderness. Having no compass, no GPS and no map to guide us to our destination was daunting, but Willie assured us that there was nothing to it; in the morning the sun should be on our left arm and on our right in the afternoon. We were just going for a stroll in the Okavango.

* * *

Our two-week hike would take us from the extreme northern tip of Chief's Island right across Moremi Game Reserve and pop us out at Xaxaba Camp on the Reserve's southern boundary, where we would reprovision. Chief's Island is a large tongue of land which traditionally was the local chief's personal hunting ground. When the tribe decided in the early 1960s to stop hunting and conserve the Moremi area, the chief threw in his island too. Once we left the Reserve we would have roughly the equivalent distance to walk to Maun, passing initially through a hunting concession and then, once we had crossed the buffalo fence, finishing the final section in cattle country.

The initial stage was easy going, apart from the weight of our backpacks. We moved over reasonably firm ground through short grass which provided good visibility for all of us, except for one little pup who had to leap over the dumpy tufts to see anything. He loved the freedom and soon settled into periodic leaps interspersed with short trots, as his legs were too stubby to keep up with our normal walking speed. When he saw his first herd of impala his exuberance took over and he gave chase. The graceful antelopes' initial surprise at seeing a tiny ball of fur that did not reach to their knees in hot pursuit eventually gave way to panic as their collective will broke and they set off in headlong flight, with Django's little cranium bobbing through the grass right behind them. He ignored our feeble, laughter-filled efforts at calling him back and soon disappeared from sight. It was a long 10 minutes before he proudly returned with a satisfied grin across his jowls, but he walked straight into a stern lecture from Salome, who explained at length to him why he should not chase the wildlife. Whatever he did or did not understand from her admonishment, he knew the tone and never again chased any animal, other than scrub hares and spring hares.

We clung to the edge of Chief's Island for the first half of our hike. Here in the northern section the terrain gradually changed to deep sand and tall acacias, with no sign of water anywhere. As we wandered through the bush, we saw groups of languid giraffe striding through the grass, quitting one clump of candle-pod acacias for what looked like an almost identical copse some distance off. From Django's lowly perspective the giraffe must have seemed colossal and they intrigued him so fully that he would watch them with unwavering attention for as long as we were prepared to allow him.

I too was content to study the giraffe for long periods because I understood what had caused them to move to such a set pattern, and it is one of the truly amazing stories of the bush. Unknowingly – merely by nibbling on an acacia bush – the world's tallest animals had just triggered one of the most advanced chemical defence systems on this planet.

When Gondwanaland fragmented and Africa split from Australia, the Dark Continent landed up with all the hard-hoofed animals while

Australia got the soft-footed bouncing beasts which presented no threat to their trees. Africa's acacias (named after the Greek for 'point') developed thorns to protect themselves, while Australia's mimosas never needed defensive spikes. This makes it all the harder to understand why some nerds in Australia seized the name 'acacia' for their spineless mimosas and left millions of Africans wondering what they should call their exceedingly thorny specimens.

The reason that Africa's acacias (and I will continue to call them that) developed thorns was because they had all sorts of hefty animals – elephant, giraffe, black rhino – and any number of large antelope eager to devour their foliage. Thorns, they figured, would keep them safe ... but, because the animals needed to eat, they in turn evolved a toughness to their mouths which allowed them to chew contentedly on spikes the size of six-inch nails. I imagine this forced an emergency meeting of acacias at which the agenda had tabled a single item: what more could they do to defend themselves against these hard-mouthed vandals?

The trees ingeniously decided that every time some outsized raider chomped on them they would respond by increasing the tannin level in their leaves, making them so bitter to the taste that the offender would quickly move on. However, nearby trees were then likely to be targeted until they too increased their tannin and there would be nothing to prevent a beast from returning to the original tree to start the process all over again. So acacias formed a pact whereby the first tree to be nibbled would not only raise its own tannin but would release pheromones on the breeze to alert its neighbours so that they could also turn bitter, even before they came under attack. This would encourage the browser to move some distance before trying again – just as these giraffe were now doing. It is such a wonderful story of evolution that I wish I could claim that our acacias were unique in working this out, but it would not be true. There are species of North American oaks that have developed the same defence against caterpillars – a threat which, I must say, seems decidedly wimpish by comparison.

The routine for our walk was established on that first day. It all started at first light when we would roll out of bed. The first one up would light a fire and put the billycan on the boil while everyone else swiftly packed up camp, usually in silence, appreciating the fresh morning scents and early bird calls. Django would stretch, shake out his slept-in fur, trot off a respectable distance to do his morning's ablutions and find a quiet spot to watch the sunrise while he waited for his daily dog biscuits.

Breakfast was modest – usually tea or coffee and a rusk, accompanied perhaps by a bowl of oats. We would then strap on our backpacks and set out while it was still cool, making it easier for us to keep up with Willie's long strides and fast pace. After about five hours of brisk walking we would rest under a shady tree during the heat of the day, when there was time enough to make tea or even have a cooked lunch. Afterwards we would relax, mull over the morning's events, read, catch up on our sleep or pick prickly grass burrs from our socks until mid-afternoon.

Django would lie panting with eyes half closed, snapping at sweat flies that irritatingly tried to extract moisture from his eyes, nose or mouth. The only time he rose was to follow the shade as it moved around the tree or if Salome excitedly exclaimed, 'Oh, look ...!' as she found an interesting insect or a delicate, flowering sedge to photograph. While the rest of us emitted sleepy grunts, Django would enthusiastically leap to his feet and trot over with ears cocked, head tilted keenly and tail curled, to investigate whatever had intrigued her.

After the day's heat had dissipated, we would hit the trail again for a further three hours of non-stop walking, interrupted only when Django found something of interest to show us. His interests were varied and included dung, insects, snake tracks and smalls that we could only guess at. Each time that something caught his attention he would trot over to it and check it out and then stare at us, willing us to come and have a look.

Dusk was the time to find a suitable lair for the night and set up our simple camp – preferably not under rain trees, which tend to drop large branches, nor under sausage trees, which regularly shed huge missile-shaped pods heavy enough to kill a human. Marulas were best avoided too, as they were in season and the enticing smell of their ripe fruits attracted elephants from afar.

Our basic evening meal was slapped together quickly, and as we had little light other than the fire, we ate early. The girls would discreetly find a bush behind which they would spread the day's sweat a bit more evenly over their bodies before retiring to bed under their respective mosquito nets. Willie and Victoria shared one, Django joined Salome and me under our double net and the two girls slipped in on either side of Eric, stating that there was no way that they were going to sleep alone in the African bush. Try as I might I could hear no murmur of objection from Eric.

Most evenings we collapsed, too tired to chat for long around the campfire, and that was when I appreciated Salome's foresight in insisting on bringing her mattress. It is surprising how much comfort a piece of foam no thicker than a pocket calculator can bring to a night in the wild. I spent the remaining nights surreptitiously trying to edge her off it, but always landed up firmly back on the hard ground. I soon learnt to loosen the soil with my hunting knife – having foolishly coerced Salome into leaving the spade behind – and softened the bumps with grass or palm fronds. Django would scatter sand on our sleeping bags when he scratched a hollow for himself, as near to the tops of our heads as he could get. He gave the definite impression of being the most comfortable of all of us.

*　　*　　*

That first day we came across no water at all and our bottles were all but empty when we set off the next morning. After five hours of struggling under the backpacks, we found a small pan – a shallow depression, seasonally filled by rainwater but which usually dried out in the hot dry months – that contained roughly six inches of churned, grey sludge. Algae and some vegetation grew in it, which was a good indication that no decayed animal or rampant virus had poisoned its contents. Django started lapping at the edge, which was another good sign, and trusting his judgement, I dipped my water bottle into the murky liquid. I ventured a sip. It was 90 per cent elephant urine, yet it tasted like chilled champagne.

'I've drunk much worse than this and survived,' Willie assured us. 'Come along. It may be the only water we find for a while.'

We all filled our bottles, and with various expressions of dismay, headed off to the nearest shady spot for a rest.

'Willie, has anyone ever walked this route before?' Salome asked.

'I doubt it, except for maybe some river Bushmen from a long time ago, and they were not likely to try it in one go like we are.'

'So no one, so far as you know, has ever survived this walk?'

'Probably not,' Willie concurred, his customary chuckle playing about his lips.

*　*　*

That evening we came across a recently dried sandy riverbed and decided we should sleep nearby. Willie and I would scout for some water while the others set up camp and put supper on the boil in what was left of the bottled urine. With Django at our heels, we two set off and headed towards a bed of phragmites reeds, a sure indicator of damp ground, because they soon perish if denied moisture. This patch was bright green and healthy.

'Must be water here somewhere,' Willie stated. 'Let's take a look around this clump.'

We had pushed into the centre of the reeds, hoping to find standing water, when Willie whistled softly.

'Trouble!' He pointed to a fresh track in the sand.

I instantly saw what it was and whispered hoarsely in a highly alarmed state, 'A bloody dagga boy!' This is a local term for an old buffalo bull, given because the mud they wallow in gives them the appearance of having been freshly covered with plaster, or *dagga*.

'Yes,' agreed the hunter and murmured in Setswana: '*Kwatale!*' This loosely translates as 'Run for your life!'

The buffalo's acrid presence was in the air and, startled that I had not picked up the scent earlier, I became finger-tinglingly alert. So intent had I been on finding water that I had allowed my other senses to dull – an inexcusable error in the bush. I wondered why Django had not warned us. Perhaps the pup was still too young and inexperienced to understand the dangers presented by this friendless black bovine who had been excommunicated from his herd and had watched as his old mates were picked off one by one by lions. He would have survived solely by being the most fearsome of his era.

'Make sure your rifle is cocked and the safety is off; if he comes for us he'll come quickly,' Willie whispered softly so as not to alert the beast. 'He's heading in the direction of camp and the wind is in our favour, so we'll need to follow right away. Watch my back. He could appear from anywhere.'

I levered a bullet into the chamber, slipped the safety catch to 'off', and followed Willie cautiously along the narrow path into the thick reeds as he started to track the old bull. Django sensed our tension and was instantly watchful but showed none of the nervousness that I felt. Anyone who has worked in the bush will enjoy telling you, over a cold Castle, that there is no more dangerous animal than a lone bull, nor one more cunning. Famed for their habit of doubling back on the trail of anyone stupid enough to follow them, buffalo have won many a battle by charging out of a thicket in close-quarter ambush.

Discussing the dangers presented by a dagga boy in a cosy pub is one thing; encountering a monstrous killer in dense cover was altogether a different matter. There was no point in trying to peer past Willie to catch a glimpse of the old bull; he could well have been just a metre away, on either side of me, planning my execution under his ton and a half of short-tempered ferocity. It was also of little comfort that they often do not take out the first person to appear but wait for someone further back. That someone in this case would be me. There was no one else – except Django, and, unlike me, he was too nimble for an aged buffalo. We moved stealthily through the insufferably thick reed bed. I jumped at every sound. Even Willie looked concerned. Django strutted with ears erect and tail held high in anticipation, sniffing the air with eyes half shut in concentration as he absorbed the smell and seemed to file it away for future reference.

Then, inconceivably, Willie stopped for a chat. 'Did I tell you about the time when we were hunting a buffalo? It was a lot like this,' he glanced around, 'when he charged. I tried to shoot him but my gun jammed. There was not much time to react, so I had to throw the rifle aside, literally grab the charging bull by the horns and leapfrog over its back. It turned around and came for me again. I ducked behind a tree. Finally, my client managed to shoot it. That was an adrenalin rush, I can tell you.'

I was surprised that he had any adrenalin. 'You are not helping here, Willie. Come on; let's make sure that they are safe at camp.'

We pressed forward; the reeds began to thin at last, until we could discern trees through the tall sturdy grass.

'There he goes!' Willie suddenly exclaimed.

I looked over his shoulder and not 20 metres away the great beast lumbered painfully into the bush, as if in agony with an arthritic condition. My heart was aflutter at the idea that he was moving away, not charging full tilt in our direction. I could not picture myself calmly facing down an assailing monster intent on trampling me underfoot, and coolly using its massive horns to vault over its vast back. I always saw myself ending up as a bloodied blob.

Mercifully, he was also heading safely past our camp, so we let him be and returned to the reed bed to see if we could find something to drink.

'You can put the safety back on before you shoot me,' chuckled Willie. 'That hair trigger could catch in the reeds.'

I felt humiliatingly like an amateur.

*   *   *

There was no surface water in the reed bed. Django started digging in the cool sand where we had found the buffalo and settled, panting, in the little depression that he had made for himself. After making sure there were no other surprises lurking in the reeds, we took his lead and in turn started to hollow out the coarse beach-like sand with our hands. About half a metre down, clean, sweet liquid started to filter into the hole. We called the others and enthusiastically poured out the remnants of murky urine as we filled our bottles with fresh water. Whilst we scooped up the precious liquid, more would trickle in, refilling our mini-well, so we decided this warranted the effort of moving camp closer to the seep for the night. Gratefully we used the sand-filtered water for our cooking and still had enough left over for each of us to take a sponge bath. Even Django had a potful poured over him, which he happily accepted and then proceeded to shake silver droplets all over our bedding. Our gaiety concealed the lesson of just how vital water is for survival.

Willie celebrated our good fortune with a large stick of biltong – dried, seasoned meat, developed in the days before refrigeration for journeys just like ours – from his private stash. Thinking of the soya stew that awaited me, I looked on enviously as he shared this treat with Django. Salome was concerned about the effect the high salt content of the dried meat would have on him, especially when we could not guarantee that we would have water in regular supply, but Willie shrugged off her concerns and sliced a large chunk for the happy pup, who accepted the offering gently from the grizzled hand with the Bowie knife. He never snatched at food and his innate dignity never allowed him to beg.

With a soothing liquid sound in our ears like champagne being poured, coming from a secretive Burchell's coucal roosting in the reeds, the tough hunter started to reminisce about growing up as a mixed-race child in a poor family in Francistown. His father had died when he was young and his mother had to make sacrifices in order to bring up the family in an era when there was no great wealth for the majority of Batswana. The Phillips family lived in a small house on a dusty road in Francistown, which was then Botswana's biggest, but by no means liveliest, town. There was nothing for a kid from an impoverished background to do. Every day was just as boring as the one before it and only the buzzing flies showed any energy.

He smiled wryly. 'One day, for a dare, I lay down between the railway tracks while a train thundered over me. It was the noisiest thing I ever heard, and the scariest, because the cowcatcher fixed on the front of the locomotive was slung so low that I was convinced it would catch and kill me. Luckily I was a skinny kid or it would have.'

Many people left Francistown as soon as they could and Willie was no exception. As a teenager, he found a job as a crocodile hunter with Bobby Wilmot in the Okavango and for years he hunted the giant reptiles in the dark of night for the price of their hides, lashing them to the side of his dug-out canoe, or mokoro, before poling them back to camp.

'In those days there were plenty of big hardwoods to make a decent-sized mokoro – not like today when they make them out of useless softwoods, like sausage trees, because there is so little good-quality timber left. The more tourists, the faster the hardwoods disappear. Someone needs to come up with a different idea – maybe a fibreglass mokoro would work,' he mused. 'Anyway I did all that work in deep water in the dark and I never learnt to swim. There's really nowhere to practise because the crocs will eat you, so I was happy to have a big, stable mokoro under me.'

The sun having set, we all drew nearer to the crackling campfire. Django inched closer to Willie and, with head resting on forepaws, seemed to follow the gentle banter. I reminded Willie of a story that I had heard at the Duck Inn. One glorious day a crowd went to the river to party. They were fooling around in a boat and Willie fell into the river. As he could not swim, he ingeniously sank to the bottom, held his breath and calmly made his way to the shore on hands and knees. However, with his face immersed in water, he did not at first realise that he had reached the gently shelving bank and kept on crawling, butt in the air, in full view of his howling friends. Only when he finally lifted his head to breathe and opened his eyes did he see his mates doubled over with laughter.

'At least I came out of there alive. I doubt that any of them were sober enough to save me,' he grinned.

Willie moved on to become a highly respected professional hunter in an era that was dominated by great white hunters, many of whom had migrated from East Africa during the political unrest in that part of the continent. It is a funny thing about hunters. You might imagine them to be a band of brothers, united in their desire to kill as many animals as they can afford bullets for, and allies in the defence of their profession, but it is not like that at all. Instead they squabble incessantly, mostly over who practises the highest ethics, which seems to me like serial murderers arguing over whose crime is the least heinous.

I never heard anyone question Willie's ethics: his judgement, perhaps even his good sense on occasion, was open to question, but his ethics never. He once challenged me to hop from the head of one hippo to the next in a narrow section of the upper Savuti Channel, where the creatures were so densely packed that the dare looked almost feasible. I had nightmares for months afterwards about the possibility of disappearing down the gullet of a hippo that had yawned unexpectedly. Had I accepted the challenge, Willie would eagerly have joined in, so questioning his sanity was not entirely out of order.

One of the cardinal rules of professional hunting is that it should be conducted exclusively on foot because there is no manly fulfilment in running down an animal from a vehicle. Yet many a flabby and obscenely wealthy client from a distant land has waved sufficient incentive in the direction of the pro hunter to ensure that he could kill an animal from a position of safety without getting dust on his costly Guccis. This criminal method was used regularly by renegade hunters to slay the breath-haltingly exquisite leopard. The hunter's truck would trundle through the bush along dirt tracks where fresh spoor was easy to find by a skilled tracker – invariably a Bushman. He would then leap down and follow the cat's path while the client clung to the bucking seat on the back of the vehicle. The pursuing truck would drive the prey relentlessly from one bush to another until the pitiful animal, exhausted and terrified, would turn on its persecutor and charge. This gave the fat man the chance to shoot it with his high-velocity rifle, before alighting and straddling the dead beast with weapon in one hand and a bottle of single malt in the other, ready for the photograph that would hang prominently in his dining room.

Sickened by reports of this behaviour, Willie hung up his guns and became one of Botswana's most passionate conservationists. This path led him away from his dusty childhood environment to the stately palaces of Europe, where he was able to meet the patron of the World Wildlife Fund, Prince Bernhard of The Netherlands. His mission was to ask this eminent statesman to encourage the Botswana government to realign certain controversial sections of the buffalo fence, so that its boundaries would include and protect a major sable antelope breeding area.

Though this barrier has been the saviour of the Okavango Delta by preventing the invasion of cattle herds, this was not its original intention. In 1958 Botswana suffered an outbreak of foot-and-mouth disease on an unprecedented scale, and, in the wake of the decimation of the domestic beef herds it was decided to build a fence to keep buffalo, and their diseases, apart from vulnerable livestock. In no time, however, the recovering cattle herds had devoured every blade of grass right up to the fence and the farmers were clamouring for the government to move the artificial obstacle northwards, to allow them more grazing. Admirably, the government resisted this pressure and when the cattle threatened to encircle the wire and enter the Okavango from the open-ended north-western side, the authorities decided to extend it. Willie had no objection to the extension per se – he simply wanted it realigned to include one of his favourite areas in which the regal sable herds flourished. This noble black and white antelope with sweeping horns is listed as a threatened species and Willie saw in their loss of breeding grounds a further threat to their very existence.

'Unfortunately no one listened,' he sighed, as he finished both his reminiscence and the biltong, lit his pipe and leaned back on his pack, stroking Django's head.

We ate a joyless supper of vivid orange spaghetti and soya mince whilst sitting on the ground around the campfire. Django, his belly filled with biltong, gave me a sympathetic stare before settling down at my feet. I think, overall, I would have taken my chances with a Duck Inn burger if given the option, but as I did not have that dubious choice, I pushed the food around my plate a bit and then offered it to Django, who gave me a pained look and moved over to lie next to Salome.

Again, we went to bed early. We did not have light to read by so I tried unsuccessfully to make myself comfortable on the lumpy river sand. I attempted to roll Salome off her mattress, failed once again, and counted jackals. It was a noisy night in the bush. A pair of side-striped jackal yelped mournfully, as if they had sampled the soya mince and noodles that I had discreetly scraped from my plate. In the distance there were sharp cracking noises that sounded like someone testing Willie's .468, loosing off at irregular intervals in the night air. These signalled the progress of elephants, snapping acacia branches as they smashed their way through the bush. What use was a sprinkling of tannin pheromones against those giants, I wondered?

Then I heard the single low growl of a lion. It was difficult to gauge the distance. A full-blooded lion roar travels for many kilometres as a quiet, muffled sound, while equally, a low contact call from close by can seem to emanate from the far side of the universe. I listened for a while but even the jackals stopped complaining and, incrementally, I fell asleep.

I sleep lightly in the bush – especially so here, uncomfortable and only covered by a mosquito net, which did nothing to keep the moon-light out – and some time later I awoke instantly and fully at the sound of Django growling softly behind me.

'What's up, boy?'

I tried to see what he was looking at, as he seemed to be staring right past the glowing remains of our fire to where Willie and Victoria were sleeping. He stopped growling the moment I spoke to him, content that his job was done, but he remained intensely alert. I thought I could make out movement and wondered if Willie or Victoria had gone for a leak. Then I heard Willie cock his .468. He too was awake and clearly concerned.

Whatever it was, it was coming towards us. I nudged Salome out of her dreams and groped for my rifle.

'What's wrong?' She was battling to surface from a deep and comfortable sleep. 'I told you to bring your own mattress.'

'I'm not stealing your mattress. There's something in camp,' I whispered.

'What?'

The shape grew larger and clearer.

'Don't know but it's coming over here. Look!' I pointed.

It was a lion, a huge male. To a puny human lying on the ground under nothing but a mosquito net any lion would look big, but this male would have appeared enormous even from the back of an elephant, which was a place I would have happily exchanged my current position for. He towered over the glowing embers, sniffed them uninterestedly and kept on, making his way toward us. I was never more grateful for a weapon, though I had no confidence that I could shoot straight in the dark and I was acutely aware of Victoria and Willie directly behind the intruder. I cocked the rifle, which, in the still of the night, made a noise like a 10-pound hammer against a tin roof, and released the safety catch. The beast could not fail to hear it. He stopped in mid-stride and stared at me for a very long time. Django resumed his soft menacing growl.

'Shut up, you fool dog,' I thought. 'This is not Buford. This is the real deal.'

The lion started to pant heavily. If that was a sign, I had no clue what it meant. Was he relaxing, assured that I presented no threat, or was he exercising his throat in preparation for his next snack?

What he did next was something that I least expected. He lay down next to the fire.

'What's he doing?' Salome asked softly.

'It looks like he's joined us. He's lying down on our side of the fire. I hope he likes cold soya mince otherwise you can deal with the complaint.'

I giggled at my own joke and recognised the tension in my voice. The rifle in my hand was trembling slightly, I noted with detached interest.

'Why don't you scare it off by firing a shot in the air?' Salome asked.

'He's come in peace. If he wanted to cause trouble he would have done so already,' I whispered in reply. 'To shoot now would cause panic and create a dangerous situation. If we leave him alone he will leave us alone.'

Nevertheless, for the next three hours Django and I sat bolt upright. I clutched the hunting rifle and he stared transfixed, interested but not nervous, whilst everyone else slept soundly, including – judging from the snores wafting from Willie's side of the campfire – the great ex-hunter himself. At daybreak, our royal guest stretched, rose with some apparent stiffness, and, emitting small grunts, padded so close past us that I could smell his foul breath as he strode into the bush. Django was silent and motionless until the great cat had disappeared from sight and then permitted himself a low growl. Cramped from holding the rifle, tired and hungry, I waited five minutes for the lion to clear off before I finally set the firearm down and rolled out from under the net to start making coffee.

Our American crew had slept soundly and they did not want to believe that a potential man-eating carnivore had spent the night no more than six paces away. They even accused me of making the prints around the fire myself.

'How do you do that?' they insisted. 'It's such a neat trick. Please show us how to do it.'

Willie, propped up on one elbow, sucked on his pipe, grinned, and then finally said, 'People think that if they build a huge fire they will be safe from predators. Fire intrigues lion and hyena; it pulls them in, so if you lie too close to the light they will find you. It is better to make a big fire and lie in the darkness. That way you can see what's out there.'

Sage advice indeed, I thought, then wondered why it was that we all – Willie included – had slept so near our own fire.

*   *   *

We needed to find a river that day. Since there was no guarantee of chancing upon another seep, I suggested we veer west to the Boro River – this was the middle one of three main tributaries in the Delta. We had kept to the east of this channel since heading out from Mombo. Despite the course adjustment we had found nothing by noon and all our bottles were depleted by the time we stopped for our midday break. It was not good to be thirsty and completely out of liquid with no idea how far we were from the nearest water.

The two American girls were taking strain. Dianne had bought new boots for the trip and had developed blisters on the first day. Already these had new layers of blisters on them and we were about to run out of plasters for her feet. Sarah was struggling under the weight of her backpack and complained incessantly of being tired, thirsty and filthy. Tearfully they struggled in the thick sand, holding up our progress. Willie was unsympathetic, which made me feel uncomfortable and annoyed Salome. He wanted to proceed across Chief's Island, a shorter route, but through an area where there was only the sparse shade of the silver-leafed terminalia, a species that is a sure indication of deep, waterless sandveld.

'Where the heck is the river, Willie?' Salome demanded as we settled down for our lunch break. 'We need to find water soon before we all die of thirst.'

'Not in the Okavango,' Willie was dismissive. 'You can't die of thirst here.'

'We haven't had much more than elephant pee since we left Mombo, and now we don't even have that. We are out of water, Willie,' she retorted.

'Don't fuss, man, we'll find some this afternoon.'

'I'm worried about the girls. They can't go on without water and I simply will not allow them to walk any further until we know we have a place to pitch camp near water for the night. They need time to re-cuperate. This is becoming serious. Can't you guys go and look for the river?' she insisted.

I recognised the tone: there was no arguing with it, so I volunteered to scout around for water after lunch while the others rested. I felt sure that the river could not be far, although the normal telltale reeds and papyrus were absent. Also, dispiritingly, the bushes, the palms, the birds and the few mammal species that we had seen looked as dry and dusty as they had for the last three days. We could still be many kilometres from the waterway, judging by the terrain and its thirst-inured inhabitants.

Victoria took charge of lunch. Orange noodles and soya mince, somehow carefully preserved from the night before. I rose quickly.

'I'll go and look for the Boro while you eat,' I volunteered.

'Don't you want some lunch before you go?' asked Victoria.

'No, I must be going. Don't know how long it may take.'

'I'll come with you,' Willie said, giving the pot of soya much the same look that Django had the evening before.

Django jumped up; he cherished walking as deeply as he despised the food on offer. We headed due west.

'We'll have to do something about that soya,' Willie said with feeling. 'I'd rather eat ticks off a dead hyena than that bloody stuff.'

'Do we have a lot more?'

'Tons,' he said despondently. 'The packet looked good and it's light to carry so I bought plenty.'

Django glanced up at him incredulously, then dropped his gaze to the ground and looked a lot less cheerful, though I may have imagined that.

After an hour and a half of trudging in the heat of the day we were still without any sign of water. We were not, I should mention, looking for a puddle, but one of the Delta's major tributaries, with distinctive reed beds all along its course. I realised I was starting to dehydrate – my lips were cracking and I was finding it harder to concentrate, which is not a healthy situation in the wilderness where attention to detail can mean the difference between life and death. When I pulled at the skin on my forearm, it took an age to retract – a bad symptom. Even Willie admitted that he could use a drink and Django was uncharacteristically lethargic. I wondered distractedly if it was possible to die of thirst in the Okavango after all.

The flatness of the floodplain across which we were toiling had an almost imperceptible slope. We pushed on and, as we crested the modest rise, at our weary feet lay the Boro. There had been no sign of it until we were right on its bank. We were, I realised, standing on a peat build-up that would one day play its role in eradicating unwanted salts, but which on this occasion had served merely to conceal the precious river from view.

'Looks good, doesn't it?' Willie said, a relieved grin transforming his face.

'Fantastic. I'm going straight in,' I yelled happily. 'Come boy,' I called to Django.

The river, which in full flood would have been far too wide and powerful to consider swimming across, was now shallow enough to wade through without getting wet knees. This explained why we had not come across any water before. It was nowhere near high enough to breach its banks and fill the floodplains but, crystal-clear, it was flowing strongly. Nothing at all could have looked more welcoming.

We thankfully set aside our rifles; I unlaced my boots while Willie slipped off his *velskoen* and we dashed into the inviting water, clothes and all. With reckless disregard for the possibility of crocodiles in the vicinity hoping for a meal of something squishy, we splashed about. Django lapped at the water's edge with such gusto that I expected him to explode. At one point his stomach was bulging so much that for him even to waddle was a challenge, so he slid into the river and lay in the shallows in perfect bliss, with half-closed eyes.

Once we had cooled off, drunk our fill and replenished the water bottles, we returned to our party as conquering heroes. We helped the girls with their packs and, with Django leading the way, headed back to the river, where we frolicked, soaking tired limbs and sore feet until it was almost dark before we selected a nearby spot to set up camp. That night we made merry with tuna and rice for supper. I marked the occasion with a second cup of coffee. There was no way that we could have carried alcohol, but a celebratory splash of scotch in the coffee would have been welcome.

'How do you find your way around here? It all looks the same,' Eric asked of Willie.

'I use the sun and the wind – it always blows from the east – but mostly I use the airplanes. They either come from Maun or are on their way there. It's really easy.'

'Well, I haven't been able to figure out the sun during the middle of the day. I would be completely lost out here if you had to rely on me.'

'No, you wouldn't,' Salome commented dryly. 'In no time you would have little green signs everywhere pointing "Maun 145.5 kilometres thatta way".'

* * *

The vegetation changed as we moved south. Taller grey-green fan palms replaced the bottle-green date-bearing ones of the northern delta, where we'd nearly died of thirst. Since the season's floods were due only in late May, more than a month off, we were now hugging the river as we crossed vast dry plains.

Dianne and Sarah were cheerful, yet agreeably reserved and Django favoured them with an individual greeting at the start of each day in his own restrained way. By Willie's standards the walking was not particularly taxing; our packs were lightening by the meal and we were fitter. While we maintained an energetic 35 kilometres a day, there was still plenty of time to rest, but the girls continued to struggle – so much so that whenever we had to plough through a patch of thick sand Sarah would latch herself onto the straps of my backpack and have me drag her in my wake. I had never seen myself as a tractor before, but by the end of three days' hauling I was considering a name change to John Deere. Though Dianne declined a tow, her blisters had worsened and she was now hobbling painfully. When she took off her boots to show us, I wished she had not. Her heels and most of her toes were covered in huge puffy blisters that, remarkably, had not yet popped, and her feet looked as though they belonged to the Michelin Man. How she walked on them at all, I could not understand. I would have walked on my hands before I put boots on, if my feet had looked like that.

We stayed close to the Boro over the next few days, which meant that, while we were doing something of a detour, we would not have to waste time looking for water again. The game was far more plentiful now along the river's edge and Django was maturing as a bush-wise dog. One morning we were walking on a dry watercourse between two tree islands when he suddenly stopped right in front of me and stared into the bushes on his right. He sat down, shivered slightly, and raised his right front paw – pointing, comically limp-wristed, towards the thickest clump of trees.

'Hey, what's up, little fella?' I asked. He just gave me one of those looks that implied that I was crassly stupid; could I not see?

I could not; but whatever it was, it was clearly upsetting him, so I said to Salome, 'I'm going to have a look in that clump and see what the problem is.'

'Be careful. He hasn't done this before.'

I set my backpack down and took the rifle. I made sure it was loaded but decided not to cock it.

As I approached the dense mass of toothbrush bushes, I could not make out anything unusual lurking within. The lingering scent of a creature long gone must have spooked Django. I became more casual as I neared the spot because there was obviously nothing there, and as I started to turn and wave the all clear to the others, the bush exploded in my face and a snarling spotted bundle of fur burst from the foliage. It took me a split second to recognise it as a leopard and another to know that I was in no position to defend myself and that I was fortunate that it had bolted past me. Our smart little dog had smelled the big cat and told me not to venture anywhere near. I made a mental note to listen more attentively next time and to remember that leopards are such masters of camouflage that, if they choose, they can entice you to step on them before you know they are there. How is it, I mused, that impala have so far avoided extinction?

* * *

Eric spotted the lions the next morning. He was watching a warthog that had turned, its tail pointing skywards, and fled across an open floodplain as we approached. Intent on avoiding us, the fleeing animal did not pay attention to where he was headed. Suddenly he found himself in the midst of dozing lions. Opportunists that they are, they immediately became interested in the stocky porker, who veered away, glared accusingly at us, and then proceeded to extricate himself by facing the most attentive of the lionesses and backing off slowly from the big cats, who clearly had decided that he was not worth the effort.

'Wow, I was sure we were going to see a kill,' Victoria exclaimed.

'That warthog was clever,' Willie explained. 'He never ran. If he had bolted they would have killed him for sure. Lions chase things that run away but they don't attack animals that stand and face them. Typical of all cats, they need to panic their prey into flight and then they leap on to their backs. If you have the courage to stand and face down a charging lion it will stop short.'

The theory is good, I thought, until you try to visualise standing dead still metres away from a charging mass of growling fury. A growling fury, I might add, that was intent on dining on you. I had no inkling that this would nearly be our fate that very afternoon.

Lunch was taken in the shade of a huge sausage tree and we continued on our way after the heat had drained from the sun. A low, threatening growl was the first indication that, like the unwary warthog, we had blundered into a pride of lions. The sound came from bushes mere metres to our right. We stopped as one, frozen. Nothing seemed to move in the dense undergrowth and there was no further sound. Even the birds were quiet.

'Cubs!' Salome whispered urgently, pointing at some tiny pugmarks. 'They have cubs.'

This changed things; the lionesses would be protective, more likely to charge. Willie cocked his rifle before moving slowly forward, trying to see where they were.

'Remember the first law of the bush regarding lions?' I asked the three girls and Eric.

'Don't run!' they chorused, nervously.

'Good, as long as you remember that you'll be fine.'

'How can we forget?' whispered Victoria with a nervous smile.

'It's a good time to remind you, especially with cubs around,' I cautioned again.

We inched forward behind Willie. The tracks went into thick vegetation. The pride had chosen the cover to rest up in during the heat of the day. Crouching down we could see one lioness in the grass under an acacia bush.

After a while, Willie pointed: 'Come, let's carry on along this path.'

I looked at the dense thicket ahead and shook my head.

'No, Willie. That's too close for comfort. Let's go into the open to the left. The other lionesses and cubs could be anywhere and we might find ourselves surrounded. If we move into the open they can't surprise us.'

Our guide considered my proposal for a moment and I expected him to be obstinate, but he acceded without comment. We managed to circle into open country and were about 30 metres from the protective mothers when they charged. Across the tawny grass four lionesses rushed at us, snarling and growling, cubs at their heels.

Without time to think, I found myself in front of the girls, my arms outstretched, imploring them, 'Don't move, don't move.'

Out of the corner of my eye I saw Django, watchful but motionless. He had taken his cue from us and did not run. Then, to my relief, I noticed the cubs scamper away from us into the safety of the thick scrub. As quickly as the charge started, so it was over. The lionesses came to a standstill less than 10 metres from us, snarled and ran back to their offspring. Neither Willie nor I had raised our rifles. The old hunter flipped the safety to 'on' and looked at Sarah.

'You didn't take any pictures. What was wrong? Light bad?'

'I didn't have a chance to think about my camera,' she said, her face flushed. 'Never mind, I have just had an experience that I'll remember for the rest of my life.'

She turned to me, 'You know, even with you in front of me telling me to stay I still wanted to run. It didn't seem right to stand there when those lionesses were charging.'

'Glad you didn't do that,' chuckled Willie, 'or you would not have had long to remember anything.'

That night, as we watched Eric preparing rice and soya mince for dinner, Victoria asked if we were not worried that Django could have been taken by the lions.

'No,' was Salome's reply. 'He must be free to have fun and if he dies while living adventurously then so be it.'

She told them how Django had narrowly escaped a drab and pampered existence as a lapdog and everyone agreed that he would have been miserable in that other life. Django, himself, lived as though he were familiar with Henry David Thoreau's *Walden*, who came 'to see if I could not learn what it had to teach and not, when I came to die, discover that

I had not lived. ... I wanted to live deep and suck out all the marrow of life ...' and he required no urging to suck deep on that marrow.

* * *

Next morning we took a glorious stroll along the banks of the river in golden light, with herds of zebra and wildebeest cavorting on the plains, baboons contentedly searching for grubs and bulbs, and impala and lechwe in huddles down near the water's edge. It was idyllic and when the river turned to the west in a large meander, we were happy to fill our water bottles and continue on a southerly route.

By afternoon we realised we had wandered further from the water than we had intended; dusk was deepening before we sighted it again and now a challenge confronted us. Grazing between the river and ourselves was a herd of at least 300 buffalo and we desperately needed to cook that night's choice soya stew.

'We'd better give them a wide berth, Willie,' I suggested. Nothing in the world would have convinced me that it was a good idea to walk straight up to the seething black mass in front of us – except, maybe, Willie.

'We'll walk through them. In a herd they're just like cattle,' he chuckled.

'Willie, the whole trip you have been telling us how dangerous buffalo are. Now you want us to walk among them. Isn't that a bit nuts?' asked Dianne as she shuffled from one painful foot to the other. Sarah nodded earnestly in support behind her.

'Come on,' Willie said and, without further comment, he started walking towards the milling mob.

So our merry little band of three men, four women and a dog named Django walked into the heart of a huge herd of one of the most dangerous animals in Africa. I clutched the rifle firmly to my breast after checking that there was a bullet in the breech and another ready to replace it. As I slipped the safety off, I wondered what use two bullets would be against 300 charging beasts.

Willie held his rifle over his shoulder without a care in the world.

As we approached the herd they parted for us, just as Willie had said they would, feeding all the while, and closed in again when we had passed. I was profoundly impressed and unutterably relieved. I had learned a new trick from the hunter. Old, solitary bulls, however, are a completely different matter compared to a herd of mixed sexes and ages, and I urge you not to walk up on a dagga boy with the expectation that he will calmly step aside for you – unless, of course, you plan to perform agile vaulting techniques.

We found an area to camp beyond the buffalo and near the river, but it being a low-lying soggy spot, the only suitable site was on an abandoned termite mound surrounded by a few palms. The herd lay down on the damp floodplain, lowing and snorting just as cattle might. It reminded me of the time I had inadvertently placed a new group of tourists in the middle of a cattle paddock, after having mistaken it in the dark for an open clearing. When daylight came we had found curious cows peering at us and pondering just why we were sprawled so comfortably in their dung.

Lulled by the sounds of hundreds of buffalo, we settled down to sleep.

'Buffalo are a lion's favourite food, right?' Salome enquired playfully just as I was trying to nod off.

'Yes, they are. I just hope they leave them alone tonight because we could be trampled if that lot should stampede in our direction.'

'Good night, darling,' she murmured and promptly drifted into dreamland.

With thoughts of stampeding beasts in mind, I found I was no longer sleepy and lay awake for hours listening to the occasional moo before I finally fell into a fitful slumber.

I was fast asleep when the stampede started. It was sudden, without warning. There was no moon and in the inky darkness there was no way of telling which way it was headed. It sounded as if they were all coming straight towards us. I shouted to Salome, and anyone else who could hear me above the din of thundering hooves, to hide behind the palms. At the same time I grabbed for the rifle, but it was caught up in the mosquito net, which itself was precariously tied to a feeble palm frond. The frond gave way and the net came down around our heads. Salome and I were trapped, like Goofy in a dogcatcher's net, but Django had made good his escape and was watching us from outside the constraining web.

Salome switched on the torch to get us untangled, and I couldn't figure out if that was a good or a bad thing. Would its beam attract or deflect a stampede? Finally, we managed to rid ourselves of the netting, I located the rifle and we took cover behind a palm – the same one behind which everyone else was already gathered. I felt decidedly exposed at the back of the queue but relief came when the noise of the buffalo receded into the night, and I thanked all the stars in the sky for the reprieve.

Just as I relaxed, the thunder of disappearing hooves was drowned out by a wild bellow so nearby that it sounded almost on top of us. I leaped into the air involuntarily. A series of ferocious snarls followed hard on that initial bawl. The frightening sound rolled in the dark. The snarls were so savage that they made the agonised bellows of a dying animal sound like Christmas hymns by comparison. Lions – a large pride of them – were killing a buffalo right outside our camp and the sound of the fight chilled me to the bone. It was so raw, so primordial, that every gene I had inherited from the apes and the hunter-gatherers jangled me into a state of red alert.

Even Willie was not chuckling; he stared intently into the darkness, rifle held at the ready. Salome was uncharacteristically silent as she clutched Django to her breast. I assumed she was terrified, until the dim light of the stars illuminated the smile of delight on her face, and I saw she was completely rapt. I avowed then that I would never fully understand her driving thirst to grasp and explore any thrilling experience.

Victoria was expressionless; her upper English lip clamped firmly to her lower English lip. It was hard to tell whether she was waiting for a tube train at Piccadilly Circus or death in the tan grass of the Okavango. The two girls were clinging to each other and shaking like hospital jelly. Eric, inexplicably, seemed completely relaxed as though he were at home with his family having steak and waffles for breakfast.

Bellow followed roar and roar followed bellow for a triple eternity. At one stage it seemed the wounded buffalo was drawing his tormentors right up to our camp, but luckily the struggle then moved away from us. After what was probably an hour and a half the bellowing stopped. It was replaced by a series of snarls and growls and the tearing of hide and flesh. The lions were enjoying the spoils of their victory and Salome, Django and I had nowhere to hide other than inside the flimsy shelter of a badly holed mosquito net. Finally, we all decided that no sleep was to be had. We stoked the fire and, disregarding Willie's earlier warning, huddled close to it, sipping on mugs of coffee and swapping hushed stories until the call of the Heuglin's robins and the red-billed francolins announced daybreak.

*　　*　　*

We broke camp early and Willie predictably set off straight towards the lions.

'Why is he going that way?' Sarah tugged on my arm very nervously. 'The lions are still there.'

'Perhaps he wants roast leg of buffalo tonight instead of that nice soya stew,' I ventured hopefully.

Bushmen had taught me that man could scavenge on a kill by driving lions off a carcass. The Bayei, a tribe of river people who had fled wars in western Zambia to settle in the Okavango, also used this scavenging practice. It needs some fortitude, I can tell you, to walk calmly up to a snarling lion until his nerve breaks and, with whisking tail, he abandons his meal. He usually watches intently as you slice a chunk of fresh meat from his hard-earned prize. However, on the two occasions that I had been a party to this type of raid, there had been only a single lion left on the kill and he had fed well by the time we moved him off. Now there was a large pride – I could make out six or seven of them with at least one male amongst them – and they were all active around the carcass, eating greedily, squabbling intermittently and lashing out at each other with paws the size of my head. Willie, fortunately, was not intent on plunder; he just wanted to enjoy the action from the safety of a clump of trees, with the wind in our favour. I offered a silent prayer of thanks to the gods of discretion.

Django watched the whole show with unbroken interest. He did not take his eyes off the scene for a second; maybe he too hoped for a break from the monotony of soya mince and rice. We waited until the lions, satiated, settled down in the shade near the dead buffalo, and then Willie said, 'Time to start the day. We have a long walk ahead of us. Dianne must be at Xaxaba tomorrow. Those feet of hers could turn septic.'

Dianne at this stage was hobbling in great pain, though she bore it without complaint. I would have grumbled at every aching step. Eric and I shared the contents of her backpack but, short of carrying her, there was not much more that we could do. She and Sarah had decided that they would fly back to Maun out of Xaxaba Lodge – the first and only sign of human habitation that we would encounter. Willie had also sent some provisions ahead to the camp which we needed to pick up. The stock of soya stew was, after all, dangerously low. By nightfall Dianne's feet looked liked tenderised steak. We had run out of plasters, all the blisters had broken open, and her feet were cerise in colour and seeping blood. How she was to walk the next day, I had no idea.

As we neared Xaxaba we saw the first blue and black flags planted by tsetse fly control teams, whose efforts were supported enthusiastically by Paul Rawson, owner of the lodge. 'We must rid ourselves of these pests or they will chase the tourists away,' he had told me some time before.

The hardy, cross-winged insects, carriers of the dreaded sleeping sickness disease, had been the guardians of the Delta, holding man and his livestock at bay. Now we were to put our faith in the government's will to maintain the protective fences after they had destroyed the custodial flies. Cloth traps, dyed in colours believed to attract them, had been placed strategically and over the past two years the night skies above the Okavango had been filled with the hum of low-flying crop-sprayer aircraft tasked with destroying the tsetse. I pondered the wisdom of eliminating such an integral element of this environment and at the same time discharging toxic chemicals that killed not only the targeted flies but also untold numbers of other creatures, including sizeable fish.

To reach Xaxaba we had to ford the Boro River, which at this point formed the boundary between Moremi Game Reserve and a hunting concession. The crossing was far wider, deeper and darker than the welcoming, clear section with its sandy beach where we had cavorted a few days back. The river here was downright unfriendly and treacherous.

The ford overlooked a lagoon, which led off a wide sweep of the river. The surface was dotted beguilingly with water lilies, while reed beds lined the sides – but it was prime real estate for crocodiles, affording them murky water in which to hunt and shallows on which to rest. Both Salome and I had seen monsters lurking here over the years. This was where a guide at the lodge had rescued a family of local fisherpeople whose boat had caught fire one night. Terrified of the dark waters, they had chosen to remain in the vessel and burn to death in preference to taking their chances in the shadowy depths – and they would have done so had it not been for the timely intervention.

The water was too deep to wade through without taking our backpacks off and holding them high above our heads. This presented two problems. One, it was difficult for Willie and me to be ready to offer protection with our rifles and two, it was not possible to carry Django. He would have to swim. We all knew that nothing attracts a crocodile quite like a paddling dog.

'Is there nowhere else to cross?' I asked hopefully.

'You know as well as I do that the river is much the same for kilometres in either direction. We have no choice. For what it's worth, we had better go separately and cover each other,' Willie suggested.

'You go first. I'll cover.'

Willie looked at me. Crocodiles are attracted to movement and noise and will often position up too late to catch the first offering, but in good time to claim a straggler. What made this crossing point distinctly more difficult was that the group would have to round a stand of reeds and would temporarily disappear from a watcher's view. If anything should happen there, they would be beyond help.

'I suppose I can shoot straighter than you,' he said.

'Mmm, well, I know I can swim faster than you,' I retorted.

I had seen a crocodile attack once and knew how little chance we stood if one of these creatures chose to target us. I had stopped with my clients on the shore of a lagoon in Moremi for a mid-morning tea break. Impala that had been feeding quietly nearby suddenly started leaping all around us and one hurdled right over our vehicle. Wild dog had appeared from the tree line and were herding them to the water where the antelope would be trapped. The hunting pack cornered one of the young male rams. Without hesitation it bounded into the lagoon and started swimming for the safety of the opposite side. It was about halfway across when a tidal wave, erupting from the far bank, indicated a croc had launched out to meet it. In horror, we watched as a V-shaped ripple closed in on the hapless prey. The relentless beast made a single lunge, the terrified antelope disappeared from sight and there was no further sign of its existence, save for a few waves lapping at the shore.

Willie stepped into the gloomy water with an eager dog and four reluctant women snaking behind him. Eric brought up the rear. Standing on the bank with the rifle at the ready, I pointed it in their general direction, looking for a bow wave. If I saw one, I might have a second to react, maybe less. I reminded myself to shoot just in front of the swell if I were to stand a chance of either killing or deflecting an attacker. However, if I aimed too far ahead of the croc, the bullet could hit one of the very people I was trying to protect.

The first section was shallow and I watched as Django jumped through the lily fronds, but very soon he was swimming hard to keep pace with Salome. I could just make out his head bobbing between the lilies. Then the group disappeared from sight and all I could do was search for a telltale surge of water from the dark depths. When they reappeared, they were shoulder deep in the water, with their arms at full stretch above them. Nowhere could people – and a little dog – be more at risk than they were then. Fortunately, they did not appreciate that they were too far from me to guarantee accuracy if a croc should launch an attack. My relief when they all reached the far bank without incident was indescribable.

It was my turn. I felt terrifyingly vulnerable and isolated as I waded into the water, with six pairs of worried human eyes and a single pair of canine eyes following my every step and willing me across. With the backpack and, even more tellingly, the rifle held high over my head, I focused on Willie, who was a disconcertingly small speck in the distance, with his weapon at his shoulder. There was no way that he would be able to see a crocodile from that distance, let alone shoot it; and it certainly did not help that he seemed to be aiming right at me. My heart was thumping and my knees were weak as I descended into the deepest part of the river. As I forged on it lapped at my chest, dark, menacing and just the kind of place where I tell people never to go. It felt like an eternity before the riverbed started to rise towards the far bank and the muddy waters receded around me. I stumbled onto higher ground.

'Bloody hell! That was fun,' I exclaimed with feeling.

Willie chuckled.

Salome gave me a long silent hug and Django came over and pressed his nose to my ankle with feeling.

*　　*　　*

The lodge at Xaxaba catered for wealthy tourists – mostly upper-class English and bejewelled Americans, whose clothes were so crisp and new that they looked as if they needed a visit to the Duck Inn.

They were sitting down to afternoon tea when the jungle spewed us out in their direction. Feeling conspicuously out of place, we approached the dining area from the long, straight earthen ramp that led to the boat and mokoro launch site. The guests stared in dismay at the soggy apparitions that materialised from the perilous swamps, all set to disturb their genteel activity by dribbling muddy water over the spotless floor.

We walked past the most delicious-looking teatime spread – black forest cake, fruit cake, scones, cucumber sandwiches and home-baked biscuits. I had no idea where all this came from – certainly not Maun. Not a single one of the pampered elite stopped to think, 'Hey, these guys have eaten nothing but soya for the last week. Let them tuck in. Bring on some more.' Instead, the employees, obviously embarrassed by our less than upper-class appearance, ushered us out of sight as quickly as they possibly could around the back, and on to the staff quarters.

The girls flew out and we picked up the waiting supplies, which would have to last us for the final four or five days until we reached Maun. I glanced inside the bag and there, nestled under the powdered milk, was more soya mince.

Our diminished party was subdued as we left this isolated haven of civilisation and headed off to find a humble spot to camp for the night. The absence of the girls was a part of the reason, but walking away from that luxury was disturbing. While carefully avoiding a peep in a mirror we had all revelled in the use of a flush toilet and a washbasin. A night spent in a bed with crisp white sheets would have been heaven.

There was also something troubling Willie.

'I have a problem, Peter,' he confided. 'My girlfriend has her husband out from England to sort out their divorce and I do not want to reach Maun before he has left. There was a message for me at the lodge that he would still be around for at least a week. I need to take it slowly from here on. Victoria says that she's in no rush either and will hang about with me. If you want to go ahead we'll see you in Maun.'

I was not sure how Willie did it, but he was forever in a romantic tangle of the type that sells so many cheap novels.

We stayed together a few more days, at one stage walking into a hunting concession of ill repute where those flabby and obscenely rich folk that I mentioned earlier part with indecent amounts of money to kill animals from the rear seats of hunting trucks. Oddly, their food was generally little better than our fare; high-paying hunters were not treated to black forest cake and could count themselves lucky to be served bully beef stew. Why the animals did not cross the river to the safety of the game reserve I cannot explain. Bizarrely, we saw more animals outside the park than on the inside – perhaps they knew that it was ten days before the hunting season opened, or maybe they understood that they were safe from us as we were on foot – hunting here only happened from a vehicle.

The next few days drifted into each other in a pleasant and relaxed way. We were now exploring the southern reaches of the Okavango between the Boro and Kiri Rivers. The walking was tough as we were generally on thick sand, but we were all fit and blister-free and had settled comfortably into the routine. My early concerns about Victoria had proved unfounded; she had not only retained her delicate complexion despite the harsh sun but showed a steely reserve and had blossomed on this trip. She even seemed less vague.

Django had matured on the walk and could recognise the different smells that assailed his nose as he trotted around in the bush confidently checking on who or what had left interesting scents. One morning he let out a deep, ferocious growl. I recognised its urgency and swung around. It sounded as though Buford was charging across the plains, but instead of the Pit Bull, two hyenas were approaching us in their typical sneaky, zigzag manner. They cunningly pretended that they were not at all interested in Django. They looked at the ground and took a few steps forward, then stared into the distance to their left. Moments later they again stole surreptitiously towards us, before stopping to sniff the ground. A few more paces brought them nearer, as all the while they looked elsewhere. In this distracting manner they managed to inch themselves ever closer to us, attempting to express indifference so that their little prey would be unaware of their plans. They did not fool Django, however; the nearer they came the louder he growled and the closer he stuck to me, so much so that I was confident I could chase them off if they lunged at him, but Willie decided that they were quite near enough and drove them away by waving his arms at them and advancing threateningly. They sloped off, looking backwards over their shoulders, disappointed that there was not going to be a little growling snack on their menu.

The time finally came for us to part ways and go on ahead of Willie and Victoria. Eric decided to join us, as he had some signposts to paint. We still had a full day and night to pass before we would reach the buffalo fence and beyond that lay some 24 kilometres of desperately deep sand through cattle, goat and donkey country. We said our farewells at dawn and left Willie and Victoria to enjoy a leisurely lie-in. I was now in charge of our downsized gang as we went in search of an unfamiliar gate some 34 kilometres distant.

We walked harder than we had done before and rested for shorter one-hour stops. For us the real Delta experience was over and we felt in need of home. The bush was very dry here and we had no wish to be caught again without water. We nearly were, and once more were reduced to drinking elephant waste from a small pan that we gratefully came across. Django, after we had filled our bottles with the smelly muck, decided to take a refreshing dip and emerged black and dripping mud, but visibly cooler. We were almost tempted to follow suit.

Late that afternoon Django found a rotten carcass. To celebrate his prowess, he proceeded to roll in it and stank so objectionably that we suggested he keep Eric company that night. Eric wisely declined. We pitched camp in the dark and moved our whiffy pet to the bottom end of the net so that we could sleep.

The next morning we discovered that we had overnighted surprisingly close to the access point through the buffalo fence. It took only 20 minutes to reach the first vehicle track we had seen since we left Mombo, and a further half hour before the gate came into view. The veterinary officials who staffed the post were more than mildly surprised to see us strolling down the road but were very generous in their offer of a ride into Maun. We had a brief conference about the ethics of not completing the walk on foot, decided unanimously that there was no dishonour in skipping the trudge through cattle posts, and gratefully accepted.

We were now in country settled by Herero – a cattle-proud tribe that had fled the German army in Namibia during yet another of those Teutonic wars many years ago – and we had to squeeze into the back of an open government Land Rover pick-up between four bulky Herero women, clad in their traditional billowy Victorian dresses. They too had hitched a lift into town, along with their goats and chickens, which were going to market.

While we waited for the driver and his assistant to finish loading their personal effects, including some unbearably smelly dried fish, into the back of the vehicle, I made sure that we all refilled our water bottles from a galvanised iron tank. We chatted excitedly at the prospect of being at the Duck Inn for lunch and drinking the first beer, dripping condensation from icy glasses, since we had left Maun two weeks before.

The driver must have wanted a beer even more than we did, or perhaps he simply had a death wish. He took off with the back wheels spinning and then raced recklessly along a narrow twisting track with a visibility range of about 10 metres before the next blind bend. The bushes on both sides encroached right onto the track and whipped us mercilessly as we clung to the open sides of the vehicle. At least this indicated the route was little used and there was less chance of unexpectedly encountering oncoming traffic.

Django could not cling, so he slid from one billowy dress to another, as did our backpacks and Willie's hunting rifle. It was exhilarating for about 30 seconds, until it dawned on us just how life-threatening an accident at this speed would be. Our mood changed to one of sheer terror. I considered various scenarios and promptly wished I had not. This was cattle terrain and even a lone cow wandering quietly down the road would have spelt disaster.

I tried to shout to the driver but the wind hurled my voice back to the buffalo fence. I made as much impression as a farting fly at a Rolling Stones concert. Hammering on the cab would surely persuade him to stop and I tried that, but it meant letting go with one hand. As soon as I released my grip I swung violently across the vehicle and nearly over the side, the shoulder of the other arm almost wrenched from its socket. I regained my composure and tried again, waiting for a straight section of road, but such was its winding nature that 10 minutes had passed before I could stop the driver. I am sure we had covered half the distance to Maun in that short time. He could not believe that we preferred to walk instead of making an attempt on the 'buffalo fence to Maun' land speed record.

We were on foot again, and were exceedingly relieved. It took us the rest of the day, without a break and with very little of interest to see, before we trudged into Maun, weary but alive. The beers at the Duck

Inn were as icy and the welcome as warm as we had imagined they would be.

Bernadette handed over a card to each of us – Django included – from Dianne and Sarah. Both were glowing in their praise – Django was awarded the distinction of 'Superdog', Salome was nominated 'Supermom' for the care she had showed them, and I – for having dragged them through the sand – was 'Superman'. Eric declined to show us his card; I do still wonder what honour they bestowed on him ...

5

FRONTIER TOWN DOG

Django enjoyed being back in Maun. He had returned from his expedition a fully fledged bush dog, with the air of a cowboy, yet he found himself having to revert to town life. This began with tolerating, possibly even enjoying, his first shampoo bath from Salome. He sat quietly through the lengthy process; perhaps he too had tired of the pervasive smell of the rotten carcass that he had so proudly conquered in the Okavango and worn as an invisible, but decidedly malodorous, cloak. Then he promptly went outside, dried himself in some cattle dung, and suffered a repeat session – this time with a lot less enthusiasm from both parties. Salome brushed and transformed him temporarily, if not entirely convincingly, into a smooth city slicker, and round his neck she tied a jaunty bandana – a red and white one – that he wore with aplomb on visits to town. At home he dressed more casually, in his collar.

It was also time for him to go to school. Salome started to teach Django the standard commands – 'sit!', 'heel!', 'stay!', 'let's go!', 'nooo ...', 'wait ...', 'go see!', 'what's that?', 'shhh ...', 'rabbits!'... (he never quite understood the technical difference between rabbits and hares) and his favourite, 'oh look!' There was also 'where's Peter?' which abruptly altered my lifestyle as I could no longer hide from the endless list of chores that my wife drew up for me. I added other important instructions of my own like 'fetch Castle' and 'don't tell Salome'.

It would take only one clear, softly spoken instruction for him to understand a concept and never forget it, and he was far too dignified for us to even consider asking him to perform demeaning circus tricks such as 'roll over' or 'beg'. His grasp of the spoken word and the rate at which his vocabulary expanded taught us how adept animals are at communication.

The drought finally broke that summer and we slopped around inside our barn for many days and nights while dry sand turned to mud, empty pools overflowed and plants burst into verdant life under the relentless drumming of tropical rains. Django first experienced the intensity of an extreme downpour one morning while driving to town, when he and I were caught in a thunderstorm. The rain pelted down with such violence that it seemed as if all the horses of the Apocalypse had descended, their hooves thudding deafeningly on the roof and isolating us from the outside world, while the narrow track became a veritable river. I could see no further than halfway down the vehicle's bonnet. To try to drive on would have been irresponsible as there was no guessing what lay in front of the wheels, so I was forced to stop in the middle of the road and wait in trepidation in case someone less cautious should ram into us. Luckily, no one did and we stayed there unharmed until the storm abated. Instead of showing anxiety Django was fascinated by the drops thumping on the car and kept trying to peer through the windows to see what was causing the noise and to get a view of our flooded surroundings.

From an early age, Django loved going to the movies – or, more correctly, coming back from the movies, for that was the hour of the scrub hare. Chasing this speedy quarry through the darkened night was the only temptation that he would never be able to resist. The movie house was at Island Safari Lodge on the Thamalakane River, originally owned and managed by Tony and Yoey Graham. Every Friday night was movie night and for a town that had no TV and little else by way of entertainment apart from drinking, this was a weekly highlight.

It was a movie theatre of rare distinction for it doubled on cinema

nights as a pub and restaurant, with beers and orders for Yoey's sig-
nature chicken-in-a-basket dispensed to patrons during the show. An
antiquated projector threw jumpy pictures onto an uneven, darkly
stained wall and some 150 wobbly plastic chairs were scattered in irregular rows, many waiting to collapse beneath unsuspecting patrons.
Occasionally one did, causing the most entertaining domino effect,
as subsiding chairs and flying baskets merged with uneaten chicken,
greasy chips and wildly flailing bodies.

Throughout the movie you could find your view of the screen
blocked by the silhouetted form of a waiter delivering orders to the
people in front of you. This usually did not cause a problem because
many of the movies were Kung Fu in style, with not much of a plot to
miss. It was prudent to sneak in a quick round while the waiter was
nearby because he was a busy man on a Friday night.

Each film was interrupted at least three times while Tony changed
the reels. This allowed extra time to go to the bar to order more chicken
and beer, which the waiter would only deliver once the movie had
started to roll again. Django wisely slept through most of the showings
unless he heard goats – either through the distortion of the loudspeaker
system, in which case they sounded like they were calling from the
bottom of the ocean, or from live ones on the lawn outside. Only then
would he leap up, ears pricked and ready for battle. For the rest of the
time he dozed, secure in the knowledge that he would wolf down as
many chicken remnants as he wished before the journey home.

For the convenience of the safari guests we introduce to the bush,
our vehicles are open-topped to offer them the best game viewing
opportunities. This suited Django perfectly, for he could stand on the
seat behind us, as he did for most game drives, and stick his head
out into the breeze. During daylight excursions he would snap end-
lessly at any passing branch – occasionally, to his consternation,
snagging an acacia thorn. At night, however, his focus would be on
livelier prey. The road from Island Safari Lodge to our home at the
Old Bridge wound through open bush that teemed with scrub hares.
As soon as he spotted one dashing off into the dark he would give a
delighted whimper, leap off the vehicle and disappear in hot pursuit.

We would stop, call out, conduct a futile search in the dark and then retire to the vehicle to wait patiently for him to show up again. It was judicious to have a take-away basket of chicken and a six-pack of Castles on hand to see out these protracted journeys, which should not have taken more than 10 minutes, but often stretched to hours while we indulged Django's only shortcoming. He would eventually trot back to us, head high, tail wagging proudly. As far as we knew, he never caught a hare and I am not sure that he seriously tried. The fun was in the chase.

Django coursed for his scrub hares on Lodge property where Tony had been able to convince the tribal authorities – the custodians of the land – that he intended to develop a private game park within its boundaries. Although this never materialised, he did keep a cheetah in an enclosed area near the buildings. Django was with us one morning as we walked past this pen, something that we had done many times before. It never occurred to us that the little pup trotting behind us on his first visit might attract the interest of this large cat. And attract its attention he did. The cheetah charged at full pelt across the enclosure before it hit the diamond-mesh fence with an explosive force that caused us to leap backwards in a state of sheer terror. It is not often that one experiences at first hand the petrifying velocity of the world's fastest land animal. The wire barrier was all that separated Django from certain death as the cheetah snarled and hissed and repeatedly threw itself against the obstruction in bare-fanged vehemence. Django had also leapt back, no doubt experiencing the sort of dread that comes from being totally helpless when mortal danger threatens. The ferocity and speed of the attack had unnerved him as much as it did us, and this was the only time I ever saw him turn tail and run. Ever afterwards he gave that enclosure a wide berth. Moreover, when we encountered cheetah in the wild he would obviously remember that attack, as he never took to them in the slightest way and would not even raise his head to look at another of these spotted cats that was sending the rest of us into a froth of excitement.

*   *   *

During the peak of the rains Bobby John moved to Gaborone in order to be with his long-time love, Julia, while he wrote up his doctoral thesis. He took Nari with him, of course; his house remained empty and we were alone on the property. Django was downcast for a few days after Nari's departure, but he soon made friends with a large female ridgeback called Jessie, who belonged to the new owners at Island Safari Lodge, Kay and Phil Potter. Thereafter, as soon as our vehicle rounded the bend that led to her home he would perk up, tail wagging in joyous anticipation at the thought of seeing his new pal. He no longer joined us in the movie house on Fridays, preferring to be outside staring into her eyes and bragging about hare chases.

The short, sharp rainy season was soon over, leaving in its wake a Maun refreshed, clothed in shoulder-high grass and awaiting the Okavango flood that was destined to arrive some four months later. The skies had again turned sunny and cloudless, which meant that Salome could pack her mop and buckets away and Django, who hated being indoors, was happy to be able to spend more time outside again. He loved to roll in the damp sand that the rains had left behind and would return home a uniform dull grey-brown.

Normally Salome just laughed this off, but on one particular bath-and-bandana day he had to stay indoors after he had been brushed. The change in the weather had also signalled the start of the safari season, and our small company was about to expand exponentially. Salome wanted Django to look respectable when he met our new partner, Barry McKenna, who was joining us from Perth, Australia. Spotless yet restless, Django sulked in the furthest corner of the lounge until he realised we were heading to town, whereupon he leapt excitedly into the front of the vehicle.

After two safaris to our part of Africa, Barry, a tall, youthfully middle-aged business consultant, had fallen in love with Botswana and out of love with his wife. He packed up his life in Perth, put his businesses on hold and was due to arrive that day on Air Botswana to join us.

Having turned up on time at the airport, we were not surprised to learn that the flight was late, and adjourned to the Duck for a sandwich and a beer. We would stroll across to the Air Botswana office periodically to check if they had any idea when the plane might arrive (which they had not), only to retire to the Duck for another beer. We had company during this vigil – mostly other guides, who were initially anxious over their clients' delayed arrival and disrupted safari schedules, but whose concern mellowed, in stages, from patient acceptance into blithe indifference as the rounds of beers eased away their worries.

Shortly after the government lunch hour was over, which should have been precisely at 13h45 but often dragged on for 30 minutes longer, we optimistically wandered over to the airport again, passing a man who was scuffling ineffectually in the garden in the desultory way that gardeners do in Maun. I paid him scant attention until our usually amiable dog suddenly flung himself in an outburst of fury at the fence behind which this labourer was not really labouring. Django was used to people in Botswana not doing too much by the way of hard work and it had never bothered him before, so I was surprised at the ferocity of his assault. Normally one whispered word from us was enough for him to back off from any charged situation, but not this time: our calls and instructions to come to heel had no effect. The gardener, visibly shaken by the onslaught, retreated out of sight behind the building and Django, not placated by this small victory and with hackles still raised, tried to follow him through the gate – presumably to tear him limb from limb. I had to scoop him up and carry him away, something he despised, until he calmed down somewhat, though he still cast belligerent glances in the direction of the exit.

We continued to puzzle over this as we entered the toilet-sized Air Botswana office, which was startlingly warmer than the debilitating heat outside – rather like being in a sauna, but without the chance of having some pretty girl let her towel slip. The usually accommodating Air Botswana official was having a bad tourist day and was uncharacteristically listless. Not only was the plane late and its latest ETA denied him by a faulty phone link, but he was also being slow-roasted while irate tourists with connecting flights out of Johannesburg blamed him for all their ills.

'You will hear when the plane lands. Then you will know that it is here,' he muttered, without raising his head from the desk in front of him. Realising that we were not going to get anywhere with him we gratefully retreated.

I was so relieved to escape that hellhole that I even mustered genuine sympathy for the sweltering official as I glanced up into the shimmering skies and wondered if the circling vultures had anything to do with Air Botswana.

An airport worker dressed in overalls hovered at the gate.

'How did your dog know?' he asked without introduction.

'Know what?'

'That man he wanted to bite is a witchdoctor.'

'Why do you say that?'

'I know him. He is a witchdoctor. A bad one. He likes black magic. He kills young children and animals for their body parts,' he continued, and then shook his head in wonderment while staring at Django in admiration. 'Hau! That dog of yours is tooo clever.'

I pondered what could have triggered Django's violent reaction to the witchdoctor. Did he still smell of some ravished animal? Could dogs sense malevolent spirits?

I asked Salome what she made of it.

'Dogs, as well as most other animals,' she answered, 'are believed to have higher vibrations than humans and are therefore not restricted to a three-dimensional vision of the world. They can apparently see auras, angels and other-worldly entities, in the same way that children and psychics can, and as such are far more sensitive to negative or low vibrations. It's possible he was warning or protecting you from evil intentions, knowing that you could not be aware of them because of your dense low-vibration.'

I thought about this for a moment, feeling vaguely slighted, but could not quite put my finger on why, and knowing that I had no chance of understanding any of it shrugged and settled on another beer.

*   *   *

Barry finally landed and insisted on a quick visit to the Duck to wash away the frustration of his delayed departure from Johannesburg. Tanned and slim, his thick brown hair without a hint of grey, he looked fit and much younger than a man in his mid-fifties. After the two beers that our self-disciplined visitor allowed himself, we went back to the barn where we checked him into a ramshackle building next to ours that we had previously used as our administrative centre.

As our office administration revolved around a chequebook, a cashbook, a pen, a diary, a telephone and a waste bin, there was plenty of space for Barry, his suitcase and his scrupulous business ethic. There was also room for a toilet, shower and hand basin as well as a kitchenette that we had installed before his arrival. Barry loved accountancy books, beer, pretty girls and birding, not necessarily in that order. He enjoyed nothing better than to take long walks along the banks of the Thamalakane River, dressed only in a pair of short shorts, slipslops, a floppy hat with dangling corks and a pair of well-used binoculars. After each sortie he would return with a detailed report about all the exciting, and sometimes not quite so thrilling, species that he had seen each morning.

'You won't believe how many turtle doves I saw today,' he would proudly announce.

'Mmm. How many?' I would ask, trying to look enthralled. As the most common of our birds there were always at least a dozen turtle doves picking away at the ground in front of us, or anywhere else you cared to look, for that matter.

One morning Barry invited Django on a birding walk along the river. Salome and I were selecting our reference books for a coming safari and while this promised future adventure, it couldn't help being a boring time for a dog. Django's decision to jump up and trot off behind him turned out to be a good one because that walk was filled with more incident than he could ever have hoped for. A few hours after they had left, our books were spread out over the floor and we were starting to wonder why the two of them were taking so long, when Django came charging into the barn. He tugged urgently on my shirt sleeve while repeatedly staring back at the door. He clearly wanted me to go outside but before I could stand up he was followed by a neighbour who was gesticulating madly and yelling, 'Come quickly! Barry's been attacked by a hippo. He's in the back of the pick-up.'

We ran outside, our minds filled with visions of dreadful carnage. Hippos are credited (if that is the right word) with more human deaths than any other species of mammal in Africa. In fairness, many of these fatalities can be explained as accidental mortalities because most rural Africans cannot swim. It is hard to find a crocodile-free stretch of water in which to practise, and if people are tipped from a boat into deep water by a hippo coming up for air, the chances are that they will become a statistic. Attacks generally come either from a lone bull – a 2 000 kilogram barrel on stumpy legs – that can charge at a respectable 30 kilometres per hour, or a protective mother who has stashed her newborn calf away from the pod. Either can launch a vicious onslaught and inflict appalling damage with their massive jaws, armed as they are with a pair of enormous recurved canines and another set of equally formidable incisors. I was dreading the sight of a bloodied mess, so was deeply relieved to find Barry pale but all in one piece, standing upright on the step of the pick-up and not squirting blood. I am a faint-hearted wimp when it comes to squirting blood.

He grinned sheepishly. 'I can't climb down and I can't even bend my leg because I've torn a hamstring.'

'What the hell happened?'

'I'll tell you on the way to the hospital, if you don't mind.'

We helped him down from the truck, manoeuvred him, shamelessly shrieking in pain, into the F250 and, with Django seated between us, drove him to the hospital. On the way he recounted how he and Django had been walking along the riverbank, having a great birding morning – six turtle doves had already been spotted – and Django had run ahead, exploring as usual, when all of a sudden 'a bloody great hippo' came charging out of the river straight at Barry. He turned to run, but his hamstring snapped and he fell to the ground in agony. All he could do was to lie there twitching as the creature kept on coming right at him.

When it was within a few metres and still charging, Barry had bellowed, partly in pain but mostly in fear. This stopped the attacker in its tracks. It had seemed confused, but perhaps it just appeared so because its mouth was wide open, seemingly ready to bite Barry in half. For an eternity it stood there, swinging its head from side to side, as if uncertain whether to finish him off. Django left what he was sniffing and raced to help. He bravely positioned himself between his helpless friend and the hippo, growling loudly until, ever so slowly, the beast had retreated and slunk back into the river. Our plucky dog followed it to the water's edge and stood guard while Barry lay motionless, as if paralysed. He eventually managed to inch his way up the bank on his backside, 'getting thorns in my butt', where the neighbour saw him and ran to his rescue – noting that Django did not leave his post on the river bank until Barry was in safe hands.

At the hospital, with the help of medical staff, we laid our shaky accountant on a bed and wheeled him into the examination room. Django waited quietly outside while an attractive Swedish doctor checked on the patient's condition, shook her head a lot and in the end sent him home with a pair of crutches, a handful of painkillers and a warning not to tease hippos for a while.

'I won't put a foot in that place again,' he declared indignantly the moment she was out of earshot. 'There are bloody vultures flying overhead. I could see them through the skylight while the doctor was examining me.'

'They're always there, mate,' I told him, 'just waiting for people with incurable injuries, such as a torn hamstring, to be thrown out on to the rubbish pit.'

But Barry need not have worried so much. The vultures, the authorities assured us, were not after the occasional dead person or body part carelessly tossed into the open rubbish pit so much as the disease-ridden swabs and bandages that were cast out daily.

'Already the scavengers are circling and I'm not even dead yet.'

'You soon will be if you hang around here too long. This place only has a 50 per cent survival rate for ingrowing toenails, and even those stats might have been fiddled upwards for government inspections.'

Health care in Botswana, although almost free, was dismal back then. That night over supper I marvelled at just how fortunate Barry was that the charge had not been pressed home.

Hippos, like most other feared animals, receive bad media coverage, yet I had learnt from Naas Steenkamp (notably the first Afrikaans-speaking President of the South African Chamber of Mines), that these sea-cows, as the Afrikaners call them, could be amazingly tender animals. In a conversation that took place at a lodge on the edge of Qhaaxwa lagoon where we were all staying, Naas had claimed he had an uncanny way with wild creatures and could attract one of these beasts gently to his side. Sceptical, I challenged him to prove it. That evening he went off to his chalet and after some 20 minutes called Salome and me to join him. There, bobbing in the water nearby, a metre from his swirling fingers, was a large docile female hippopotamus, which gazed at him with loving eyes, clearly infatuated. I had fully expected them to become engaged that very night.

*   *   *

For Barry, fresh from Australia, learning to bridge the cultural chasm was fraught with pitfalls in his professional role. Telex, a new staff member, had not come to work for two days the previous week, so Barry had called him in to explain his absence during that time.

'My father died,' he said.

'Again?' Barry questioned. 'According to the records he died last month when you took a week off.'

'Yes, this is my other father.'

'I see. And your real father?' I chipped in.

'He is quite well, although two cows are ill.'

Barry let out an exasperated snort, took his glasses off and sighed. He would have paced outside in the garden for a bit had his hamstring allowed it.

'I don't understand these people. Two fathers have died but his real father is tending sick cattle. What the bloody hell is going on here?'

'A cultural thing, Barry,' Salome tried to explain. 'There is an ancient social system here, based on an extended family where any adults who played a role in a child's upbringing are regarded as parents. Telex has just had two uncles die and for him they were fathers. He is not trying to pull one over you. I have four "mothers" – my own, Peter's, my godmother and Mma Mogalakwe, the local headman's wife who has adopted us as family and who has offered to build us a home on her property. If anything happened to any of them I would also be taking time off to bury my mother.'

*   *   *

We had a safari to prepare for and I needed an extension to my residence permit so Django and I headed to the Immigration Department for my monthly stamp. My work and residence permit renewal applications had seemingly disappeared (three years later I found them myself where they had fallen behind a filing cabinet in the Immigration Headquarters in Gaborone). While they had lain forgotten behind a cupboard I had to have a tattered piece of paper stamped on the last day of each month, to allow me to live and run my business in Botswana. At the best of times it was a nuisance, but if I was out in the bush on the fateful day it became a major issue. I could hardly just pop off to town and leave my clients to fend for themselves in the middle of nowhere until I returned days later. Frequently the duty official refused to stamp the form in advance and if I arrived at the Immigration office after the due date, the threat of deportation hung over my head. Nervously I stopped at the small office that had become a monthly torment. Django trotted in at my heels and, ignoring the barrier that the hinged desktop was intended to present, went straight to the back office to investigate. I was concerned that this might trigger a torrent of abuse and a negative response from the man with whom I needed to be friendly, but I need not have worried. According to the cleaner, who was the only person manning the office, the duty officer was out selling oranges.

We did some shopping and then returned, braced for the ordeal. The duty officer must have had success with his oranges, as he was back on duty – not doing much, it must be said, other than to sit behind his desk staring blankly at an upside-down piece of paper in his hand. He paid no attention to us. He made Django and me wait, without acknowledging us, or showing any sign of life. My pup lay under the bench and sighed deeply. Eventually, the officer shuffled over to the counter to attend to us and the other half dozen people who, by now, had all gathered patiently in line.

'Umm...? Dumela, Rra.'

He scowled at me.

'Can you please stamp my permit today, even though my days will only be up next week? I will be on safari on the due date.'

'No.'

'Well, what happens now, Rra? I cannot be here on the due day. I have to earn a living.'

'I don't know. I cannot help you. I can only stamp it on the right day.'

'But I can't just abandon my clients in the bush for four days to come to have my permit routinely stamped.'

'If you don't have it done on the right day I will see that you are deported.'

This stalemate was leading nowhere and I had to change tack.

'Listen,' I leaned conspiratorially across the desk, 'I need some oranges for this safari. Do you know anyone who could help?'

His eyes lit up. 'How many do you need?'

'Three bags would be good,' I answered.

He went to fetch them from a back office, charged an extortionate price, which I paid without comment, and then he affably endorsed my permit for a full three months. What a deal! I just wished I had ordered 20 bags. I might have been granted citizenship.

We returned home with the permit triumphantly. Django was going on his first safari with clients and he was going to get to hunt with the Kalahari Bushmen.

6

A HUNT WITH THE BUSHMEN

Our hunting trip was the brainchild of an American tour leader, Jack Wheeler, who asked me to make arrangements for a group of staunch right-wing Americans to witness a Bushman hunt in Botswana. No hunting with high-powered rifles off the back of a vehicle for them; this was to be the real thing, on foot accompanying the 'little people' with their small bows and poison arrows. Just the way our distant ancestors perfected it in order to survive.

Jack is a man of some achievement. For a start (at least according to Jack), he won the war against the Russians in Afghanistan. As an undercover US Pentagon agent, bearded and disguised as an Afghan, he snuck into the country and noticed that Russian helicopters dominated the mountainous regions, as the Afghans had nothing in their bag to down them. He returned to Washington with a recommendation that the US should supply the enemies of the Soviet Union with SAM-7 missiles. The Pentagon approved the idea, with the result that the Afghans won the war and drove the Russians back to the land of borscht and vodka, which made everyone, including the Russian soldiers, much happier.

Jack was a hero in some circles for a while, though I shudder to think what the American helicopter pilots say about him these days in the pub after a day's work. He was also the first person to parachute onto the North Pole; he lived with head-hunters in the Ecuadorian jungle, and led trips to some of the remotest places in the world.

Jack also occasionally wears a plate of food at dinner, or at least he did on the night I met him at Jessie Neil's Camp Moremi. Jessie, a peroxide blonde (washed in water flown 1 200 kilometres from Johannesburg because the Okavango water turned her hair orange) and a millionairess from Pasadena, California, had fallen in love with the Okavango Delta and established two safari camps there.

She introduced a style to her lodges that was previously unknown in Botswana. The luxurious living area, crafted with little concern for cost from imported mukwa, a beautiful natural hardwood, was tastefully appointed with chandeliers and tapestries that would not have been out of place in the White House, together with a liberal selection of costly bronzes of African wildlife. Only the finest silverware and crystal glasses were on offer, and attention to detail went as far as the staff's African print uniforms, which identically matched the tablecloths and napkins, and lent the impression that it was the tables themselves that conjured up the caviar. The overall effect impressed presidents, film stars and billionaires alike.

A sumptuous five-course meal was served, with a selection of superior South African wines and ports, from a bar that also offered a choice of almost every other brand of the finest alcohol ever produced. Jack had organised a safari for a group of ultra-conservative Americans, mostly – and this will probably not surprise you – from the Midwest. These visitors were evenly split between tough outdoorsy men and evangelical Christian couples. The macho men drank Jack Daniels, used foul language and told bawdy jokes, and the evangelicals were easily offended. Mike Gunn and I had been invited to guide the group on their game-viewing activities and to entertain them while they lolled in pampered luxury back at the lodge.

There were 18 clients in all and, with Jessie, Mike and myself to be catered for as well, even the extended dining table was stretched to its limit. While the main course was being served, the discussion turned to some of the very different foods that are eaten around the world. I mentioned that mopane worms – large, gaudy caterpillars that metamorphose into beautiful moths – are considered a delicacy in Botswana, and one of the group spoke of unusual morsels that he had tried in the markets of south-east Asia.

'Some people put really strange things in their mouths,' chirped Mike Gunn loudly.

Jack, who was seated to the right of Jessie at the head of the table, responded, 'I've met some girls like that.'

At that, one of the religious women stood up with her recently filled plate of sizzling food, strode purposefully half the length of the dining room and upended the lot in Jack's crotch, before she stormed off screaming, 'I won't put up with this any more.'

Jack made strangled warblings of shock until the heat of the food found its way through to his skin, and then he joined in the screaming.

It was bedlam. Django would have loved it.

The husband shot out of his seat to go and pray for his wife, while Jessie went pale and remained silent for a moment before remarking, 'I have never seen such outrageous behaviour,' as she cast a meaningful glance in the direction of the newly departed.

After dinner and over a glass of port, Jack, having changed his trousers, mentioned to me that he would love nothing more than to bring a group out to meet a genuine Bushman clan.

I said, 'I can do that.' Port apparently encourages me to say wildly reckless things.

He said, 'Fine, let's make it next August.'

I went to bed wondering just how I would deliver a band of nomadic Bushmen on demand.

*　　*　　*

August did indeed find us wending our way along a narrow, deeply sandy track in remote western Botswana towards Xai-Xai, a distant, minuscule Bushman village. Our party consisted of Map Ives, a fellow guide; Salome and her arty sister, Liza (more at home with a paintbrush than a soup ladle), who would be doing the catering; Shylock, another experienced guide whose major role on this trip was as translator; Mansue, my right-hand man and trainee guide, and his camp staff, our dog and me. As we were not going to be camping inside national parks, Django could join us, while Barry stayed at home to oversee the office.

The Kalahari is not a true desert as it is well vegetated and enjoys enough of Botswana's heat-induced convectional thunderstorms to ensure sufficient grazing for its game population. However, it does not retain any permanent surface water and to venture across this vast stretch of land presented a logistical nightmare to the early traders, missionaries and trekkers who came in their ox wagons to ply their trade in driest Africa. Living here for any extended period verged on the impossible, except for the most skilled bush people.

We had an 11-hour drive to Xai-Xai from Maun through monotonous but appealing countryside. Stands of medium-sized trees, mostly purple-pod terminalias and Kalahari apple leaf, broke the uniformity of the endless scrub – largely coffee bean trees, western rhigozums, various small acacias and assorted raisin bushes. Tall, yellowy, silky Bushman grass softened the terrain, lending an impression of cultivated grain fields. In patches it was a little like driving through European parkland, except that it went on, unchanging, for hour after hour with no sign of human habitation.

Our hopes of finding a nomadic Bushman clan rested squarely upon the youthful shoulders of Keeme, whom I had met on a previous trip to Xai-Xai, and who, fortuitously, had looked me up when he came to school in Maun. He was descended from a Bushman mother and a Herero father and held, I hoped, the answer to my Kalahari dreams. He could speak both fluent !Kung and Setswana and would translate what the Bushmen were saying to Shylock, who would then render it in English.

'Could you get a nomadic clan to set up a camp near Drotsky's Caverns?' I had asked him.

'Maybe.'

'I need to be sure if I bring these people.'

'Maybe. I don't know if I can find them, or if they'll do it.'

'Can you try – and let me know?'

'Maybe. I have school holidays in August. I can let you know then.'

'We'll meet you in Xai-Xai. Just make sure that you don't try to dress up the village drunks as the real thing.'

'Okay.'

I had feared another 'Maybe' here.

It was months later now, and with some trepidation we approached Xai-Xai. Jack's group of eight was arriving by air the next day and, because there were no communications with the village, we had no idea whether Keeme had succeeded in his mission. If he was not waiting for us, it might mean that he was still in the bush trying to locate the nomads, or that he had failed to find them or, alternatively, to convince them to co-operate – and that, rather than face us, he had sidled off somewhere where we could not find him. If we did not meet up, I myself might slither off somewhere safe, lest Jack and his crew do to me what Keeme had feared might happen to him.

As we had penetrated deeper into the western Kalahari, the parkland had given way to arid semi-desert terrain, leafless shrubs replacing trees and the waving Bushman grass capitulating to bare sand. When we crested the final rise before Xai-Xai, in front of us lay the semblance of an oasis where leafy acacias shaded a dry riverbed. A mixture of Herero and Bushman huts greeted our eyes, as did the welcome sight of a government-installed borehole and water tank. Donkeys and goats huddled outside the telltale circle of planted logs which kept livestock from the water point. Waiting there were regal Herero matrons, looking overdressed in their bright, multi-layered Victorian-style outfits and contrasting dramatically with the delicately featured Bushman women who were wrapped in tattered skins. Both groups were clutching 20-litre yellow vessels – old cooking-oil containers – to fill with water and then balance on their heads before trudging varying distances through thick sand to their homes. Despite the weight pressing down on their necks, their graceful natural poise ensured that they never spilled a drop. Snotty-nosed kids, with flies crawling unmolested about their faces, stopped in their play to watch us pull up next to the communal tap and join the queue.

Keeme, bless him, came running down the slope from the village towards us, waving joyfully and grinning broadly.

'I have found them and they are near the caves,' he shouted ecstatically. 'They will wait for us.'

'Fantastic!' I shook his hand warmly before a moment of suspicion clouded my elation. 'But are you sure that they are not the town drunks?'

'No, these are people who still live in the bush.'

'Well done!'

I sighed with relief, overjoyed that I would not have eight American outdoorsmen practising their bow-hunting skills (or whatever bush skills they may acquire in the Midwest) on me.

Keeme took us to meet the headman while Mansue and George, his new assistant, filled the water containers. An introduction to the chief or headman, with an explanation of your purpose, is a courtesy expected in all rural areas. Django unhesitatingly came along, even though there were packs of unfamiliar and potentially aggressive village dogs that might have attacked an intruder. That thought never crossed his mind: this was a new place to explore, with different smells and many strangers to convert to friends. He headed confidently straight into the middle of the first gang that he came across and after a few moments of stiff-legged, erect-tail posturing he trotted off to meet the second group, with five dogs excitedly following him. In this way he had collected a dozen or so followers by the time we reached the headman's home. Kalahari dogs were taller than Django, universally light tan in colour, many of them with twisted tails that looked as if they had been put through a wringer then left un-ironed. In comparison to his stocky build, they seemed positively anorexic even when well fed, and the difference between them and our sturdy long-haired hound was stark.

We took the chief a few simple gifts as tokens of our respect. As shops did not exist in Xai-Xai, basics like tobacco, sugar, tea and maize meal were not easily available. In addition to these staples we added a large bag of sweets to spoil the kids. The chief was Herero, not Bushman (which was a surprise in a community where the latter were clearly more populous) and, in the manner of headmen all over the country, he was seated on a low wooden stool in the shade of a tree outside his hut, available to dispense counsel to his people. He looked so comfortably sage and at peace with himself that I wondered briefly if it was a job that I should apply for, but just as quickly changed my mind. The petty squabbles and daily issues of an insular community living in an isolated village would soon leave me feeling neither sage nor at peace.

The headman was pathetically thrilled to accept our offerings and would practically have given up his only daughter for another box of tobacco. When we pulled out of the village, his wife was contentedly brewing tea for the small group which had already assembled at his home, while he sucked on his freshly filled Bushman pipe. A bushman 'pipe' is just that. It is a straight piece of metal without the bowl of a conventional pipe as we know it. It typically tapers somewhat at one end and looks like a large-calibre shell, which, unsurprisingly, it frequently is. The tobacco, often merely locally harvested leaves, is stuffed into the end and smoked rather like a metallic cigarette, with due care taken not to burn lips or hands on the heated metal. Every Bushman over the age of about six years smokes, and those who abstain are regarded as social misfits. Clearly the Herero, who lived cheek by jowl with the little people, had readily adopted this habit. When we departed a few dogs ran after the vehicle, reluctant to say goodbye so soon to their new friend.

We drove south from Xai-Xai for about an hour over fossil sand dunes towards Qwihabe caves, with Keeme on the back of the truck giving directions. He banged suddenly on the roof when we neared a dry pan surrounded by candle-pod acacias and trumpet thorns. The only shade was from a sprinkling of Kalahari apple leaf trees and a scrubby-looking peeling-bark ochna. A portion of this uncommon species, I came to discover, was used by the Bushmen as a lucky charm when hunting, or a piece of its root as a talisman when job-hunting, which is a puzzling tradition in a society that had no need for jobs.

'We camp here.'

'Why here?'

'The others have their huts somewhere over this hill.'

It was more of a grassy rise than a hill, probably an old sand dune, but we did as Keeme advised because it was as good a place as any to set up camp. No sooner had we stopped and begun to offload than Map pulled out a garbage bag which he used to line a small depression that he dug in the pan, and filled it with some precious water. Django followed him and watched his every move, then sampled and approved its contents.

'We'll have plenty of birds coming in by tomorrow,' Map predicted.

He was right. Doves were the first to find the welcome liquid, and colourful waxbills and finches followed. It added to the overall ambience. Django waited considerately until there were no birds about before using it again.

Map grew up in Francistown and had the reputation of being one of the most knowledgeable guides in the country, though he was always modest and complimentary about the prowess of his peers. He read any scientific manual that he could lay his hands on, no matter the subject – geology, grasses, hydrology, soil science, geomorphology and anything else that would help him understand how the natural world slots together. His enquiring and freethinking mind would then challenge every hypothesis that did not make intuitive sense to him, and his alternative theories were, invariably, not only original but also believable.

*   *   *

Jack Wheeler and his seven clients were on time at Xai-Xai airstrip. We picked them up, recharged our water supply and within an hour were back in camp. These were tough boys – or at least boys who talked tough. Wally, an older fellow, was in great shape, having just finished the New York marathon at the age of 61. Joel, a much younger man, was an Olympic-class water-polo player. John Perrott was a Red Adair double, only much bigger. John was a giant Texan oil-fire fighter and pipeline builder, who travelled the globe putting out conflagrations started by terrorists with political agendas, or by unthinking people carelessly flicking cigarette ends into oil wells. When there were no fires to fight, he built pipelines in war-torn countries.

However it was Fred, a toy-store owner, who was my favourite. He asked the most inane questions and never really sorted out which of the tents was his. As a result, he kept dumping his camera equipment on someone else's bed before backing out looking seriously confused. I could relate to this man. He also looked as if he would never be able to keep up with a hunt, should the Bushmen decide that we could join them, and he made me feel sleek and conditioned. The others were clones of each other, all on the wrong side of middle-aged, and they belonged in their faded Banana Republic outfits, as if they wore them daily on their Montana ranches.

Over lunch I underlined the fact that we had a unique opportunity to spend time with a nomadic group of one of the oldest peoples on earth. We needed to respect the fact that, apart from sensitive anthropologists, they'd had minimal contact with westerners and that they could feel threatened by outsiders, especially those who made them feel like dwarfs. I also pointed out that they had agreed to allow us to mix with them. If we did not ask too many daunting questions and were pleasant to be with, they would be happy to stay in our company but they'd made it clear to Keeme that should they feel uncomfortable with us they would simply move away.

A lively discussion ensued as to what questions would make them feel threatened.

'Anything personal is out,' I answered. 'A rule of thumb is that if it's a question that might embarrass you, then don't ask it of them. If it comes across as aggressive, or even if you ask too many questions about their movements, they might fade away into the bush.'

'Are you saying that we have come all this way and these guys might shove off if we ask the colour of their underpants?' Fred asked.

'That's just what Peter's saying,' Salome answered. 'Why exactly would you want to know the colour of his underwear?'

Fred squirmed, unsure of how to answer.

'Then don't ask,' I suggested. 'That surely falls under the category of a personal and pointless question. In any case, as you will see, the men only wear a loincloth made from skins and do not wear underwear. This will become blatantly obvious when you notice that they seem to have a permanent semi-erection. It's not an indication that they are particularly excited to see you, but that they have an extra tendon in their penis that causes this. Please don't ask them about it either.'

Fred pondered on that over the rest of lunch.

*   *   *

After we had eaten, we set off to meet the Bushmen. Their camp was further than I expected – almost three kilometres from ours – and Fred was sweating profusely by the time we arrived. The shelters were typical beehive affairs that were too small for Big John to squeeze into, yet a Bushman couple and their infants shared one at night. Each hut had the scatterings of a fire at the door, as is the custom. Communal fires are only for times of celebration, which typically revolve around a successful hunt. Two younger women were bare-breasted, which put a twinkle in Montana eyes, while the older women were modestly covered, which was a relief, as there is nothing to age skin faster than the Kalahari sun and Bushmen in their mid-thirties generally look 20 years older. Fred could not stop taking videos of everything he saw – especially the topless girls with pert breasts. Then he wandered off in the bush for a pee and nearly got lost.

Django took to these people immediately and even dropped his characteristic reserve for a while as the younger children played with him. This clan had no dogs with them, unlike the villagers and the Bushmen in the Central Kalahari who hunted with hounds from the backs of donkeys. As they had never seen a dog like Django, everyone pleaded with me to give him to them. My immediate answer, of course, was an unconditional no – except, perhaps, for a small hesitation when the young women fluttered their eyes at me.

Our translation process was cumbersome and undoubtedly not wholly accurate. Fred asked a question because he was confused; Shylock translated it into Setswana for Keeme, who posed the question to one of the little people who then, probably, replied with the answer that he thought Shylock would want; then Shylock embellished that for dramatic effect – and Fred was further confused.

'Do you see how well cared for the young children are?' Salome mentioned. 'Look how that baby is passed from one to the other. Everyone handles the child so that it grows up feeling totally secure within its clan.'

'Not like us in America,' responded John. 'We stick our kids in front of the TV and ignore them because we're too busy making money. Then we wonder why half of them can't name a single Asian country, or which of our presidents it was who led us during the Second World War.'

*   *   *

That evening there was an air of excitement and expectancy. The cacks of barking geckos mingled with the sound of clinking ice and swirling Jack Daniels as we sat around a blazing fire – which was being fed by Joel, who proved to be our group pyromaniac. Django growled a soft warning as two figures appeared from the dark – they were Bushmen from the nearby camp. We were sitting on folding chairs and they came and joined us, squatting down easily on the sand as they do at home. Wally and Joel immediately jumped up and offered their chairs but the Bushmen chuckled and shook their heads.

'Not for us,' they said and frowned at our wasteful fire. They traditionally used a few small branches that they fed slowly into the blaze and thereby utilised a limited resource with ecological sensitivity. Joel looked suitably chastened.

The two introduced themselves as Noishay, a small man with a wizened face, and a younger man, Qui. We discussed with them what we would do the next day. Water, they answered, was a priority if they were to stay here any longer, so the men would dig a well while the women went foraging for food. We would be welcome to join in both activities.

'Will you go hunting?'
'Not tomorrow.'
'Maybe the next day?'
'Maybe.'

Once the programme had been sorted, Noishay became fidgety and could hardly restrain his excitement. He had a story to tell and when he could no longer contain himself, he suddenly started laughing.

'I want to tell you about a leopard.'

Storytelling is the way Bushmen have passed on history and important family relationships to following generations. His eyes were alight with animation. Django moved under my chair as usual at the mention of a leopard, but watched the storyteller with interest.

'This leopard had been coming into the kraal, where the chief, a Herero, kept his cattle at night, and killing the calves. He called for me from the bush and asked me to get rid of the thief. He sent his strong young son to help me. We tried to stay up at night to catch the calf-killer but he was too clever for us and never came near the cattle while we were there. Then we thought to use a gin trap, you know the one with the big metal teeth. We borrowed one, chained it to a tree and set it.

'That very night the leopard came back and triggered the snare, which caught it by the front leg. This thief is stronger than we think and it breaks the chain and runs away with the snare. The chief said we must go and find it and bring back the trap, so his son and I, we take the rifle and go to find the cat.

'We followed it through the bush for a long way but it was easy to follow. The leopard was bleeding and dragging the snare. It was like following a big road,' he laughed.

'We finally find it in a hole in the ground. We talked to the leopard and laughed and shouted because we wanted the animal to charge so that we could shoot it and go home. I had the rifle and was ready to fire and the chief's son threw sticks into the hole. Then the leopard came out at full speed. I pulled the trigger and nothing happened. It was a misfire.'

He burst out laughing as though this were the funniest thing that could ever have happened.

'The chief's son and I, we turn and run. I am older,' Noishay proudly pointed to his chest. 'We run, first me, then the Chief's son, then the leopard.' He gesticulated with his hands and fingers the order and manner of running. 'Then I trip over a log and fall. There was no time to stand up, so on my knees I start to crawl away.'

His laughter increased as he crawled frantically in front of us in the sand to demonstrate his dramatic escape attempt. Django leapt to his feet, eager to join in.

'The chief's son went running past me and I feared for my life because then it was the chief's son and then me and then the leopard. The angry cat goes past me like this,' Noishay smacked his two hands together in the universal symbol of a flash, 'and then it is the chief's son and then the leopard and then me.'

Again, his laughter was unrestrained.

'Then the leopard catches the chief's son and pushes him to the ground. The young man lay still like he was dead and the leopard lost interest and disappeared into the bush.'

Noishay and the chief's son decided that they had stretched their luck far enough and went back to the kraal without the snare. Some months later, he told us, they found it lying in the bush. Perhaps the leopard had died; possibly the leg had rotted off. Noishay seemed to find both eventualities enormously amusing.

'Can Django come along tomorrow?' I asked Noishay before they left.

He looked at me with a puzzled expression to see if I was being serious.

'Of course he can.' He turned and took a few paces and then looked back and stated solemnly, 'Maybe he will be the only one of you to come back.'

*   *   *

We left for the Bushman camp shortly after sunrise to find the women already waiting for us. Only the two older ones were going gathering because the younger females were staying behind to take care of the children, much to Fred's disappointment. Then he discovered that he had forgotten the video film, so he spent the morning complaining that he had to carry a goddamn camera that weighed a ton and he couldn't even use it.

We meandered in the bush for three hours, Django delightedly sniffing at the turned earth, and we watched as the women transformed barren-looking vegetation into a smorgasbord. Desiccated beans, once opened, provided succulent nuts for roasting; tubers of one type provided drinking water while another would be used to wash hands. Leaves were collected to make into tea or eat as spinach, others to smoke. The fruits of the raisin berry bushes were plucked for the children to snack on and sour plums – which, I can vouch, deserve their name – were gathered for their vitamin C and moisture content. Roots provided a starch staple, while harvested grass seeds supplied the grain requirements. We were laden with food when we returned to their camp and the Americans were duly impressed.

'I never had any idea that there was so much to eat in this desert,' Jack commented. 'They are better off than the Afghans for natural food, I can tell you.'

'I bet poppies would grow well here,' said Map, known for his cultivation of interesting plants.

'You don't need these guys getting involved in hard drugs as well as booze and tobacco, from what I hear,' replied Jack.

Map nodded vigorously in agreement. Bushmen, as with aboriginal people elsewhere in the world, are particularly vulnerable to addictions – alcohol and tobacco being the primary problems – and if hard drugs were to be accessible and affordable, their effect would be devastating.

After lunch, we went to visit the men at their new well. They had chosen a fossil riverbed to dig in and by early afternoon were shoulder deep in the hole, having used only digging sticks, which gave an indication of how soft the sand was and, possibly, how short the men were. They had just struck water and were busy filling tsama melon shells. These hardy gourds formed the first manner of trade between whites and Bushmen, when the bush-wise little people stockpiled them for the early explorers' oxen and other livestock, and without them the traders could never have crossed the waterless Kalahari. It was curious that they still used melon shells, which were not exactly efficient, when the villages were littered with discarded plastic bottles, but these people seemed to be purists. Either that or they were putting on a show to impress. We tested the water. It was not sparkling Perrier; the liquid was cloudy and tasted salty, but it was palatable and, in the desert, life saving. Django lapped enthusiastically enough at the sample offered by Keeme.

Qui climbed out of the hole and went over to a patch of sansevieria – known as 'mother-in-law's tongue' – a long-leafed succulent with an aptly sharp point. He picked a number of the plants and showed the group how to make rope by separating the filaments and then, by rolling them on their legs, weaving the strands together.

'Can we try it?' asked Fred somewhat surprisingly.

'Yes, sure,' I replied, eyeing his hairy legs. The strands, I knew from painful experience, became entangled with leg hairs and, like Elastoplast, excruciatingly ripped each hair out of its follicle by its roots as they were being rolled. Rope making is better left to people who, like the Bushmen, don't have hairy legs.

'Jesus Christ,' yelped Fred after such a moment, 'that is sore.' His leg, the sudden focus of attention, showed a bare patch amongst a tangle of brown hairs.

Salome peered at it with interest and said, 'Could be more effective than waxing. Can I test another small section on you?'

Fred's answer was decidedly indecorous.

We accompanied the men back to their camp and helped them carry the precious water-filled melon shells. The Americans were brimming over with questions and started asking how long the clan would stay, where they would go next, where they found other clans with whom they could marry, how long their lifestyle could be maintained, how many children each had and if they would be able to support more.

Suddenly Shylock turned to us. 'This gentleman, Noishay, says that they will not be here tomorrow. He cannot understand why you don't use your eyes to see how they live and not ask so many questions. He fears that you wish his people harm and that he must keep them safe. He is very serious.'

That stopped the questions immediately. These huge Montana men looked bashful and they stared at their own feet, their hands held to-gether as if a teacher had just scolded them. I asked Map to take them back to our camp while I sat down with Noishay, Shylock and Keeme, with Django in close attendance. Over the next two hours I explained, again and again, that while the Americans are stupid and do not understand how people live in the Kalahari, they did not mean to harm or offend.

Finally Noishay accepted my explanation. 'Yes,' he said, 'I can see that they are not clever and do not understand our ways, so we will stay – but if it happens again there will be no talk.'

He then invited us to walk with the hunters early next morning. They would be heading off after their tea to look for signs of fresh tracks. If there was evidence of game the hunt would take place on the following day.

Back at camp we set new rules. No questions would be posed to the Bushmen that were not first filtered through Map or me. Then Shylock would consider each question before transmitting it to Keeme, who would only ask the Bushmen if he approved it. Everyone was hugely relieved that the little hunters had relented and that the show would go on. The clients even unanimously embraced my description of themselves as being stupid.

After yet another of Salome's gourmet dinners we relaxed around the glowing embers and a sense of peace settled over the gathering. Even Django seemed unusually restful as he lay quietly next to my seat, staring into the fire.

'Aren't the stars amazing,' Jack commented. 'They're never like this at home.'

The night was ablaze with twinkling lights, and the glorious sweep of the Milky Way added to the splendour in a manner that very few places on earth can emulate. The Central Kalahari sky is one of the world's best for stargazing, because it lies deep in Botswana's heartland where the local atmosphere has suffered little human-induced pollution and there are more visible stars on offer than just about anywhere else.

'If you listen quietly,' I said, 'you can hear them whisper to each other. That, at least, is what those beautiful people just over the rise believe. They spend every night under stars like this and are the only people outside of accepted science to have their own acknowledged constellation – "Grus", the Stork.'

'Why do you call them Bushmen?' Jack asked. 'I thought that San was the politically correct name.'

'I met a man in Ghanzi,' I answered, 'who could speak three Bushman languages, as well as English, Setswana and Afrikaans. I asked him this question, and his answer was that each clan would like to be recognised by their individual names – such as Red People, Pale People and so on. They did not understand where the word San came from and, if we insisted on grouping them as one, then the term Bushmen would be preferable.'

The hunters arrived as we were finishing breakfast next day and we headed due west towards the Namibian border, where we soon encountered some unexpectedly rocky terrain. I reckoned this area must be geologically related to the range that housed the Aha Hills, just north of Xai-Xai. It was not the hills, however, that held my attention that morning, but puff adders. I had never seen so many in one small area; it was as if they were holding a convention.

I was right behind Qui and bumbling along as I normally do, with my head down looking at the ground in front of me, when Django, who was exploring, suddenly darted past me and nipped the little Bushman sharply on the ankle. This was so out of character that at first I could not believe what had just happened. Qui could not believe it either; he stopped and instinctively raised his spear threateningly at Django – just as I spotted a coiled puff adder lying on a rock where the Bushman had been about to step. He had been looking into the bush for signs of animals and would have stood on the viper.

Puff adders are arguably the worst of all snakes to encounter, because they lie dead still and hope that neither prey nor predator sees them. Their lightning-fast strike, whether in attack or defence, is swifter than almost any other snake in the world. If Qui had trodden on this one with his bare foot he would almost certainly have sustained an agonising bite, as the potent, tissue-destroying, cytotoxic poison settled to its task of rotting away the flesh. I pointed to the snake behind him, and, after watching it slither slowly away, he turned to Django with a broad smile of gratitude and uttered a series of happy clicks as he bent down to pat his rescuer, who became the toast of the moment as everyone crowded around him offering praise in different tongues.

Django had treated this particular snake with more obvious alarm than he had displayed when confronting the cobra at our barn. I could not make out if it was the sluggish nature of the portly adder, with its attractive yet somehow threatening markings, or if he already knew, from some previous experience that I was unaware of, about the speed of its strike – whatever the reason, he showed deep respect for it.

Puff adders, because of their stationary hunting style, are responsible for more venomous bites than any other snake in these parts. The good news is that death generally does not occur within the first 24 hours, so we might have had time to rush Qui to Maun for treatment, but there have also been many spectacularly quick deaths caused by this species, and he could quite conceivably have died even before we'd been able to get him back to camp.

En route to hospitalisation he would have suffered extravagant swelling – I once witnessed a victim's arm that looked like a balloon about to burst, and merely touching it caused intense, excruciating pain. Dizziness, loss of consciousness, severe blistering and perhaps gangrene would follow. Without professional treatment, death would be certain, and probably welcome.

I stopped bumbling, as did Qui and the others, and walked with my eyes out on stalks. It was as if we were in the middle of a B Grade movie: every rock seemed to harbour a puff adder – even the one that I wanted to sit on when we stopped for a smoke break. I wanted to stand still and shout for mommy to pick me up, but because I was supposed to be the fearless leader I just whimpered inwardly while shooting nervous glances about me. Django was also unusually skittish and looked carefully before he leapt over any rock.

To relax my mind I concentrated on watching the Bushmen light their cigarette pipes. They did not have corner stores to buy matches, so they carried their own lighting material with them in the form of two rubbing sticks – a male made from a straight hardwood and a female cut from a softer wood and into which the hard stick was twirled – and some dry grass seeds. In much the same time that it would have taken you to find your matches and strike one successfully, these little guys had whipped out their makings, twirled the sticks and had some of the grass seeds smouldering. In the past I had diligently persevered with their system but all I had landed up with were hands that were so badly blistered I could barely touch a steering wheel afterwards.

Eventually the hunters found fresh gemsbok tracks that elicited exuberant clicks, and spotted some tiny steenbok footprints which drew less animated chatter. More pleasing for me was the creeping certainty that we had passed puff adder koppie. Then we saw giraffe spoor that was only a few days old and Noishay announced, with an expectant smile, that we would hunt at dawn the next day.

We would need to find fresh poison for the arrows. Qui, who had taken a liking to me – thanks no doubt to my dog – explained that old poison was kept moist by wrapping it in a cloth bandage which they dampened frequently, but that it never had the same potency as a freshly made concoction. He showed us how to dig for the poison grub, with the unmemorable scientific name *Diamphidia*, and which was found only under a specific tree – aptly called the poison-grub commiphora. Once we had gathered eight of these small, hard grubs – the minimum needed for a single arrow – he demonstrated how to extract the venom, and once he had primed the tip with the deadly mixture he allowed only me the honour of handling the now lethal missile.

I was not at all sure that I appreciated this honour to the extent that I should have, because one mistake could have seen me dead within hours. I approached the barb with much the same caution as I would have, had it been a puff adder. An animal as large as a giraffe will succumb to this poison, even if only glancingly struck, so I held the arrow for just a brief moment before I quickly set it down and stepped gingerly away, making sure that Django did not go anywhere near it. I do wonder how many people, unaware of its potency, may have died unnecessarily after carelessly or ignorantly handling this deadly poison.

Qui also allowed us to try a few practice shots with his bow and poison-free arrows. The miniature bow reached only to my waist from the ground and the arrow, made in three separate parts, was small and light. The whole assembly wobbled wildly, a little like getting bubbles to go in a straight line, yet these hunters have the skill to be able to aim and discharge it even after stalking and getting to within the 15-20 metres of the prey necessary to have a reasonable chance of accuracy.

If they manage to pierce the hide, the outer two pieces of the missile that are not attached to the arrow head are designed to fall away, so that the embedded and poisonous barb stands less chance of being brushed off when the victim stampedes through the bush. It is an age-old system that indisputably works.

We reached camp before lunch and Noishay invited us to join the clan that night for some dancing as a pre-hunt good luck ceremony, and to thank God ('Gaoxa' in !Kung) for saving Qui from the snake that morning. My, was I swollen with pride. There were no thick T-bones in the camp freezer, so I sneaked a rump steak instead and cooked it for Django – he was a 'rare and hold the spices' steak eater, although he did appreciate a good cheesy sauce. My gesture incurred Salome's ire.

'Did it not occur to you that I cater according to a plan and do not carry extra steaks for you to dish out whenever the whim takes you?' she admonished me.

I went without steak that night, but Django was grateful. He kept a worm's eye open for legless reptiles from that moment onwards, and was disappointed when he was not rewarded so richly for finding harmless bush snakes.

*　　*　　*

That evening, before supper, we set off with Keeme to see the dance. We were transported back in time to an era when our common many-times-great-grandparents invoked the spirits through trance dances. It was a celebration of life, unchanged through 20 or 30 centuries, as the women chanted and clapped rhythmically, the beads on their wrists and ankles rattling in time to the beat. The men kicked up the dirt while performing a circle around the fire in perfect unison with the women, and their own chanting was a deeper, different sound, but to the same rhythm. Tears welled in my eyes as I realised how privileged

I was just to be there – in fact so deeply moved was I, that I hugged a tree.

The world's oldest people, ancestors of all of us, were performing possibly the oldest surviving dance in human history. No doubt the excitement of our presence helped oil the fires in the hearts of the dancers, yet they were largely oblivious to our being there. They went on to perform a series of other routines and Keeme interpreted each one – many of them told of heroic stories like that of Noishay and the leopard. They danced, trance-like, for over an hour but, as far as I could tell, none of them entered a full-blown hypnotic state on this occasion. Fred did. He was mesmerised by the dancers, especially the young women, and cursed when he ran out of film.

After the ceremony, Noishay told us that they would be down at our camp at first light and we had to be ready, because that was the time to hunt. Django, he reiterated, would be welcome; casting a disapproving eye at my belly, he stated that in his opinion Django, Wally, Joel and Map, maybe, would keep up. The rest received a shake of the head. Women were not welcome on a hunt – they brought bad luck – so Salome and Liza would have to stay back at camp.

Over supper we went through the strategy for the expedition. Firstly, Map would not join the hunt, as he was to drive ahead to Tsodilo Hills to set up camp in readiness for us when we flew in afterwards. Secondly, we did not know when the chase would end. If we wounded a large animal like a gemsbok, giraffe or eland it could take three days for the poison to take full effect. Therefore, everybody had to be prepared for a hike of up to three or four days, as well as sleeping out in the open. We might miss visiting Tsodilo Hills, but we would have had the experience of a lifetime.

'Oh, and there is an essential thing,' I said. 'Do you notice how light the Bushmen travel? They are barefoot and, apart from a tiny loincloth which scarcely covers their genitals, they carry absolutely nothing else other than a hunting bag, which they sling over their shoulder and which holds a bow and some arrows, a spear and a digging stick, plus their smoking gear.'

I did not expect our guests to be quite so extreme – a loincloth on

Fred would have been severely off-putting, but I urged everyone to be sensible about what they took along. 'If you err, then err on the side of extra water. Trim the rest. OK, guys?'

'Yes, Peter, we hear you.'

Well, if they did, they certainly did not listen.

Django and I emerged from our tent ready for the big event, our dog in the barest minimum – a collar for serious bush work. I was kitted out in shorts, shirt, boots and a cap, to which I added my survival knife, a compass, a pocket maglite and sunscreen lotion, plus two bottles of water – I did have to share with Django, after all.

Wally and Joel were the next out of their tents and they were sensibly dressed in lightweight longs, boots, a shirt with pockets that held sun lotion, lip salve, compass, some energy bars and a small camera each. Around their waists they each had a Swiss Army knife and two water bottles. On their heads they had what my mother would call sensible hats.

Big John was next and he had a few more things to carry, but I was not too worried about him. He was strong enough to carry me. Progressively the other intrepid hunters emerged, each more heavily laden than the one before. Map chuckled and I wore a mask of consternation.

Fred and Jack were still preparing. To my surprise Fred beat Jack to breakfast. He looked like a packhorse, but, in fairness, much of it was video equipment. He had brought every accessory that Canon have thought of – wide-angle lenses, telescopic lenses, filters for each, battery chargers, extension lighting, spare batteries, spare films, lens shades, racing stripes, the list seemed limitless. Fred was mystified by all this stuff, so he brought it all in case he left something important behind.

Then Jack came out of his tent. Map chuckled again. I burst out laughing.

'Where are you going, Mary Poppins?' I asked incredulously.

Jack looked like Michelin Man and could hardly walk. He had trousers with zip-up pockets all the way down to his ankles and each pocket bulged. His shirt pockets strained with the contents that he had shoved in each, and on top of all this he wore a press-jacket with 32 pockets, each of them stuffed. On his back was a large backpack, the pockets of which were also crammed to bursting point, and the final touch was an umbrella peeking out from the pack and not from a pocket.

'Expecting rain?' Map asked, looking up at a cloudless sky.

'No. It's for the sun.'

'You have no idea how fast these little fellows walk in the bush, do you?' I said.

'We might have a slow time when it will be useful,' replied Jack and steadfastly refused to shed any of his gear. He opened his jacket to reveal packets and packets of some new Californian energy product that he was to endorse.

'Just remember what you take, you carry. Don't ask me or any of the staff to help you. Understood?' I made sure that they each nodded.

Salome and Liza had prepared breakfast and packed lunches – sandwiches, energy bars, assorted snacks and boxed fruit juices. Most people took two of everything; I picked up two small packets of peanuts, an energy bar and a pocketful of dog kibbles, while Jack and Fred took three of each item on offer, and then found that they had no space to store it all, so they clutched the packets like primary school kids.

The hunters arrived, talking quietly among themselves, and indicated that we should go. Noishay looked at Fred and Jack and shook his head in silent wonder. We set off straight away with the little Bushmen in the lead, followed by me and the giant Americans, and Shylock and Mansue at the rear to pick up any stragglers.

After just 10 minutes, Fred started to grumble. 'Why are they walking so fast?'

I laughed. 'Fred, they haven't even warmed up yet.'

The Bushmen were incredibly light on their feet – they were little guys who carried next to nothing and weighed less than the load that Jack bore. They danced around the bushes like Fred Astaire on a polished floor, whereas our Fred had already given up skipping around and instead went straight over the bushes like a Sherman tank. The thorns grabbed at him, tore his trousers and tripped him up. He was already having a miserable time and we could still see camp behind us. I was glad that Shylock and Mansue were there to mop up. We could not afford to lose Fred – we might never have found anyone like him again.

'Are these little bastards trying to kill us?' he gasped.

'They haven't found a fresh track to follow yet. And when they do, they'll pick up speed – you wait and see,' I told him.

'Can't wait, I'm sure,' he replied, puffing.

Just then the hunters came upon a promising gemsbok track and started jabbering excitedly before they burst into a charge down the slope in the direction that the antelope had taken.

'Oh shit!' Fred yelped, as he fell over a small bush and sprawled heavily.

I could not help it, I doubled up with laughter. The sight of fat Fred flopping in the wake of nimble Bushmen was too much. By the time I regained control of myself he had lumbered to his feet and we set off in hot pursuit. After 20 minutes of wild dash through the bush, there were only the Bushmen, Wally, Joel, Django and me (which surprised me beyond belief, trust me) left in the chase. The gemsbok had been sighted, but it whiffed our scent and, alerted, ran off. There was no point in following the prey any further, and it was an hour before Shylock and Mansue had rounded up Jack, Fred and the rest of the team.

When they joined us, I asked Jack how the energy powders were working.

'The stuff is killing me,' he admitted. 'I wish I could dump it here.'

Fred came sidling up to me. 'I can't lug this camera any more. Will you carry it for me?'

'No.'

'Please, buddy.'

'I did warn you.'

He looked at me helplessly. 'If I give it to you, will you take it?'

'Maybe.'

'Maybe? This thing cost a goddamn fortune and you say maybe?'

'I don't want to die out here carrying stuff I don't need to survive.'

'Well, I can't give it to you anyway. It belongs to my brother and I would have to buy him another one. Otherwise I would.'

'OK, let's go!' I called, ending the pointless exchange.

'We've just arrived,' Jack grumbled.

'Quite so, but our hunters have been held up for an hour waiting for you to unfurl your umbrella.'

The Bushmen, with playful smiles, stood up and set off at a brisk pace. They were enjoying the game. So was Django, who showed no sign of weariness.

I was walking right behind Qui when he stopped and, with one fluid motion, hurled his spear. I had not even seen the steenbok standing in front of the rain tree. The assegai shaved the top of the tiny animal's back and stuck harmlessly in a branch, while the antelope escaped to safety – an inch lower and we would have had a kill.

We had walked for another two hours before we came upon a patch of the tsama melons that provide much of the water requirements for man and beast in the Kalahari. The hunters each picked a melon, chopped them open with their spears and drank deeply, with obvious enjoyment. I opened one with my knife, took a swig and spat out the foulest, most bitter liquid I had ever put into my mouth. The Bushmen burst out laughing. How could I not know that that one was not ready, they wondered. I asked them to show me how to select the right ones, which they attempted to do, but try as I might, I could not understand the difference at all between a bitter and a ripe melon; they looked identical to me and even felt the same. Since it was blatantly obvious to them, they must have decided that, like the Americans, I was a little on the stupid side.

The melons, even the ripe ones, were no great hit with the Americans either. I had a feeling that most of them were ready to call mommy. We had walked hard for six hours and now it was time to sprawl, which they did – like beached whales, and, like beached whales, they did not want to move. I checked with the Bushmen; there was no point going on, as the day was already hot and the hunting hour had passed. Maybe tomorrow, they said. I left everyone to rest a while and then asked who was ready to walk back to camp. Nobody was, so I allowed them more time. Still they beached. I decided I should fetch a vehicle to ferry them back, so Django and I walked back to base.

Salome and Liza had just pulled out for a drive, equipped with a picnic box, a book for Salome and a sketchpad for Liza, and were obviously set for a long afternoon of leisure.

Having heard that we had whales to collect and needed both client vehicles for the job, the girls had to forfeit their afternoon of tranquillity and help me with the transport. As we loaded them, Liza offered to walk back with Fred and Wally. Fred was, once again, ungentlemanly in his response.

'Wow, that sure was something,' Jack said over a beer back at camp. 'I did some stuff in Afghanistan but it was never like this. No wonder these guys aren't fat. They have to work for their food, and I really mean work.'

Fred was in a funk and clutched his brother's video camera protectively to his bosom. He had lugged all that heavy equipment through the bush for six hours and I doubt that he had managed even a single minute of filming. In addition, he had nearly given an expensive camera away.

We were all in bed and asleep by eight o' clock, and in the night it rained. It never rains in the Kalahari in August. Jack could have used that umbrella if we were still out hunting.

7

HOME OF THE GODS

The next morning, with lactic acid playing havoc with our legs, we limped and groaned our way up to the Bushmen's camp to say our farewells. Big John expressed his concern about the future of these unique people, and though I knew that we are all related at some distant point, it was hard for me to see any connection between this giant and these small folk.

'What does the future hold for them? I mean, can they really survive in this state in the modern world?' he asked me.

'I think you know the answer to that, John. You tried some tsama melon. Which would you prefer to drink? That, or fresh water at the turn of a tap? You also saw the food they eat and how much work it takes to gather enough to live on. Their cousins in Xai-Xai receive provisions from the government every time the rains fail. Also, the authorities are embarrassed to have these people living, as they say, "like animals", dressed in skins, and they want to bring them into the mainstream of society. To treat them differently would be deemed a racist act in a country with a constitution that bars racism. There is no chance of the Bushmen staying like this, I'm afraid. In 10 years' time there will be no nomads left. In 20 years, few will have retained the skills to survive for a week in the bush. In 50 years' time they will be engineers and professors, living in cities around the world, married to Swedes and Chinese, and their culture will be a footnote in history.'

John looked pensive.

I pondered privately how long it would take our clan to rush to Xai-Xai to tell their mates, over a *chibuku* beer or two, about the strange people who had popped in for tea. I had no doubt that these particular nomads could survive indefinitely in the bush, but I was equally certain that they would have close contact with those who chose to live in the established villages. They were caught in transition between the old and the new, and I wondered how long it would be before the new won their hearts.

Rain forests have been sacrificed to the pile of books eulogising how gentle Bushmen are, how they possess supernatural powers and how they are the finest botanists and trackers to grace this earth. I have some breaking news. Bushmen are simply people.

They like to party, they love to hunt – and they are generally very good at it. Some are bright and others are not, some are happy and pleasant and others are not. They laugh when they are happy and cry when they are sad. Some are gifted at identifying plants that have a use – food or medicines are obviously vital, but if they do not bother to give names to plants for which they have no use, no one makes a fuss. Above all, I find, they really enjoy not being on a hunting licence.

References abound that it was as recently as 1936 that the last licence to hunt a Bushman was reportedly issued by the South African government in Namibia. Whether this is the truth or some kind of desert-legend, is a matter of some controversy. I, nevertheless, can picture a keen sportsman, Teddy Roosevelt, say, swaggering into a licensing office to buy a permit to hunt a Bushman.

'I'll have an elephant,' he might drawl, 'a rhino, two leopards, a lion, an impala and one of those little rascals – what do you call them...? Oh, yes, a Bushman.'

And he could then go out and legally chase down a person as though he were hunting duck. I wonder how many of these trophy hunters would have hauled their treasures to a taxidermist and asked for the mount to be stuffed. Perhaps they would have named them, as

Roosevelt did with his favourites. The President's dead elk was 'Boom', a wild turkey was lovingly called 'Pow-Pow' and a massive blacktailed buck, with an impressive head that spanned over 120 centimetres, was 'Pop-Pop-Pop', presumably after the number of shots required to end its life.

'Here's "Willie-Wally the Warthog". I nailed him when he was rooting for food on his two front knees,' our hunter might boast to his dinner guests over a glass of port. 'And next to him is "Bang-Bang" the Bushman. I bagged him from 30 metres while he was squatting behind a bush. Great shooting, I thought, but his wife did kick up a fuss. One would think I was poaching without a licence the way she carried on.'

I dearly hope that that sort of thing never happened and I am not for one moment suggesting that the venerable President would have hunted people, but for a man who was besotted with birds and who set aside an astonishing 93 million hectares of wilderness for posterity in his own country, he did palpitate with excitement at the idea of shooting big game. He travelled clear across North America and as far afield as Africa to gratify his hunting bloodlust. On his modest African safari he hired 265 porters to carry back the trophy elephants, lions, rhino and the like that he had blasted.

At the Bushman camp our friends gave Django the fondest of all the farewells. He had never asked them one stupid question, could keep up with anything they did, and was not hobbling around that morning as if his legs were in irons. Moreover he was a real hero, having saved a hunter's life: the clan promised that he would be revered in a new dance and so become part of Bushman lore. I have no idea if that really happened, but I would like to believe that my dog is thus immortalised.

For all of us, it was an emotional departure. Somehow these folk with their simple lifestyle and easy manner had touched the heart-strings of our wealthy conservatives from the far side of the world. The Bushmen looked saddened to see us leave – perhaps because their source of entertainment was drying up – and there were tears in many American eyes. Fred had the moistest of all: he had left his spare film in the camp again.

In acknowledgement of the special experience Keeme had organised for us, we prepaid his school fees for his final year and placed an amount in a trust for tertiary education, should he desire it. I never asked him to organise a similar trip again. I felt that for his people one exposure to the western world was enough.

We set off to Xai-Xai in reflective mood.

Within minutes of our arrival at the airstrip a pack of happy dogs had gathered to greet their friend, but not a single person from the village showed even a passing interest in the rest of us. Django joined me in the back seat of the waiting Cessna to fly to Tsodilo Hills. Salome was left to pack up camp and get back to Maun, to meet up with us for the charter flight that would take our party out of the desert and on to a search for river Bushmen.

We were heading for the birthplace of man – at least according to !Kung legend ... and they should know if anybody does.

* * *

Flying into Tsodilo Hills, it is easy to see why this would be such a revered place. As far as the eye could see, with the very weathered exception of the nearby Aha Hills, the land was table-top flat, receding into a hazy distance without an undulation to break the horizon, except, that is, for three hills that tower above their surroundings like giants wading through a vast shallow lake. Scattered behind them are a few much smaller rocky outcrops. The !Kung believe that this is the spot where they were lowered on to the earth, which might be something for Erich von Däniken, a man who explained all of Earth's mysteries in terms of aliens, to take a closer look at.

The airstrip was an adventure on its own. Nobody maintained it and the wheels of donkey carts, the occasional government truck and the even more occasional visitors' vehicles had rutted the runway. We bounced alarmingly as we landed, lurching from side to side with both wings alternately coming perilously close to clipping the ground. Django gave me a pained look that said, 'Cut it out!' as though it were my fault. I did not relish the prospect of taking off from there again in two days' time.

Map was there to meet us. Now that sounds just as it should be, but to achieve this he, with George as his assistant, had had to negotiate 15 hours of bush trails, mostly through desperately thick sand, and he was the only driver. A major breakdown anywhere on the way could have spelt disaster. For a start, we would not have had any toilet paper for our camp.

In front of us brooded the Male, largest of the Tsodilo hills. By world standards it is a teenage pimple, but in the Kalahari it's a veritable giant. It is high enough for the British SAS to have used it for rock climbing experience in the past and it demands respect, having claimed an SAS trainee who plummeted to his death. Next to the Male, smaller and more open, is the Female. She, as the most fertile of all the hills, is adorned with about 1 500 rock paintings, some quite exquisite, many others rather plain. Intriguingly, a good number of these are difficult to explain.

Actually, they are all a puzzle. We can really only guess at what they might symbolise, because the last artist who may have been able to tell us was shot. He was strolling on somebody's farm during the middle part of the last century, fingering his little selection of paints and, no doubt, planning his next masterpiece when he was spotted and gunned down for trespassing.

The people who have devoted their entire lives to trying to unravel Bushman art don't help a lot, frankly. They tell us that the !Kung Bushmen were not rock artists, and that these paintings must have been created by the |Xam people from the Cape who were hunted to extinction in the period following the arrival of the Europeans, so they cannot help much in this debate. However, they do not tell us how the |Xam travelled to Tsodilo, 1 900 kilometres from home, and how they created so many paintings, which span a great length of time, and then disappeared, to leave the !Kung scratching their heads in appreciation of their artistic skills. I unloaded this information on the group and then took Django and my developing headache for a walk.

A short distance from our camp was a painting that gave me a greater headache. It was of a whale, not so eyebrow-raising in itself – but this one is over 600 kilometres from the nearest ocean, which washes on to the wild and inhospitable Skeleton Coast of Namibia. To reach this puzzling piece of rock art from the sea requires the crossing of the Namib Desert, one of the planet's driest. Perhaps this confirms the theory that the |Xam did come all the way up from the Cape after all, to teach the !Kung about the lovely beaches and the whale-spotting opportunities they were missing.

The David Livingstone of Tsodilo Hills was Sir Laurens van der Post – the man who brought the Bushmen to world attention. Significantly, he told of inadvertently angering the spirits en route to the Hills by taking part in a hunt without asking the clan's permission to enter the sacred area, as well as by taking water without permission.

These acts dishonoured the gods and everything started going wrong – the camera equipment repeatedly and mysteriously packed up, bees attacked their camp with monotonous regularity, and fear entered the old soldier's heart that the deities would start to tamper with his Land Rovers and leave them stranded. To placate them he wrote them a letter of apology, persuaded the entire group to sign it and buried it at the foot of his favourite paintings. They then left in a rush – just in case – although the local clan had told him that the gods were no longer annoyed with him and that he was fortunate; in times gone by he and his party would all have been killed.

Despite the relenting of Gaoxa, I still offered a silent prayer to the Bushman divinity, just in case. We never suffered a single misfortune.

I went back to camp and poured myself a weak lukewarm scotch. The ice had melted and the beer was warm.

'Will it rain again tonight?' asked John, eyeing gathering storm clouds.

'It never rains in the Kalahari in August. I thought I had already made that clear,' I replied, looking skywards nervously.

Our tents hung like mosquito nets from a tree and were not waterproof. Map, who usually slept in the open by the fire, decided to share my accommodation because he believed, correctly, that it was going to rain and, incorrectly, that he would stay drier in the tent. Somewhere during the middle of the night he wished that he had slept elsewhere. It poured heavily and the hanging contraption did not exclude a drop of rain, which was neatly retained like a baby's pool, by virtue of its waterproof groundsheet. The water trapped inside the tent was almost deep enough to swim laps. Django, who had slept in the car, was bone dry and very perky in the morning.

After breakfast we took a walk around the Hills, still a bit stiffly, I confess – the night's soaking had not helped – and saw the famous Van der Post panel with its fine giraffes and eland. I wondered briefly whether I should see if I could unearth his buried note, but decided, as there was every chance of annoying the gods, I would not.

!Xowie was to be our guide. He was the head of the clan of 40 or so who lived at the Hills on a more or less permanent basis. Despite the first signs of grey in his beard he was probably only around 40 years old and every bit as fit as the youngsters. I had met him on regular visits to the Hills over the past five years, but had cemented our friendship when Salome and I had spent a week on our own there over New Year's Eve two years before. While the world partied, we had climbed to the top of the outcrops and, on a moonlit night, looked out over the endless Kalahari and listened to the stars whisper to each other. Of all the fresh new starts to life that a new year encourages, none was as poignant as that one.

!Xowie welcomed me as an old friend and then greeted Django in much the same way that Willie Phillips had – reserved but with restrained respect. Django liked this man at once.

'Today I want to show you the secret waterholes. Come.'

I understood the implied honour and trust. I had clearly not displeased Gaoxa.

'Can I bring my friends?'

He hesitated. 'Yes, but they must do as I say.'

We walked north along the western side of the Female and saw paintings in abundance that I never knew existed. It is likely that the oldest of these are 26 000 years old, possibly more, and that they form some of the oldest examples on earth. !Xowie suddenly left the path and started to scramble up a steep rock face. We all followed. Halfway up there was a birdbath-sized waterhole.

'This one only holds rain water, but it doesn't dry because the sun doesn't reach it.'

He went on to show us one after another. These desert hills literally bubbled with water if you knew where to look.

'They will fill again. We can drink as much as we like.'

'Should we not ask Gaoxa's permission before we drink the water?'

He stared at me for a long time. 'You are ready. I will show you the secret pool.'

We went off to perform a strange ritual. There is a permanent pool on the western side of the hill that is said to be occupied by a monstrous horned snake. This was true, our guide told us; he had seen it himself.

'It is the most important place in all the hills,' he said, 'because it is the entrance that God uses to get in and out of his home deep inside the Female.'

Abruptly !Xowie veered off the path and scrambled up another steep rock face. Suddenly he bent down and picked up a handful of stones, which he threw high into the rocks above him.

'Why are you doing that?' I asked.

'To warn the huge snake with big horns that lives in the water here.' He raised his arms as high as they could go to indicate how big the horns were. 'You must let him know that you are coming or he will catch you and eat you.'

'How big is this snake?'

'He can reach from here to the road and maybe further.' (The road was 100 metres away.)

We cautiously approached the area above where he had thrown the stones. A cave was set in the rock and its floor sloped at an angle of 45 degrees, allowing rainwater to wash in and run down to a pool at the bottom. The approach was steep and had been worn smooth by the hooves of animals that had gone to drink there over the millennia. To reach the water we would have had to walk very carefully and I did not want anyone to land up in the dark liquid with a monster like that on guard.

!Xowie kept us at a respectful distance.

'The snake with horns protects the entrance for Gaoxa,' he explained. 'No one is allowed in that cave and we must take care not to go too close in case we anger our God.'

Django could clearly sense or smell something there that made him feel uncomfortable; he came and sat close to me, pressing against my leg. I remembered how he had sensed the bad witchdoctor in Maun and wondered what could have triggered his apprehension in this revered place.

Instead of resting during the siesta period after lunch, I left Map in charge of camp and returned with Django to the cave. The legend of the giant snake intrigued me, and I wondered what we would see if we approached stealthily and did not throw warning stones.

We saw the horned snake.

After quietly climbing to within sight of the cave we were electrified by the sight of a python sunning itself on the rocks next to the entrance. This was not just any python; this was a massive specimen that I would guess measured a full six metres and was large enough to take an adult human. Perhaps that is what Django had smelt earlier – no wonder he was nervous. Pythons are regarded by the Bushmen as intermediaries between worlds and this one seemed to be doing just that as it guarded the entrance to God's home. They are also the custodians of water, and this one was lying right next to the largest waterhole for 40 kilometres in any direction. This serpent would be 25 years old, maybe older, and would have used the pool for a long time – longer than !Xowie and his people had been around the Hills, so it was unsurprising that old myths were reinforced. I could see no horns on him, but his 'spurs' – vestigial femurs from a time when his ancestors walked on legs – would leave clear scrape marks in soft sand.

Pythons, herpetologists say, rarely attack humans without provocation. I am one of those rare people who has been attacked by a python without provocation. As a 17-year-old, I was walking alone in the bush along the banks of the Limpopo River in South Africa when a huge python dropped from a tree some distance away, and then crashed through the brush aiming directly at me. I felt targeted and paid no heed to the injunction 'Don't run whatever you do.' I fled as fast as I could, which in this case was, happily, quickly enough. I was on the menu that day but the food proved too fast for the diner.

I wanted a close-up peek into the python's lair but I was not keen to attempt to outrun a monster down the slippery rocks, so I tossed a few small stones in its direction and watched as it slithered into the water. When my eyes had adjusted to the gloom in the cavern, I saw the second part of the myth. In the pool was a dead male kudu with his large spiralled horns protruding above the surface. The unfortunate animal had obviously gone to drink, slipped, its feet unsuited to the hard, smooth surface, and slid into the water where it had drowned because it was unable to get enough purchase to pull itself clear. On the other hand, as it was still bloated, this particular specimen could not have been the original source of the myth.

Having had the good fortune to see both the massive snake and the horns I did not overstay my welcome – it would not be good to upset Gaoxa now that I knew where he lived and understood his security system. I returned to camp to write him a little note.

In the afternoon we went to see the proof of man's arrival on this planet. When our first ancestor was lowered on to the Hills, cattle were sent for him to eat. Proof of this is embedded for posterity in the rock, where an animal had stepped on a malleable surface and its print had fossilised into the rock face. Some say it is not the footprint of a cow but that of a dinosaur. For me, the remarkable thing is that at some recent geological point the rock was impressionable enough for a large animal to leave its mark.

Having shaken our heads in wonderment yet again, we visited !Xowie's people – the local !Kung family who had been brought to the Hills as a tourist attraction 10 years previously by a commercial tour company. Though I was very happy to be related to the Bushmen near Xai-Xai, I was forced to reject any relationship with these squalid characters. They had lost pride in themselves and their ancestors while sitting, literally, in the shadow of great achievement. The huts were the same but the people were filthy, their karosses torn and soiled, and litter from tourist handouts lay discarded where it had fallen. The last group to visit were apparently Italians who could not resist handing out lipstick to the women, with the result that when we arrived, hoping to see some dignified relatives of our 'wild clan', we found listless men selling cheap 'authentic' trinkets and jaded women, their faces smeared with bright red lipstick. Django would not even enter their compound and lay patiently on the opposite side of the road until we were done. And done we were.

There was much tut-tutting in the evening over the plight of these poor people, as well as those at the Xai-Xai cattle post, and how we could save the wild Bushmen. I felt another headache coming on and went to bed. During the night a gust of wind howled through the caves, creating a sound that resembled a weird incantation in the hills – the departed soul of a witchdoctor, the local people would say, but I knew better. Gaoxa was wishing us a safe trip to the Okavango on the morrow.

*　*　*

The next morning we flew to Jedibe in search of the river Bushmen – or, more accurately, in search of the man who claimed to be the only living river Bushman. His name is easy to remember, Keikanamang (see, I told you), and he lived in an area called Xichera. To find him – the last of his kind – luck would have to be on our side, but at worst, searching for him would mean for us a day floating about in the Okavango. The truth is that there were other river Bushmen living in the Delta as well as in the Caprivi, most of whom had assimilated with the local Bantu tribes and were not easily distinguishable.

The airstrip in Jedibe village was in better condition than the one at Tsodilo Hills but it was disconcerting to have people and their livestock strolling on the strip as we landed, seemingly impervious to the danger of having their heads lopped off by a spinning propeller. Salome had flown in too; Django was thrilled to see her and set about telling her of all his experiences. It was remarkable to see him stare unblinkingly into her eyes, willing her to pick up on his telepathic messages.

That afternoon we were scheduled to take a three-hour mokoro ride starting at three o'clock, having reserved the whole of the next day to search for Keikanamang by power boat. We had tea at a precise 2.45 pm then climbed aboard our *mekoro* (the plural of *mokoro*) dead on time. Not even Fred dared to be late.

Apart from our group there was a honeymoon couple who had been at the lodge for the best part of a week.

'What is the little doggie's name?' the woman schmaltzed, as she rubbed her husband's forearm affectionately.

'Django,' I told her.

'Django of the Okavango?' she asked.

Up to that point, it had never occurred to me that Django rhymed with Okavango. I started to mull over the coincidences – born in Okavango River Lodge, he had already experienced the Okavango by plane, car, boat, mokoro, canoe and on foot. He had swum in it, crossed crocodile-infested channels and trudged across its drier inner regions; he had camped and lodged in it and slept under its stars; he had befriended its inhabitants, feasted on its fruits and even peed on it. This was his Eden.

'Yes, he is indeed Django of the Okavango,' I answered, my chest puffed with pride. Django grinned self-consciously and then rose, stretched, trotted over to a bush and lifted a leg as if to show he was without a doubt master of this domain.

A mokoro seats two adults comfortably, except in the case of Big John, who needed a boat of his own. Salome, Django and I shared one, and I had packed all our camera gear, because I wanted to photograph the water flowers that were blooming in profusion. It was a blissfully restful afternoon as we floated lazily past a cornucopia of aquatic plants, while Django stood in the prow and did his best to catch them all, often nearly overbalancing. Purple water lilies made stunning images in the bright sunlight – they also, apparently, are hallucinogenic when soaked in red wine, and according to the ancient Egyptians, act as a relaxant when boiled in water. The Okavango was so peaceful that I required neither of those properties right then.

Django stared down at his own image in the clear water, his furry face and its cheeky curl framed by blue skies and white clouds. Water lettuce streamed on the current, its yellow flowers floating on the surface, and Django willed me to pick one and offer it to someone to sniff. Once their nose was presented to the flower, a quick squeeze on the bulb would turn it into a water pistol for the unwary, and my dog, who had bitten into a passing one and been surprised when it squirted in his mouth, loved the reaction of astonishment that this always caused. Small fish darted about and ubiquitous dragon and damselflies, flying in tandem, occasionally landed on his nose. Water chestnuts, with their distinctive coarsely-toothed, diamond-shaped leaves, offered their hard triangular nuts to be eaten raw, while the kernel could be roasted. Their faint white water 'snowflakes' looked as out of place in this down-to-earth environment as would fine china at a sports pub.

Then a tiny painted reed frog with remarkable wild dog patterning hopped onto Salome's chest. She has a frog phobia – something she cannot explain and tries hard, usually unsuccessfully, to deal with. I expected a sudden violent reaction – one that could easily cause the mokoro to tip and throw us and our gear into the river.

'Steady girl, steady,' I said as calmly as I could. 'It's only a small harmless painted reed frog and we have all our expensive camera equipment here.'

'Then get it off me,' she demanded in a quavering voice.

'I'm going to turn around slowly and grab it. Just don't budge,' I pleaded.

She did not move, seemingly frozen in her fear, and I picked up the beautiful mottled brown-and-white frog and placed it on a passing reed, with a recommendation that it should be more careful about whom it leapt upon next time.

As the sun sank lower, reflections mirrored the still, backwater ponds. Perfect double images of the papyrus, reeds and bulrushes, fringing the darkening skies above, floated past as frogs started their strident evening chorus. Tall chimney-sweep miscanthus, their long stick-like stems topped with brown seed tufts, bent over in the current to make surreal drawings on the water. Pygmy geese bobbed gently on their reflected doubles while black crakes, with their psychedelic bills and bright red legs, darted in and out of the papyrus. Even Django stopped his game to watch the idyllic scene play out before him. Our poler, also clearly moved by the moment, hummed softly. A fish eagle announced its territory from a nearby bush and the waters and sky turned to flaming orange as the sun set behind the tall riverine trees. Fish, possibly the start of the barbel run, churned the shallows around us as we pulled ashore. Nothing could have been more tranquil.

*   *   *

Next morning we set off on our search in two powerboats down papyrus-lined channels. Django stood at the bow like a figurehead, eager to see what each twist in the winding river would bring. The wind whipped through his shaggy coat and water sprayed into his face. And we found Keikanamang. He was living on an island with his family. Taller and darker than a !Kung, he probably had some Bantu blood and, because his wife was of the local Bayei tribe, the children running around would be far from pure Bushmen. Quaintly, he had a fridge on his island. It was an electric fridge, far from a power source, so it just stood there quietly rusting – a beacon of aspiration. He had laid out his fishing nets (with undersized holes, I noted) and we had to be careful not to foul them in our boats' propellers as we nosed our way in towards the shady clearing where he was working. Drying racks made from silver-leaf terminalia branches covered much of the glade, indicating that fishing in this remote part of the Okavango was good, though it probably would not be sustainable – even for him and his clan – if he continued to net illegally and for commercial purposes. If someone wished to take a photo of Keikanamang or his family he would hold out his hand for payment, and if they asked a question, out shot the hand again. After a while I tired of the charade and went to join Django, who after a quick inspection of the drying racks, had retired to the boat. Once the others had seen enough, we moved off to a sandbank to have a swim and a picnic. The lunch provided by the lodge was impressive – home-baked bread, cold meats, salads, boiled eggs, muffins, cakes and a variety of soft drinks, beers and wine. We feasted in paradise.

That night we lingered, chatting, after the meal and Django lay quietly between Salome and me, listening and taking in the changed atmosphere. Over farewell drinks Big John, bless him, returned to his subject and reiterated that he was going to try to save our Bushmen.

I found it hard to be positive about this – powerful forces for change, I feared, would rout his earnest efforts. In this situation globalisation will inexorably take its course and our Earth will be left the poorer by the cultural extinction of its oldest people.

8

WHERE SMOKE THUNDERS

Django's first international boundary crossing was a momentous occasion in his young life. Of course, he already had his own travel documents just for journeys inside Botswana, to pass through the many veterinary fences that crisscross the country. Current rabies inoculations, the three-in-one parvo jab and quantum and galaxy vaccinations were required, which could presumably have prepared him for intergalactic space flights. A vet then had to clear him and issue him with a 'permission to travel' document, which, in turn, required a State Veterinary Officer's stamp – and even then this permit was only valid for a single internal trip. The red tape became infinitely more complex, however, when we needed to cross an international border – although, thankfully, that permit was valid for three months.

Our pup had had to learn how to buck the bureaucracy occasionally. It required no more than a nod towards Salome's outsized handbag, which she kept at her feet, and he would leap inside its cavernous interior, to hide there until we had passed through a checkpoint. An 'OK, boy!' was enough for him to emerge from his concealment and resume his former position. This time he would be accompanying us to Zimbabwe, however, and we had made certain that his passport was up to date and correct in every detail.

Border crossings in the 1980s were remarkably challenging. No matter that our own documentation was in order, the vehicle was demonstrably mine, that we were not smuggling or exceeding our foreign exchange quota, that we'd had all our prophylactic shots, and that Django's papers were current, I still dreaded putting us into the hands of a person with the power to make life miserable for no evident reason. At that time the best that could be said of relations between South Africa and all her neighbours was that they were locked into a diplomatic war of attrition, with apartheid still firmly entrenched and ferociously defended. Crossing into Zimbabwe on South African passports was always uncomfortable.

To compound the problem, a group of saboteurs from South Africa, posing as safari operators, had recently been arrested after illegally crossing into Botswana from Zimbabwe. As I was a known operator of safaris, I was treated with a certain suspicion by border officials, who saw it as their patriotic duty to be as obstructive as their seemingly un-limited powers would allow them. Their eyes lit up whenever they fell upon a hapless South African safari guide – and if he was escorting an entire family of these denizens of that hated haven of apartheid, their expressions would glow in eager anticipation of an early taste of heaven.

This time I was accompanied by my wife, her mother and brother, and we were to be that early taste – this, despite such regular use on my part of the Kazungula border post between Botswana and Zimbabwe that I practically lived there. Victoria Falls was an essential component of the safaris I had guided over the past seven years, and at least twice each month I had been subjected to the whims of the customs officials at this tiny, forgotten frontier post. Kazungula was the furthermost border from the Botswana Customs and Immigration Headquarters in Gaborone, and was apparently used to rid Head Office of their drunks and misfits. There, not pitching for work or misappropriating signifi-cant sums of national funds were not considered as grounds for dis-missal, while displaying overt rudeness to foreign visitors or being paralytic while on duty were hardly concerns at all. Head Office relied on lethargy and the unreliable telephone connections to ensure they were not bothered too often.

Perched out in the blistering sun, the cheerless, shoebox-sized Botswana Customs and Immigration building gave the unsettling impression that it had been designed as a medium for pitiless and abnormal punishment. No more than four people could shoehorn themselves into it at the same time – and even then they could not raise their elbows to wipe the perspiration off their brows, let alone find space enough to fill out the forms. If there were more than four victims hoping to cross, the dawdlers would find themselves outside in the midday heat, at toasty temperatures that were unimaginable in most parts of the world – and they were, perhaps, the more fortunate because it was 10 degrees warmer in the shoebox. In the middle of the room was a battered counter that looked as though it had been the victim of an artillery attack during the siege of Mafeking. The top was so deeply gouged that it was not smooth enough to use for filling in the immigration form without poking holes through the flimsy paper. The hinges for the flap, through which the officials had to exit or enter, had long since disintegrated and as a consequence every time an officer left or staggered back in, they invariably dropped the heavy plank on somebody's toe.

The first tactic of the authorities in their war of attrition was invariably to slouch at their posts like toads in semi-hibernation, and watch dispassionately through half-closed eyelids at the room crammed with eager tourists, all flushed with the prospect of new adventure. Rising slowly, the officials would make a point of stretching each limb from its dormancy before taking their departure from the pokey room, dropping the trap door on someone's shoe. They would disappear for 20 minutes, presumably for a cooling beer or two, while the temperature inside the hothouse soared at a rate that matched rising tempers. When they returned, their beery breath mingled with the odour of people confined in a sweatbox for far too long. The next ploy was to set about rejecting all the completed papers because they were full of holes. Everyone would be forced outside to find a flatter surface on which to fill in a new form – inevitably a vehicle bonnet, which by that time was hot enough to be used as a soldering iron. The newly completed forms would then be reluctantly but speedily processed, as it was time for another beer. Once done with Immigration, it was the Customs officer's turn – if he was there and not outside enjoying a cold one.

'Vehicle papers?'

'Insurance?'

'Money?'

'How much? Show me!'

'Open the boot.' 'What is this?' 'A wheel spanner!' 'What do you do with it?' 'Why did you not declare it?'

This could take from 10 seconds (if he was thirsty) to two hours (if he was bored and in need of entertainment).

Finally, having worked their way through the border post, victims would climb muttering into their vehicles, and drive a few hundred metres via no-man's-land into the arms of Robert Gabriel Mugabe's new Customs and Immigration force. Here, the customs officials' specialty was to search every single item in the vehicle, as well as the trailer, while paying particular attention to ladies' lace underwear – which would be held high between two fingers for all to admire. After an hour and a half of this baiting, they would tire of it and an unexpectedly cheery official would bid punch-drunk tourists an enjoyable stay – having just spent a considerable part of the day ensuring precisely the opposite.

Over the years I had avoided conflict here, due possibly to small incentives. Newspapers, even weeks old, were welcome gifts, as were cigarettes, milk and freshly baked bread. My crossings became quicker, even pleasant at times, as the costs soared from a cold coke to a case of them. Nevertheless, I was the envy of many of the other guides.

* * *

Prior to this family visit, I had twice crossed the border uneventfully over the past four days. Furthermore, Salome was now allowed to travel freely beyond Botswana's borders for the first time in six months because her revalidated work and resident's permits had finally arrived. This being Django's first international sojourn, his passport – the record of his many inoculations – had been packed, together with his bandana, water bowl, blue blanket, a selection of chewy toys and some dog biscuits. I confidently looked forward to the crossing.

We pulled up to the Botswana border in sweltering heat. There was a desultory individual, whom I had not seen before, reclining on the steps to the sweatbox nibbling at a plate of stiff maize meal and a few oily sausages. Django looked at the food with undisguised interest. He was clearly hungry. The Immigration officer set the dish down, forced himself to his feet and moved unsteadily into the customs post. He was wearing an unbuttoned regulation navy jacket as issued by the Immigration Department but none of his other garments distinguished him from the drunks who spilled out of local pubs at closing time. His associate from Customs then came out from the closet-sized room at the rear of the building that passed for their office. He was more formally dressed, but the way that he and his companion had twice staggered into the counter suggested a recent familiarity with a substance that perhaps Head Office would not have approved of. The combined alcoholic aroma emanating from the two put me in mind of a party I once went to where everybody had a half-jack of brandy emptied over them at the door to ensure that they would not dare leave the celebrations before the sun rose, in case they ran into a police road block.

'Dumela, Rra, I'm back already,' I began, squirming up to the Immigration officer, 'but today I'm off duty and taking my wife and her family to see the Falls.'

He threw a bleary stare vaguely in my direction, but failed to focus on anything, swayed gently and said nothing. I handed the passports over and he peered at them blankly, as if he could not for the life of him remember what he should do with the documents. Then, as if a light bulb had suddenly come on in his head, he opened mine.

'Where is your residence permit?' he slurred.

'Oh no!' muttered Salome in a stage whisper, as she clutched her head in distress. 'I forgot mine.'

'Wonderful,' I spat from the side of my mouth as I handed over my permit.

He stamped the passport and picked up Salome's. 'Permit?'

'I'm afraid I haven't brought it with me, Rra. It's only just arrived and I haven't got used to carrying it with me yet. We never used to have to carry them separately before because they were always stamped in the passport,' my wife answered.

He didn't look up. He simply started counting the days that she had been in the country, lost track and started again and lost track and started yet again. Giving up the uneven struggle he said, 'You have been in Botswana more than 90 days. You must get out of the country.'

He picked up a large red PROHIBITED IMMIGRANT stamp.

'Yes, I have been in Botswana for more than 90 days. Look at my passport and you will see that I had residence permits stamped in it that were valid for the last four years. It is my renewal that I have left behind, because before that we never needed to carry our permits. It was stamped in our passports until the recent change of law.'

'You are in the country illegally because you cannot show me your permits,' he insisted and fumbled for an empty page to stamp.

'Wait! Don't stamp, please. Could you kindly phone Salome, a lady who has the same name as me, at the Immigration office in Maun? She will tell you that I have a permit because she personally delivered it to my house last week. She knows me well because there are very few people in Botswana with the name Salome.'

'Where's your permit?'

'I told you; I left it at home in Maun.'

'Then you don't have one,' and he raised the red stamp again.

'I do. Really I do. Please just phone Maun Immigration. They will verify it for you. Please, Rra,' she pleaded. 'Why can't you just pick up the phone and dial? It will only take a minute.'

'I can't do that. And you can't come back to Botswana.'

This was all too much for Salome – she had been kept a virtual prisoner for six months, unable to travel until her permits came through, and now she was being thrown out of the country, seemingly for ever. She started sobbing. If this was supposed to soften the heart of the Immigration officer it failed dismally, as he seemed to consider it a victory. It did soften mine, however: I tried to put my arm around her but she shook me off. Django nudged her calves but even that did not console her.

'Don't worry,' I said comfortingly. 'I'll get your permit sent to Kasane while we are having fun in the Falls. Just give me the vehicle papers and I will clear them.'

She looked at me with weepy eyes. 'They're left behind with my permit in Maun.'

'Well then, the car stays here,' announced the Customs officer, who had clearly enjoyed the show.

I lost it. I thumped the war-ravaged counter with my open hand, which I instantly regretted as I felt a sharp pain shoot through my wrist.

The office fell silent.

The Customs officer sat back gleefully in his chair, looked directly at me in a moment of clear-headedness and said deliberately, even calmly, 'Aah, now we have a real problem.' He caressed a small section of the counter lovingly. 'You have assaulted government property and I am going to have to report you.'

'I have assaulted what? You couldn't damage this thing any more if you dropped a bloody great atomic bomb on it.'

'Aah, now you are swearing at me.'

'I am not bloody well swearing at you. I am swearing at this stupid counter.'

'Aah, now you are calling me stupid.'

'If the shoe fits, wear it.'

'What is wrong with my shoes?'

The Immigration man suddenly spied Hans, Salome's brother, standing behind me, arms folded across his chest, with a short-back-and-sides haircut of the kind favoured at the time by the Afrikaans universities. 'You are a South African policeman. I think you are a spy.'

'No, I'm not,' Hans retorted indignantly. 'I am a Mathematics student at the University of Pretoria.'

'Students in South Africa have long hair. You are a policeman. I will call the CID.'

This was an interesting twist, I thought. Salome was to be deported, but would have to walk because the car was impounded and had to stay in Kasane; I was about to be frog-marched off to the police station to face charges of insult as well as malicious damage to property; and Hans was apparently to be handed over to the CID as a suspected spy. It couldn't get much worse.

At that critical moment, Django entered the room with a sausage in his mouth. The Immigration man stared speechlessly as his lunch was, with some delicacy, dropped at his feet in what looked like a peace offering.

'That dog,' he finally stammered, 'is eating my food.'

'No, he's not,' I pointed out. 'He has brought it for you.'

'In his mouth? I can't eat that now.'

I had to agree with him. Our staff would not even wash a dog blanket without wearing gloves because they consider dogs diseased.

'I will kill that dog,' he spluttered.

'Not before I kill you.' Even as I spoke I knew I shouldn't have said that.

'Ah ... ah ... ah. Now you want to kill me.'

Absolutely I did, but by shutting up I showed my first acumen of the day.

Then redemption came in its unlikeliest form. My diminutive mother-in-law, Marda, who all this while had stood wide-eyed behind us clasping her handbag to her solar plexus and watching in growing horror as her family was sentenced to various forms of banishment, decided to enter the fray and with a wrathful vengeance elbowed her way to the counter.

'Do you know, young man, that I am a Seventh Day Adventist, and that Lady Ruth Khama (the former President's widow) belongs to our church and she will definitely hear all about this? Where I come from people don't drink when they are on duty and they are respectful to visitors and you should be ashamed of yourself and furthermore ...'

Salome and I both tried to stop her, expecting the worst now, but she silenced us with a stern matronly look. For a full 20 minutes she lectured two increasingly sheepish officers. They even threw furtive glances of sympathy my way, before they meekly ushered us all out of the office and into our vehicle without pressing charges or resorting to the giant red stamp.

I nearly kissed the old dear.

A hundred metres down the road I saw a Zimbabwean official saun-tering towards us with a sneer on his face that implied 'Now it's my time for fun.'

'I have had enough for one frigging afternoon.' I snarled. 'Don't you dare try it!' And he didn't.

When we reached the town of Victoria Falls we phoned Barry in Maun and asked him to locate the missing permits and papers and fly them to Kasane, the nearest town. Only then could we settle down to enjoy ourselves.

*　　*　　*

Django revelled in his visit to the Falls. He did not fuss about its name, or its title as one of the seven natural wonders of the world, but im-mersed himself in the experience. There was no entrance fee to this heritage site and, indeed, no figure of authority interested enough to chase him away. Our dog trotted around bursting with curiosity; he admired the majestic views and lingered longer at the Devil's Cataract than any of the others. That, of course, may have had something to do with the two smartly attired Japanese executives who, as soon as they saw him, smiled broadly and called him over to share their ham-burgers. With a glance back at me for approval, he indulged in a tasty snack. He then followed them to the wet and slippery edge of the preci-pice where, in true African style, there were no unsightly barricades to prevent careless visitors from tumbling into the seething cauldron of the Boiling Pot far below. As he peered downwards, his ears drooped in alarm and he took a cautious step backwards. Not so the Japanese. They took photo after photo, each getting progressively closer to the brink until, one after the other, they fell over the rim. That did not really happen, of course, but Prince Charles, with a royal touch of morbid humour, deemed it a most picturesque venue for committing suicide. Human suicide apparently happens here on a sufficiently de-pressing scale for all records to be suppressed, but every four years on average a hippo gets terribly disheartened, or alternatively too close to the edge, and tumbles over the lip – and even the occasional elephant takes the plunge in front of a crowd of tourists as they yell, 'Don't do it, don't do it!'

The Zambezi, once it plummets over the Falls, decants itself into a narrow gorge with towering vertical walls and then, in a wild dervish dance, it surges and crashes over a series of rock formations, creating the wildest rapids in the white-water rafting world. That, at least, is the claim of the professional rafters who spend their lives running rapids on major rivers around the world. The constricting gorge, with its serpentine twists and turns, alternatively exposes or hides its rocky bottom as the floods ebb and flow.

The next morning Hans decided to try white-water rafting and Django and I climbed down the gorge to see him off. Our two senior Japanese businessmen were being ushered onto one of the rafts. They were wide-eyed with alarm but seemed unable to escape. The bar later that afternoon buzzed with the news that some glitch of translation had them white-water rafting when they had in fact booked the guided champagne breakfast cruise above the Falls. It is the ultimate decadence to glide in the calm headwaters just upstream of the roaring cataract, with a man to steer you from danger and to ply you with glasses of South Africa's finest sparkling wine, chilled to perfection and interspersed with plates of delectable treats. The image of these two grave gentlemen arriving in their elegant business suits saying 'Ah ... boat trip' and finding themselves plunged into raging torrents in their fine attire had us falling from our bar stools.

Having seen Hans launched, Django and I went for a walk into town. There he saw his first train, which alarmed him when it hooted loudly at us as it thundered across the road, and he took a few cautious backward steps. It had never occurred to me that a train would be a novelty for my little companion, but in Botswana there were no railways north of Francistown. I enjoyed a cup of good coffee at Wimpy while Django demolished a bowl of milk, courtesy of the waiter. With drinks finished we wandered around the modest supermarket, admiring how well stocked it was in comparison to Maun's stores. Then I felt a nudge on my ankle and looked down to see Django staring up at me.

'What's up, boy?' I asked.

For an answer he trotted down the aisle and stopped in front of a basket filled with rubber balls. Then he looked up at me again, clearly inviting me to buy one for him. His joy when I reached down and selected a colourful one was obvious. My dog had learned to shop.

After wandering around the craft market it was time to rendezvous with Salome and Marda at the Victoria Falls Hotel for morning tea and cakes, and it was here that Django met and charmed Oddwell, the legendary doorman, who presided, with attitude, over the grand entrance to this celebrated establishment. He was a giant of a man, impeccably attired at all times in a bright red tailored coat, plastered with lapel badges donated by guests from around the world. His outfit was his pride and joy and he would gladly explain the origins of all the shiny metal decorations to anyone who had a morning to listen to him. Each one held a special meaning for him, and when he heard that Django's ancestors hailed from Nepal he selected one from that country, removed it from his breast and pinned it on our dog's bandana. No greater honour could have been bestowed.

'This is a fine dog and he deserves to wear a button from Oddwell!'

The booming voice followed us as Django proudly trotted through the imposing high-ceilinged foyer and into the extensive and immaculate gardens, where tables groaned with an endless display of cakes, éclairs, muffins, scones and, inevitably, cucumber sandwiches.

*   *   *

That afternoon Django became a hero again: he saved my wife's life. Marda had elected to enjoy a quiet afternoon reading and I happily found the pub filled with friends, pulled up a bar stool and joined them. Salome decided to take a long walk along the Zambezi with Django, and to do some birding. Her inquisitive companion enthusiastically scrambled among the trees and rocks with her, exploring a section of the riverbank that few ever penetrate.

It was a couple of hours later, when I was in good form chatting freely to anyone prepared to listen to me, that a visibly shaken and ashen-faced Salome appeared at the door with Django, who seemed unusually chipper. She came inside and sat down heavily next to me; the young dog lay on the floor between us.

'A long pink gin and tonic, please,' she ordered from the barman.

Once it arrived and she had taken a large gulp, she turned to me and calmly said, 'I nearly died on that walk.'

The bar stilled attentively, even though she was not speaking loudly.

'I shudder when I think how close it was. We were walking along the riverbank, when we came to a small bay bordered by hippo grass. The path followed the edge of the grass and Django was sniffing around there, just ahead of me. Suddenly he stopped and pointed with his front paw, as he does. I knew by the urgent way he kept looking back that there was something there that worried him greatly. Thinking it was possibly a monitor lizard, I moved up behind him to see, when a black mamba reared up less than a metre in front of us. It was enormous and it towered over him. I froze in terror – I could see we were too close to escape if it struck. Django stood his ground and never took his eyes off the bloody thing, while I managed to back away slowly. I couldn't call him for fear that he would be distracted and give the snake the opportunity to strike. They seemed to be summing each other up, somehow assessing their own chances of success if either were the first to attack. Finally the mamba sank back into the grass and retreated.'

She took another gulp from her glass. 'I would have stepped on it if Django had not warned me and I probably would not have made it back here.'

As she stopped speaking, the bar erupted as people told increasingly vivid and troubling stories of mamba attacks, each of which highlighted just how lucky Salome was to be alive. I listened for a while and then went to the kitchen, where I ordered a large T-bone steak, medium rare, for my hero.

Salome had not been melodramatic. Black mambas, I mused, have a well-deserved reputation as the most fearsome of the snakes in our region because they can inject large amounts of a powerful, fast-acting neurotoxin with such speed that the victims are often not aware that they have been attacked. Because they can raise themselves upright and remain perfectly balanced with only one third of their body on the ground, strikes are often inflicted above waist height. Once bitten, the victim feels dizzy within minutes, salivates but cannot swallow and starts slurring and falling over a lot. So far, it doesn't sound too different to a night at the Duck – but breathing problems rapidly ensue, followed by palpitations, paralysis and death.

I turned back to the kitchen and ordered a cheesy sauce for the steak.

* * *

The 'Flight of Angels' flip in a small plane over the Falls was another new experience for Django. The 15-minute flight affords a stunning overview, not only of the Falls and the deep gorge below the drop but also of the flatness of the plain that surrounds this spectacle, but for any pilot who flew it day in and day out, it must soon have lost its attraction. The routine was rigid and dreary for the bored aviator, who would have done this four times every working hour for most of his stint in Vic Falls. After a laconically delivered, expressionless, staccato introduction, he would trundle down the airstrip and, once airborne, turn towards the Falls, bank sharply to the left, complete two circuits, bank sharply to the right and perform two more, so those on the other side of the plane could take their pictures. Finished with the Falls, he would fly straight and level upstream to allow 195 seconds of game viewing before turning back to the airstrip on the edge of town to pick up the next group.

When I asked our pilot whether he minded if Django came along, he became animated and so delighted to have any break from routine that I thought for one alarming moment he might hug me. I was placed in the co-pilot's seat with our dog on my lap; he immediately placed his front paws on the dashboard before transferring them to the door the next moment, as he peered out of both windscreen and side window with equal intensity.

When we banked sharply to the left I shut my eyes and held on for dear life. Not so Django. He strained to see from that perspective, and had no sense that airplanes should not fly with one wing directly above the other. So enchanted was the pilot with his enthralled little passenger that he gave us an extra circuit on each side.

Then came a suggestion: 'I haven't done this for a while, but would you like to follow the gorge for a little way downstream instead of going over the Park?'

The unanimous answer was yes.

He dropped low towards the ground, banked sharply again and with one wing virtually in the gorge we did some impressive low-level aerobatic flying that had me turning shades of green, and my mother-in-law clutching her handbag ever tighter. Hans was clearly tense, while Salome lit up with the thrill of it. Django simply continued to leap from window to window to get the best view. The hairpin bends of the gorge made the flight challenging because they were tighter than the turning circle of the average plane (and ours was certainly average). The pilot would pull up at the last instant to avoid rocks and trees that almost filled the view through the windscreen, and then gain a minuscule amount of altitude before banking again in such a way that your stomach was left screaming towards Lusaka in the north, while your mind was trying to cope with the sharp turn to the South Pole. I learned two very valuable things that day. Firstly, the gorge is stunningly attractive from a falcon's perspective, and secondly, let sleeping pilots lie.

*   *   *

The time came to go home. Tension in our vehicle rose perceptibly as we neared the border. The Zimbabwe side went smoothly, but Salome sat on her suitcase in no-man's-land and refused to cross to Botswana until such time as I had fetched her permits from the Kasane officials. I went ahead to the Botswana post, where they greeted me like an old friend, with warm smiles and hearty handshakes.

'Where's your wife and family?' the Immigration officer asked.

'My wife is waiting on the Zimbabwe side until I go back with her permits. Her mother and brother also chose to stay. It is just my dog who came with me to check if there are any more sausages.'

He scowled briefly at Django and then said cheerily, 'Tell her to come. We phoned the office in Maun and they gave us all the permit numbers and confirmed that she is legally allowed to live in Botswana.'

It was not easy to convince Salome to return with me. Understandably, she was less than effusive in response to her former tormentors, but we passed through the border post without further problems. I don't think they were prepared to risk another sermon from my mother-in-law.

9

RHINO BUST

Perhaps there should be a sign discreetly placed outside the furniture shops in Maun: *'Beware, Furniture Shopping Could Be Hazardous To Your Health.'* I say this because Salome came home one day, her usual poise in shreds, after a morning's shopping in town.

'You won't believe this! I was just offered rhino horn!' she exclaimed indignantly. 'At the furniture shop!'

Well, please excuse my surprise, but when I go into such an establishment I expect the offer of a bed, perhaps kitchen appliances or maybe even a ghetto blaster – but illegal rhino horn?

'I was poking around looking for a bedside table when the manager invited me into his office,' Salome continued. 'He asked me if I was in the safari business and naturally I said yes. I assumed he was going to offer me a good deal on some camping equipment or something, but he just blurted out that he had four rhino horns for sale and he wanted to know whether I was interested. I didn't know what to do. I was caught completely by surprise, so I said the first thing that came into my mind.'

'Oh yes ... and what was that?' I probably did not want to hear the answer.

'That I needed to talk to you first and you would go and speak to him, because we always make joint decisions.'

'What? Why did you say that? Whatever happened to "No"?'
'I didn't think of it.'

*   *   *

At least 26 species of rhino, ranging in size from that of a small pig to a shorter-necked giraffe, have become extinct over time. The latest to go was the woolly rhino, which survived until last week in geological time, having succumbed to the last Ice Age just 15 000 years ago. Only five species now survive, and are on their way out for ever, in our own short lifetimes, unless we stop poaching them.

Botswana boasts – in a very small voice, it must be said – the two species that still occur in Africa, although both are teetering over the abyss of extinction. These are the black rhino, which is not black at all, but grey, and the white rhino, which is not even vaguely white but ... much the same grey, really. The terms came from a simple mix-up of the Dutch word 'wyd' (meaning 'wide' and referring to the broad mouth of the grazer), which someone with a hearing impediment heard as 'white' – and the other species was named by a complete twit who saw the world in opposites, and so called it 'black'.

When the early European explorers reached Botswana, white rhino grazed in their hundreds upon the plains, while intrepid hunters could barely move in the forests for all the nasty-tempered black rhino that browsed there and chased them around the trees and over the shrubs. So they shot them all. By 1882, less than 30 years after Livingstone first set his boot of goodwill to Kalahari soil, all the white rhino in Botswana were gone, slaughtered in some kind of mad killing frenzy that is not easy to understand. When the white rhino was considered extinct throughout southern Africa, many hunters returned, broken-hearted no doubt, to their native lands.

However, with the kind of good fortune that they desperately needed, a small group of white rhinos was found hiding in Zululand in the early 1900s. This tiny group, given protection and the chance to breed, did remarkably well and by the 1980s there were enough to risk sending a small batch of them to Botswana to see if they could make a go of it. This they did well enough to attract the attention of furniture shop managers.

The black rhino, on the other hand, had taken another route. Their population by the late 1980s was a quarter of what it had been in the 1970s, and poaching was driving them headlong towards extinction outside of places like London Zoo, where they bred happily. Indeed, London was bizarrely destined to have a larger black rhino population than Botswana. The problem for the 5 000 or so that have made it so far is that they are split into seven subspecies, five of which have populations of under 500, and all of which are scattered over the southern, eastern and possibly central parts of the African continent, in isolated islands of dubious safety.

Every now and again in Botswana, a pilot or a group out on a game drive would spot a black rhino, but such sightings were rare. As for their 'white' brethren, amazingly, I saw 13 of them on a single game drive one morning, in a forgotten corner of the Chobe National Park. Shortly after that, Somali poachers based themselves across the river in nearby Livingstone and were too professional for our Wildlife Department. They slaughtered the population. Extinction stalked the rhinos in Botswana once again, and it became a major issue in government and environmental circles.

I was disappointed, though, to learn the truth that Chinese traditional doctors do not use the keratin-rich powdered rhino horn as an aphrodisiac; they prescribe it rather for fevers and convulsions. If we are going to exterminate an entire family of animals, I would have hoped that it should be for the higher cause of glorious orgasms rather than for the erroneous belief that something no more medicinal than fingernails would provide occasional relief of a few twitching muscles or sweaty brows.

*　　*　　*

The furniture shop manager had been a fool to approach a stranger, but he had handed me a golden opportunity to be a rhino poacher gang-buster. I phoned Paul Schaller, chairperson of the Okavango Wildlife Society, and told him about Salome's experience.

'I tell you what: we'll set up a sting,' he said. 'Are you prepared to meet with this crook, and we'll get General Ian Khama to send some guys up from Gaborone to entrap him?'

'Sure I'll do it.' I trusted Ian to get the job done expertly.

'It could be dangerous. These poaching types are armed and do this professionally.'

'Mmmmm. But the guys that Ian will send will also be professionals, right?'

Paul was a man of action; without delay he phoned Lieutenant-General Ian Khama and was put straight through to him. Where else in the world, I wondered, could the chairperson of a small local conservation society access the commander of a nation's defence force with such ease?

The general was acutely concerned about reports of rhino poaching, but this was a police matter, he said, not a military one. He offered to phone the police commissioner and request him to liaise with Paul directly in order to set up the sting.

'Oh, and by the way, be extremely careful; these men could be desperate,' he cautioned before ending the call. 'And Salome must be kept well out of it,' was his last emphatic instruction.

*　　*　　*

I dropped in on the shop manager to arrange the planned meeting. He was a slight man with a shifty expression, who never once looked me in the eye as he told me that his four rhino horns were worth enough money to keep both of us in a good time for a year. He could easily smuggle them to South Africa on one of the regular transport trucks that supplied his shop, but he needed an outlet in Johannesburg to take them over, and that was where we would come in. I told him I had hundreds of contacts in Johannesburg who would be interested and that I would speak to them and report back. A further appointment was set up at Riley's Hotel for Friday night at 6 pm.

The plan of action was for the cops to be discreetly deployed at the hotel to witness and record our rendezvous, and then to follow unobserved to where the horns were stashed. They would then nab the poachers and put them behind bars for a very long time. All I had to do was play it 'real cool' (Paul's words) and insist on seeing the horns before I bought them. The country's finest CID officers would take care of the rest.

The country's finest CID officers did not want anyone to know they were in the vicinity, so they set up camp where they would be inconspicuous – on the side of the main road into Maun in full view of every person who happened to drive in or out of town. Within hours half the population was speculating as to why members of the Criminal Investigation Department had decided to base themselves on the town's outskirts.

Three different people asked me what I thought they might be doing. The cops might as well have advertised their intentions on Radio Botswana. I hoped they were not tempted to shop for furniture.

Salome volunteered to join me at Riley's Hotel that night.

'No thanks. Khama said it was too dangerous and you should be kept out of it.'

'What about you? They could shoot you just as easily.'

I had contemplated this scenario quite a lot over the past three nights: 'I know that, but we have to consider our furry child. If you come along and also get shot, who will he have to look after?'

'Good point,' she agreed, with a little pat to the head of the dog that was following our conversation with the attention of a Wimbledon centre court spectator. 'But you may need back-up, so he must go with you.'

The furniture store manager kept me waiting in the car park of Riley's Hotel for an hour. This is a local tradition to establish dominance, so to pass the time I rather nervously rehearsed my lines with Django and explained what was expected of him. If I lifted my left pinkie, he was to go for the jugular. He wagged his tail in agreement.

It was getting dark before the poacher and his mate arrived. We entered the hotel and made for the garden bar, where we could sit outside around a table and within comfortable earshot of the undercover agents. Standing at the entrance to the garden was Columbo himself, dressed in a fawn-coloured trench coat with the collar turned up. A hat that could have belonged to the silver screen hero was perched on his head, and the largest pair of dark glasses I had ever seen was poised on his nose. Given that dusk had already fallen, this alone should have been enough to raise suspicions, but he then pulled out a small camera and took a close-up picture as we passed him.

'What's he doing?' the poacher asked doubtfully, blinking in the blinding flash.

'No idea. He must be a tourist,' I tried, without much conviction. 'Let's sit here.'

I chose a table in the middle of the lawn around which, at a discreet distance, was a selection of empty chairs and tables suitable for Columbo and his cronies. We sat down and ordered a round. I talked about the fortunes of the national football team, because everybody in Botswana liked to talk soccer, and the Zebras – our pride and joy on the odd occasion when they won – were enjoying a purple patch.

While we chatted, Columbo and two of his mates, who were dressed identically – it must have been the standard disguise doled out to all detectives in Gaborone at the time – came and sat nearby. They decided that they were too far away to eavesdrop comfortably and moved their table so close to ours that they invaded our personal space. Then, to my unutterable surprise, Columbo started to rock his chair back and forth on its back legs so that he was able to join our conversation by intermittently poking his head between the poacher and me.

'Do you think that the Zebras can beat Cameroon ...' – a head would appear between us; then, as it disappeared – '... away in Yaounde next month?'

'No I don't ...' and the head would come between us again '... think so.'

The poacher clearly realised that something strange was going on. I was also becoming almost uncontrollably edgy as I remembered the General's dire warning. Clumsily I tried to swing the conversation to the rhino horns.

'We haven't come here to talk Zebras, let's talk rhino horns instead.'

The head came between us and stayed there, so that I had to lean forward to see the person with whom I was having a drink.

Even the poacher was not that stupid. He jumped up and exclaimed, 'This is crazy. Who are these people?' and stalked out, his accomplice following closely, and they both threw 'You are dead meat' scowling glances at me. Django and I rose, thanked the country's finest for their expert policing and left them to pay the drinks bill.

Furniture shop managers and their ilk around the country remained free to continue their decimation of Botswana's rhino populations and were hugely successful as the species again slipped into near-extinction.

10

SALT IN THE WATER

Django had South African connections. Although he was a Motswana dog through and through, Salome and I, his human family, had moved to Botswana from South Africa many years previously and in 1994 we were determined to exercise our right to vote when the first democratic elections were to take place. There had been a new buzz in the air in the Republic since the universally revered Nelson Mandela had been restored to the world stage and we wanted to be part of it.

My parents owned a small apartment in Uvongo, not far from their home in Shelly Beach, which we rented on a year-round basis, so that we could spend a few weeks annually in their company. It would have been cheaper and less trouble if we had booked into a five-star hotel.

Winston Court had two adjoining blocks of five ground-level apartments, each with its own lock-up garage, tidy garden and, during clear weather, a glimpse of the distant sea, made possible by standing on the sofa and peering through the burglar bars. To our dismay, the constant drone of the traffic that whizzed past our bedroom window day and night drowned the sound of the waves. Yet we stayed; partly in order not to upset Mum, and mainly because we could not store all our furniture in a five-star hotel. We turned the spare room into a study and think-tank for our various creative projects and when we got writers' cramp, we would stare forlornly out of its window with no worthwhile view, except for our neighbour's flickering TV that never seemed to be turned off.

Mother Nature hid her charms on this section of coast. Sometimes we would gaze with wonder at the patience of the anglers as they stood on rocks for hours yet never seemed to pull a fish out of the sea. We attempted some bird watching, but apart from small flocks of bronze mannikins that flitted past the window, the call of the elusive purple-crested louries that would lure us outside, occasionally offering us a glimpse of their colourful feathered dress, and a troop of monkeys that sneaked through the burglar bars to raid the kitchen, there was very little to enthuse over – there was far more life in the Kalahari.

*   *   *

And so it was that we three had wended our long way from Maun to the Indian Ocean coast and Django saw the sea for the first time. When our vehicle door opened for him upon the vastness of that beach, the first thing he did was rush across the sand to quench his thirst – and found this was not what he was used to at all. The expression of surprise, then disgust, on his face as he realised it was salty, was a study. This was followed by shock, as the unexpected boisterousness of a foaming wave bowled him over and caused him to cast a look of extreme disapproval in our direction. He hurriedly quit the water's edge and it was a long while before he trusted the sea enough to take a dip.

A morning routine was soon established: we would take a brisk pre-sunrise walk along the beach, with the hissing, pounding waves as our companions, until the sun rose gloriously over the ocean, its early light glimmering gold and silver on the water. Weather permitting, there would be an evening stroll too, but for the rest of the day Django lay patiently indoors waiting for us to complete the writing tasks that we had set ourselves.

He revelled in his early-morning outings and would pee and pee until the ocean level rose, and then he'd pee some more. Not a lamppost remained unaware that the cowboy was in town. Mornings became social encounters too, as other early risers, mainly retired people, would set out at precisely the same hour every day, regardless of weather conditions, dragging their assortment of reluctant dogs behind them. A narrow path cut through the dense dune vegetation to bypass towering rocks along the beach allowed the aged to lay their societal ambush by blocking the way and engaging us in pointless chitchat about the weather. Then we would hear – yet again, as we had done every morning for the past two weeks – how the great-grandchildren muddled their footwear for example, and went to school wearing one of each other's socks. Salome, bless her, would encourage this and laugh gaily as though it were the first time that she had ever heard these tales. Then she would progress to muffin recipes, and that was when Django and I would try to escape, only to be foiled at each attempt by a stout old lady who managed, with a nimble side-step that belied her age, to block our flight.

By comparison, it was almost a relief when it was Wilkie and his obnoxious little Scottie whose web trapped us. He was an old colonial type who looked as though he came straight out of a 1950s comedy, with his erect bearing, neatly trimmed moustache and the clipped accent of a pukkah Englishman used to having his orders obeyed without question. He had worked as a civil servant in a post office in Kenya, if I recall correctly, and had come to the south coast to die. Wilkie – short for Wilkinson – was arguably more British than the Queen (which is not that hard as she comes from German stock) and had some interesting ideas about the Empire.

'We should never have given the whole of Africa to them,' he would state with some authority and a vague flourish of his walking stick. 'Kenya is a pretty place. Perhaps we should have kept that and given the rest away.'

'Excuse me for my ignorance of Kenyan history, but weren't there quite a number of indigenous Kenyans living there when the Brits arrived?' I'd asked respectfully.

'There were only a handful and I think they should take off all the rubbish they screen on TV and show more cricket.'

Wilkie would change the subject quite startlingly in mid-sentence, invariably in favour of cricket and if I was feeling particularly sore about listening to ten dozen ways to bake muffins I would engage him in a lengthy discussion about the inadequacies of the English cricket selectors. This, in turn, drove Salome mad and she would try to escape – until she found out that Wilkie could not care less if she was there or not. He totally ignored her in all discussions, as these were supposed to be conducted between men only. This infuriated my wife but did not bother our dog in the slightest.

Django got on well with most people (and nearly every dog) but he despised Wilkie's Scottie who, despite being descended from a clan north of Hadrian's Wall, I am certain would have snarled in a clipped English accent if his strangled yaps in Django's direction had been translated. Django, who was never leashed, was scornfully unconcerned by this little pooch that frantically risked garrotting itself as it leapt at him, and soon learnt not to hang about when Wilkie stopped us for another lecture on the failings of the British Empire. He used his freedom to trot off eagerly on his own, which frustrated the Scottie even further and left me wishing that I could escape as easily.

Our pet was accustomed to being welcomed wherever he went, even at the beach where the 'no dogs allowed' signs were universally ignored. Then he noticed something interesting, and I swear a gleam came into his eyes. The anti-canine signs, posted along a retaining wall that surrounded the beach, featured the image of a Scottie with a red 'prohibited' stripe painted through it. Whenever he came across one, Django never missed the opportunity to jump up on the wall and pee on his adversary.

*   *   *

Uvongo was a small town with a tiny shopping centre, but it did have an art shop, which was Django's favourite destination. It sold dolls made of seashells smuggled from the denuded Shelly Beach, and squeaky toys. He would urge us to buy a high-pitched rubber dolphin, or a Beluga whale that he personally selected from the baskets, and having convinced us, would proudly carry it away, head held high, eyes shining with excitement. Once home, he would throw his new toy up in the air and catch it again, then wrestle, shake, paw and roll with it before playing tug of war with us, all the while growling with delight.

When he eventually grew tired of the game he would conceal it in Marmalade's old basket, where he would chew it into small pieces. When Salome found the bits and pieces she would reprimand him for destroying his toy, and he soon learnt that the best way to avoid a scolding was to hide the evidence, smuggling the pieces outside and burying them in the neighbour's garden before returning with a soil-blackened nose and an air of innocence. He managed this so stealthily that we probably would never have known what had happened to his dolphins, were it not for the fact that the neighbour could watch him from her kitchen window. Despite all Salome's efforts, this was one of Django's habits that she could not break. This particular neighbour, Frances, was a happy bubbly woman. She doted on Django and set aside small treats for him, and he made it a point to pop in regularly to see her, happily announcing his arrival with a soft muffled bark. He was invariably welcomed and invited in to share a cup of tea and a cream scone, and perhaps to discuss muffin recipes.

My parents too were admirers and became almost pathetically keen to look after Django if we went to places where he was excluded. My mother complained that Dad was no longer to be found in his work-shop, as his time was spent in the garden playing ball with our pup. They had invented a game where he leapt up at a tennis ball on a string, while Dad tried to outfox him without lifting it out of reach. It was wonderful to witness the bond between a two-year-old dog and a 70-something-old man.

On the other side of us were neighbours Frik and Sarie, who hailed from Excelsior, a small, ultra-conservative Afrikaans town in the Orange Free State. It was here that a scandal had exploded during the dark apartheid years, when several highly respected town elders were exposed as engaging in sexual trysts with a dozen or more young black girls. Those among them who could not face the resulting out-rage and scorn after being named and shamed, committed suicide.

Many citizens still bore scars from the ruined reputation of their home town and Frik and Sarie were two of the most miserable people I have ever met. I supposed it was because Frik had resented the fact that he had not been not invited to the orgies, while Sarie suspected that he had been.

Rob, the chairperson of Winston Court residents' committee, phoned me not long after their arrival.

'Your neighbours have written a letter of complaint about your dog, and I am afraid he can no longer stay.'

'They wrote a letter? Why?' I asked, not comprehending.

'They brought some vicious Rottweilers from their farm a year or so ago. These dogs terrorised everybody and savaged Frances's maid, mauling her arm badly, so they were told to remove them. It's retribution for that,' he sighed.

'Don't worry, I'll speak to them,' I said, confident that I would win them over.

'Good luck!' I detected the scepticism in his tone.

I knocked on their back door and was reluctantly invited in to take a seat around the kitchen table, which I took to be an Afrikaans custom, and hoped it had nothing to do with the fact that they did not want me any deeper in their home. I quietly explained to them that Django was not a dog in the sense that we know most dogs; he was quiet and discreet, did not chew arms off maids, never soiled the grass and just a week earlier had alerted me in the middle of the night to the fact that someone was trying to break into their apartment. He had, I said, saved them from being cleaned out, and deserved their gratitude.

With a smile I sat back, satisfied that they would surely agree to Django's continued residence, but I could not have been more mistaken. Sarie, who was obviously terminally ill and should have been at a more magnanimous, gentle stage of life, was the more insistent about turfing him out. Unmoved, her face assumed an expression of vicious spite as she baited me.

'If our dogs couldn't stay here, then why should yours?'

To address the issue of the expulsion notice, an extraordinary meeting of the residents' committee was called. The complainants having returned to the Free State by that time, this august gathering unanimously resolved that since Django's behaviour was always impeccable, he was an asset to the community. This being so, it was minuted that he be declared an 'Honorary Person' and thereby allowed to stay for as long as he wanted.

When his new elevation was publicly announced, we invited our dog's supporters to a celebration at the seafood restaurant around the corner, where a place was immediately laid at the head of the table in his honour. I must be honest, so I will admit that he had a problem handling his honorary knives and forks.

All the above recognition was not without precedent in this crazy country, because South Africa was used to changing a person's standing in law. Often, when an influential dignitary who was embarrassingly non-Caucasian arrived – especially a visitor from a powerful ally – the government would feel compelled to afford that person the status of 'honorary white', thereby insulting the guest along with most South Africans. We hoped that Django's kin were not similarly angered.

Ironically, once we were declared free to stay at Winston Court, thanks to Django's new enhanced status, we realised that it was time to leave. Our work on the book was finished for the moment, Maun beckoned and I needed to teach our safari staff some muffin recipes.

11

CHOBE BECKONS

We held an urgent family meeting to discuss the planned tarring of the road to Maun.

'This is the end of Maun as we love it,' I said. 'Let's move.'

'I'm ready for somewhere new,' Salome agreed.

Django wagged his tail. He was always ready for somewhere new.

'Where shall we go?' I asked.

'I want water,' my wife replied.

'How about Shakawe?'

Shakawe is the northernmost town in the Okavango, just near the Namibian border. It has water and lots of it, and after having endured a drought in Maun we were more than ready for lots of water.

'I like the idea of a big river and certainly Shakawe is very pretty with its reeds, but I want water and animals,' my wife implored.

'There's only one place in Botswana then, and that's Kasane,' I stated.

And so it was decided. Down at the coast we created our next home, which was to be on wheels, so that we could just ride out of town, as cowboys do. It was a spacious second-hand caravan and needed tweaking – it had no double bed, no mains lights or plug points and the upholstery was faded and tired. We did the work at my parents' house, where Dad had a workshop equipped to build a space rocket.

While Salome busied herself with curtains, cushions and bedding, I surprised myself by doing an acceptable job with the infrastructure. Together we transformed her into a thing of joy.

Ahead lay a journey of 2 000 kilometres, which took four days before we could park the caravan under a cluster of giant jackalberry trees at Chobe Safari Lodge, and go in search of the hotel manager, John Tugwell, a big man in every sense, with a huge frame that supported a generous belly. A deranged employee, wielding a shotgun, had shot him in the chest at point-blank range one night. This would have killed most people, as the doctor who patiently plucked the shot out of his chest and belly constantly reminded him. If it were not for those extra layers of flesh he would have died – which is surely an argument that large people could embrace. To complement his size, John had an open smile and a heart the size of Jupiter. He also had a small wife, Pat, with a voice shrill enough to peel the paper off a wall and a bulldog demeanour that concealed a heart no smaller than John's. John was terrified of her. He was always doing something of which she would disapprove, like sneaking into the pub for a quick Castle when he was supposed to be stocktaking in the laundry. He would have a naughty twinkle in his eye when he tiptoed in, and a sheepish grin when caught, which was nearly always. Pat would bark at him and drag him back to the laundry, his unfinished beer left on the bar.

*　　*　　*

Kasane was a tiny village, lying on the floodplain of the mighty Zambezi, picturesquely spread out like jam on a French loaf, along the Botswana side of the Chobe River. The raised shoreline, 'platoo' in the vernacular, stands guard over a settlement significantly smaller than Maun. It boasted three grocery stores – the term 'supermarkets' would be an embellishment – two in Kasane and one in Kazungula, a sister village situated twelve kilometres downstream near the confluence of the two rivers.

One of the locally owned Kasane shops was very basic in many ways, and on one occasion caused a section of the community to recoil in horror when a housewife, while fossicking around near the bottom of the meat deep-freeze, laid her hands upon a woman's breast that had been placed there for use in some future ritual. She screamed, dropped the boob on the floor, hustled out of there and told the story three times over to anyone who would listen. People listened, and only those traditionalists who understood the symbolic importance of fertility and nurturing continued their support for the store. Rumour has it that buried beneath its entrance lie the genitals and other bits of a young boy who had mysteriously disappeared. Whenever I drove past this squalid enterprise I found myself involuntarily giving it a wide berth, often resulting in near road accidents.

Savas Stores was infinitely more cheerful, rather in the style of a corner shop in an English village, but with an African trading store character. It was owned by long-time friends of ours, God-fearing and upright Geoff and Trish Williams, who had recently moved to Kasane from Gaborone to take over the business, and they certainly would not sneak bits of dead people into their freezers. But what did sneak into their shop, whenever the chance arose, was Django. Trish had a stash of gifts for the children and, as she acknowledged Django as part of our family, she kept a packet of biltong in there for him. He loved Trish, not only for her biltong, and would wait patiently outside the glass door of her office for someone to open it. He would take the gap to greet her and remind her of her duties by nudging the bottom drawer with his nose, before staring up at her expectantly.

Our local bank was surely the only financial institution in the world where you could touch all four walls at once. It was an agency – a twig, really, rather than a branch. To change a US $10 note took 20 minutes, while the clerk scratched around to find the right forms, the current week's exchange rates, his calculator, pen, Bible and whatever else this transaction required of him. God help you if you wanted to send something as complex as a telegraphic transfer or to negotiate a loan. A good book, a flask of coffee, a packed lunch and a comfortable tent could then come in handy.

Django delighted in the bakery with its smells and tasty scraps. Owned and run by an elderly Portuguese man out of a room smaller even than the bank, it possessed a wood-burning oven, mixing bowls, bags of flour and salt, all stacked into two thirds of the minuscule space. He lived in the other third, separated from his baking equipment by a thin, tattered curtain. From this grubby setup came the most delicious light, fluffy loaves – on the days that he was sober and enthused enough to bake. Generally, bread was not available in town.

Apart from these facilities and a sprinkling of government institutions dotted around the town, a couple of bars were all that catered for locals. The pub at the Chobe Safari Lodge was the Duck Inn of Kasane, and Django loved it dearly because, though there were fewer fights, there was no less by way of entertainment. John and Pat had a long-haired mutt named Buddy who was much the size of Django, and who would come down to the pub in the evenings to meet up with him. I think it's fair to say that Buddy liked Django more than Django liked him. It is also likely that Django considered him part Scottie, though Buddy, like Django, was part Lhasa Apso. The other part was hard to tell because he was longer in the leg than our dog and had straight, light-golden hair. Pat liked anyone that Buddy liked, so she took a shine to our pet – while John liked anyone who did not make Pat bark at him, so he also accepted Django, with the inevitable result that our dog was made to feel at home there, where other canines were discouraged.

*　　*　　*

Chobe Safari Lodge was the first tourist establishment in the Chobe, perhaps in Botswana, and was built by people with the visionary talent that I admire so much in others, because I don't have it. If it had been me who had arrived in 1959 instead of Ethnee and Charles Trevor, I would no doubt have pitched my tent for a week, deeply appreciated the beauty of this wilderness, glanced at the desultory handful of villagers and the three white folk – the policeman, his wife and small son – and said 'What a place!' I would then have undertaken the tortuous road back to Livingstone, which offered the closest form of civilisation. This journey consisted of 12 kilometres of sandy road through elephant country, a ferry trip across the Zambezi into Zambia, followed by a narrow track for another 70 kilometres. If you were in the Chobe and were short of an onion, Livingstone was where you needed to go. ('Excuse me, sir, but we appear to have run short on toilet paper, I'll just pop out to the shops and get some more. I should be back tomorrow night. Hold on, will you?')

Everything had to come via this route unless, of course, it was something that was not stocked in Livingstone, when you might have to add an extra 400 kilometres to go to Bulawayo in Zimbabwe. If Bulawayo had run out, then plan on a couple of weeks for a round trip to Johannesburg. ('I'm sorry madam, but Bulawayo doesn't seem to stock Cameo cigarettes. I'll pop down to Johannesburg quickly for you. Can I get you anything else while I'm there?')

Charles and Ethnee absorbed all of this and said 'What a place!' They built a hotel and travelled to Johannesburg when Bulawayo did not have their brand of cigarettes.

Their chosen site was on a vegetable patch that had belonged to Duncan Mlazie senior, a Malawian by origin, who was the supplier of mostly traditional medicines to the small community, and the breeder of a clutch of children who were destined to play major roles in the development of Kasane. What a setting for a vegetable patch!

The Chobe Safari Lodge lies on the edge of a broad section of the Chobe, with its adjacent campsite on a sweep of the river, over which the sun sets in a kaleidoscope of oranges and pinks. All the building materials used had taken the same sandy track that followed David Livingstone's first trip to the Victoria Falls. Despite the hardships, the Lodge was operational by the early 1960s. Within a few years they had built an airstrip and opened two stores, one in Kavimba in the Chobe Enclave and the other in Kasane, which was handy because they could stock the correct cigarettes and save themselves a long trip. Charles planned to build a house for Ethnee on the river's edge, but this dream never came to fruition because of a tragedy that happened just off an island that lay close to his new lodge.

A glorious cruise on the river with two young friends was what Charles had looked forward to on that fateful afternoon – and no place offers better game-viewing and birding experiences than a boat trip on the Chobe. Unlike today, they had the river to themselves. When his boat ran out of petrol just 50 metres from the hotel, Charles pulled up on Sedudu Island to refuel. His two friends clambered out of the boat while he busied himself with the job in hand. It was shocking bad luck that they had moored right near a beehive, and its occupants swarmed all over them within seconds. In the world of bees, if one stings you it releases a pheromone that alerts the rest of the colony. If you happen to be far enough away from the hive, all the bees scoot off to defend it – but if you are unfortunate enough to be near their home, they attack with a vengeance to drive you away.

Charles shouted to his mates to dive into the water to escape the attackers, while he bore the brunt of the onslaught, tugging vainly on the starter rope to fire up the boat, unaware that he was attracting the bees both through his frantic movement and through the carbon dioxide that his heavy breathing produced. Though severely stung about his face he steadfastly refused to abandon ship. He somehow managed to haul his companions aboard, push the boat off and paddle away from the killer bees. A chartered plane eventually flew the victims to Livingstone.

The young man had wisely kept his head under water for most of the attack, but his wife, like Charles, had sustained multiple stings, and was fortunate, after a long struggle, to recover fully in a clinic in Salisbury, Rhodesia's capital city. Charles, treated in a Bulawayo hospital, survived for seven weeks, mostly in and out of a coma, before succumbing to kidney failure.

Twenty-five years later, and oblivious to this drama, we parked our caravan in view of the very spot where all this had happened. I pulled an extension lead from the ablution block, switched on the new lighting system that I had proudly built, flinched as it tripped the campsite power, and then settled into the Kasane lifestyle.

*   *   *

Sent from their newly erected tent in the campsite to wash the previous evening's dinner plates by his demure wife Alison, Roy Ashby looked uncannily similar to how I would look in the same circumstances. He was comically confused and kept reaching for a bottle of dishwashing liquid, which would promptly slip through his fingers and land in the mud. He stumbled over the plastic washing bowl, sending plates flying and, taking a quick step backwards, trod on a wine glass. Roy looked like the front-row rugby forward that he once was, broad-shouldered, powerful and now, in his middle years, rotund. The glass stood no chance. Aghast, Roy looked down at its shattered remnants, shook his head and stretched resignedly for the dishwashing liquid, which slipped through his fingers yet again.

Django watched this scene with interest, recognising me in this type of activity, and trotted down to greet Roy. They became firm friends and on the odd occasion that Django could not be with us, he was happy to stay with the Ashbys, who in turn became our lifelong friends, though it is true to say that our wives no longer asked us to do the washing up.

Roy was a pilot who ferried people into the bush in a small Piper Cherokee. He had been flying for many years, and I know that he was a lot better at that than doing the dishes because he took Salome, Django and me for a flip over the nearby confluence of the Chobe and Zambezi rivers – which is the only place on earth where four countries meet.

This interesting phenomenon had a drawback for the inhabitants of the local village of Kazungula, which came into being at a time when land ownership was based on tribal definitions. Little did its elders know that their descendants were destined to become citizens of either Zambia, Zimbabwe, Namibia or Botswana, while all were officially residing in one village which happened to straddle rivers.

The floods were high that year and Salome had an idea in mind for a postcard, so she booked a flight with Roy. I sat in the back seat with Django while my wife, who needed to communicate with the pilot, sat up front. This was a mistake, I soon realised, as she commanded him to do more circuits around the confluence than a moth around a spotlight. This on its own might not have been too bad, but Salome had thrust a camera at me with instructions to take as many photos as I could, because I was not likely to get an opportunity like this again. As I tried to focus the camera on an earth below that was revolving as if I had consumed John Tugwell's entire whisky stock in one sitting, I began to feel airsick.

'Let's go back,' I pleaded, 'I don't feel well.'

'Just a few more times,' my wife promised. 'Roy, do you think you could point this wing on my side directly over that ferry and twirl around it, holding your position above it like a spinning top?' Roy could, and did so for an eternity. Django clearly thought that this was fun, and clawed at me to get a better view of the rotating world that I was desperate not to see. I reached feebly for a paper bag and vowed that I would wreak revenge on the sadistic pilot in John's bar later that evening, when the gyroscopes in my brain had stopped spinning.

*   *   *

We agreed that the Chobe was to be our base for the foreseeable future, and it was time to set up our office under the towering jackalberries. As the river levels rose our camp was in danger of going under water, however, so we moved to higher ground. A huge stranded barge, the victim of a previous massive flood, stood guard behind our new site. We ran an electric cable to the area, installed a water pipe and tap, and were almost set. We even had semi-private ablutions that we shared with two mostly unoccupied bungalows. The telephone people came in answer to our application and installed a line. Instead of planting a neat row of gum poles, as one might expect, they wound the cable from tree to tree until it reached our office tent, which we had added to the rear of the caravan. We could hardly complain. How many tele-communications services around the world would consider providing a landline to a movable caravan? We were equipped to do business.

We learnt to trust Django not to wander too far. If we had to go away for a day to some place where we could not take him – as rare as that was – we discovered that if we left him outside the caravan he would always be waiting for us when we returned. Prior to that,

Salome had tried locking him in – for his own safety, she thought. This was a blunder, as we saw to our dismay on our return. We replaced curtains, cushions and bedding and never made that mistake again.

Our dog was now in his prime and was confident wherever he went, but he needed to make some major adjustments in his new home. In Kasane he had no goats to distract him, for which he was grateful. Instead, his new friends and adversaries were nearly all wild animals from the adjacent National Park, who wandered freely in and out of the unfenced campsite. His first challenge was from a monitor lizard, a direct if distant descendant of the dinosaurs, which had discovered the bowl of food that was left out for him to nibble on whenever he was hungry. Our dog did not like this slithery reptile stealing his food and he would charge, hair abristle. The one and a half metre mini-dragon would retreat a few paces and hiss at him, halting his advance. If Django pressed on with his attack, the monitor would try to bite him or to use its powerful tail to swipe at him, but our little fellow nimbly avoided its cumbersome defence and each confrontation would end in deadlock. Django finally resigned himself to his new companion, and would lie on the far side of the mat and watch for an opening. The leguaan added 'Hopelessly Pampered Pooch' to its regular diet of crabs and mussels, and our order for dog food at Savas Stores increased proportionately.

Much more fun for Django were the banded mongooses that lived in burrows in an old termite mound under some thorny *moselesele* bushes nearby. This troop of small, striped animals – an individual never weighs more than a kilogram and a half – numbered in the high thirties and collectively outweighed him by a significant margin. With banded mongooses you have to consider their combined mass because when threatened they group together in a tightly knit unit to provide a united front to any adversary. This Django experienced regularly, as the mongooses used to invade his territory and rival the monitor in feasting on his 'Hopelessly Pampered Pooch'. When he leapt to defend his food from these raiders, he would find himself confronted by a wall of hissing, sharp-toothed creatures that would advance on him, causing him to backpedal in alarm, so he changed his tactics and lay in wait for them, concealed in the office tent. As they moved into the open area and spread out to feed, he would charge an isolated individual and, if the little creature was not fast enough, he would bowl it over and return to the caravan proudly, his tail held high. He never used his teeth and never intended any harm. For him it was a diversion.

One day the mongooses turned the tables, however, surprising him while he sunned himself. They inched closer and closer as he slept and then three or four of them pounced as one. He yelped as they attacked, nipping him all over his body and pulling out mouthfuls of his wiry hair. This was open warfare. Django fought back but was badly outnumbered and was lucky to regain his feet and escape before he sustained serious damage. I have seen mongooses kill a large python by running at it and biting at skin and muscle, viciously tearing strips off the helpless snake until it could no longer move. They did not bother to deliver a coup de grâce or eat it, but abandoned their attack once it became clear that it could no longer survive. On this occasion Django hastily reversed into the safety of the caravan and their relationship settled into one of guarded animosity and mutual disrespect. For months they would chase each other fruitlessly back and forth over the same patch of territory, much like the trench warfare of the Great War.

That pattern continued until one particular day when Django's victory swagger back to safety was interrupted. The vanquished troop regrouped and caught him from the rear. They mobbed him, managed to knock him over, then set about an attack with intent to kill. In fear, he bit two or three of his assailants and drove them off – and from that time on the mongooses and Django showed deep respect towards each other. They left his food bowl alone, his retaliation ceased, and thereafter their interaction turned playful. Many a morning Django could be found lying in the middle of the feeding troop, while he and they kept a wary eye on each other. When a litter of young was born, the mother allowed them to play with our pet and he was always gentle with them, even when they nipped him.

Django's best domestic friend, however, was a wolf. She was a gorgeous Malamute named Mitshka who lived, on occasion, with Keven and Gonda Chadwick. The rest of the time she jumped their fence and trotted down President Drive to the Lodge campsite to visit her little friend, Django. The two of them would set off, looking like a Laurel and Hardy combination with the short male proudly leading his large lady wolf around the neighbourhood. Keven's attempts to quell her illicit forays verged on the comical, as he first raised the fence to no avail and then raised it again. When that failed he resorted to an electric dog-proof fence around his property and, while it may have worked for a dog, it had no effect on a wolf. She soared over the live wires and went in search of her diminutive beau.

Inevitably, of course, his measures prevented her from escaping and the friends were separated unless we took Django to visit her. This gave Keven and me a great excuse to watch rugby together under the guise of visitation rights for the dogs. Salome realised this of course, but sportingly let it ride and it worked a treat for men and dogs for the rest of the rugby season.

Django never fully appreciated his lack of stature and gauged no difference in size between himself and, say, an elephant, which led him into a few interesting situations. Once, when he and Salome were walking out together, he spotted a dozen or so village dogs raiding a rubbish bin in the Chobe Safari Lodge grounds. Each one of them was roughly three times his height, but because he was so stocky they were probably only twice his weight. Django was on his home territory and, outraged at the spectacle, he launched himself at the pack. He hit the first animal with his chest and this initial victim, caught by surprise, was knocked over on to its back and yelped in fright as Django went for its throat. Our dog then turned fiercely on the second member of the pack and the rest fled, tails between their legs. He looked so proud when he returned with his tail upright and a smirk on his face – he had seen off 12 bigger adversaries unaided. He checked for a steak in his dinner bowl, but came away disappointed. After all, we could not be seen to encourage bullying.

Django's next opponent was larger, and it was hard for me to make a bullying case against him. In winter, when there was no food out in the bush, animals were drawn to the Lodge gardens, which were kept agreeably lush from regular watering. The seeds of the giant camel thorn tree that sheltered us in the campsite were irresistible to ravenous elephants, and they would lean their massive weight against its trunk and shake it until the earth moved and the pods showered down. One regular visitor, a mature bull, did not stop at shaking the branches. In an orgy of devastation he snapped washing lines, ripped up Salome's garden and devoured my forest of tree seedlings; he then systematically isolated us from the outside world by disconnecting our electricity supply and tearing down our telephone line that, if you remember, had been wrapped around what he now considered as his personal camel thorn. This destruction, Salome decided, was clearly malicious and she dubbed him Stroppy.

Django became fed up with these nightly raids and decided to take control. He would charge fearlessly at Stroppy (who, we should never forget, outweighed him by some 520 per cent) and, growling and snarling, nipped at ankles that were almost too high to reach. Uproariously, he would turn the giant and drive him off. My heart could not have swelled more with paternal pride, but inevitably Stroppy recognised the absurdity of his retreat and hit back by chasing Django, who would escape by hiding under the caravan. This brought Stroppy almost to the entrance of our office tent.

Every time it happened Stroppy seemed to pull up just that little bit closer. I thought it so hilarious that I mentioned it over a beer to Darryl Dandridge, an old-time hunter, who looked at me as if I were inexcusably naïve. He told me of an infuriated elephant that had trashed a friend's caravan while pursuing an annoying dog. We had to explain to a dejected Django that this particular game had to stop.

One night, with our camel thorn in full fruit, the final confrontation erupted. Stroppy had introduced us to sleep deprivation on a scale that medieval torturers could not have dreamed of. When his extended nocturnal sojourns had interrupted our slumber for the fourteenth night in succession, I dragged my disgruntled self from my bed yet again and peered around the corner to see what mischief he was up to this time. He was on the lawn, just metres from me, munching on what remained of my seedlings – so I yelled half-heartedly at him to move on. Stroppy looked me right in the eye and, holding my gaze, deliberately reached up with his trunk, wound it around the telephone line and yanked. He used such force that a panel of the caravan was ripped off as the line broke. He had thrown down the telephonic gauntlet and stood, ears widely spread, daring me to respond.

I snapped. I will argue sleep deprivation in any court of law.

'Fuck you, you fat bastard! You are out of here!' I yelled (I become eloquent if you don't let me sleep), then leapt commando-style into the Cruiser and fired the engine. Stroppy had started to amble away, satisfied with his triumph, but I hunted him down. This was clearly a new experience for him. He did not have a clue what to do as I came up behind him, engine revving and horn blaring, so he started to scamper – tail tucked between his legs, his neck pulled back and ears laid flat. The path he chose took him towards the campsite, and he ran with mincing steps, like a chastised puppy. I chased hard, nudging his legs with the bullbar each time he slowed down. Django, unrestrained at last, joined in by snarling and snapping at those outsized feet. Around the campsite perimeter we went, past the campers in their flimsy little tents, who were startled from their sleep by the sights and sounds of an enormous beast, pursued by a driver of dubious sanity apparently intent on seeing them trampled by a rampaging elephant or finishing them off himself.

In his panic Stroppy missed the only exit while on the first mad loop, so we did another – which sent those campers who had already left their tents scrambling for cover, and the ones who had stayed in their beds diving under their duvets. I kept the pressure on him until we neared the way out, and then slowed down, but he was still running for his life and not thinking, so we had to complete the circuit a third time. At this stage I was aware of only a few distant, wide-eyed faces peering warily from behind isolated vehicles, so I halted well before the exit to allow Stroppy to take the road to safety and watched him scramble up a rocky hill with Django in hot pursuit.

Next morning the Lodge receptionists had to deal with vociferous complaints from irate campers about the lunatic who had tried to have them squashed by a rampant elephant during the night. Stroppy never returned to adjust our phone lines, however, and as of that night he also ceased his nocturnal raids on the houses on the plateau. He had returned to eat from the bush with his friends, far from the insanity of man.

*　　*　　*

My battles with Stroppy may well have left you with the impression that I do not like elephants, but this is far from the truth. I am not only a tree hugger but, because of Jock, I am a confirmed elephant hugger too. Jock allows strangers to clamber on to his back, and then he indulgently promenades them around his stretch of Africa. This he does, along with a small number of similar-minded associates, near Victoria Falls in Zimbabwe. To have the opportunity to ride Jock, or any of his three close friends (Miss Elle, Jack and Jumbo) you need to be a resident of the lodge at Elephant Camp.

My soul was not so much stirred when perched on the giant's back as it was when Django and I walked side by side in the shadow of this huge, lumbering animal. I had long admired elephants' timeless ambles through the bush, but this was the first opportunity I'd had to stroll alongside one. Then, when he later knelt down for me to wash him and caress the soft velvety skin behind his ears, which contrasted so starkly with the sun-cracked hide that covered the rest of his mighty body, I was smitten – and even more so when he gently accepted some cubes from my outstretched hand.

It was not until after dinner, however, when we went to say goodnight to our mounts, that my world changed in some irreversible way as Jock took me to a higher level of understanding. We found the elephants corralled for the evening in pens made of sturdy gum poles, which Stewart, the manager, assured us were purely for their own sense of security.

'They could bust out of there as easily as we can open a fridge door,' he told us, and looking at Stewie's own broad front I guessed that he had some experience in that line.

We fed them more cubes, except for Miss Elle who was already flat out on the ground, snoring gently. I went to Jock and he lowered his trunk and wrapped it around my torso in an affectionate embrace. I could not have been more vulnerable, yet never felt more profoundly protected. I blew into his trunk, and when he responded by blowing back, his breath gave off a pleasant smell of damp, partly fermented grain. When the others went to bed, Django and I stayed behind and we spent three blissful hours with Jock as I happily rubbed his trunk and occasionally blew into it, while he gently and lovingly squeezed me and blew back his grainy aroma.

Frequent calls are made for controlled culling to reduce Botswana's burgeoning elephant population – led mostly, it must be said, by those who stand to gain financially; but that night Jock taught me that I could never support their planned slaughter, no matter how well-argued.

I despise insensitivity to all animals, but particularly to these gentle giants. A troubling night-time visit to our Chobe site occurred shortly after Stroppy had stopped pestering us, when another large elephant wandered down the donga behind our caravan towards the tourists' camping area. As soon as they became aware of his presence excited campers started taking flashlight photographs, which clearly disturbed the old bull. He shook his head and took a few menacing paces towards them. Instead of dispersing the mob, his mock-charge – intended only as a warning – energised them further, and they buzzed noisily as they trained spotlights on him and their flashes increased. I shouted at them to stop what they were doing, but they were too pumped up to listen.

Enraged, the elephant powered up the embankment in the direction of his tormentors, grasped the nearest tent with his trunk and flung it high into the air. Fortunately, there was no one inside or they would almost certainly have been killed. He then knelt on another tent nearby and crushed it and its contents into the turf. Again there was no one at home; otherwise their mangled bodies would have had to be scraped out afterwards. Panic set in and the crowd fled to the safety of their vehicles as the bull forged on towards the heart of the campsite, searching for something else on which to vent his fury.

Django and I leapt into my vehicle to see if we could defuse the situation, and when we caught up with him we found the old boy stumbling unsteadily around the abandoned tents as if drugged. A few idiots persisted with their intrusive photography despite his obvious distress, and each time they did so he would shake that massive head, his ears slapping loudly against his face and neck. After demanding that the cameras were set down to calm the charged atmosphere, we drove slowly up to the bewildered beast and gently herded him away. He was neither resistant nor aggressive as we soothingly urged him onwards and as he neared the exit he lurched to his right into an enormous pile of garden refuse. It was then that we realised he was suffering from night-blindness, and the camera flashes had irritated his eyes, inflaming his anger, so we coaxed him further into the darkness and relative safety of the surrounding bush. Soon after this incident, the erection of an electric fence around the campsite ended all elephant visits, and another nail was driven into the coffin of an era.

What the new fence did not prevent, however, were visits from hippos, because the live barrier did not extend along the riverfront. A young female, Esmeralda, took to sleeping peacefully in the campsite amongst the tents during the day, unfazed by the bustle, and would only become active when darkness fell and campers were heading for the bathrooms before going to bed. One evening Django accompanied Salome when she went to brush her teeth, and as she was about to leave the ablution block his low growl alerted her to something untoward. Picking up on his signal, she peered out cautiously, and there, blocking the doorway, was the vast bulk of Esmeralda. Without Django's warning, my spouse's name might have been added to that ever-growing list of hippo-inflicted injuries.

Django asked for a little more rump and less cheese.

12

DESERT DOG

'Django's going to Namibia. Our clients have confirmed their booking for September and I have permits for him to go through all the Parks.'

With this good news a beaming Salome welcomed me back from a safari.

'How did you manage that?'

'I applied to head office of the Namibian Ministry of Environment & Tourism in Windhoek and it came through this morning.'

'I don't believe it. I wonder who screwed up. I bet no dog has been permitted for the Namibian Parks before.'

'So what? We have his permits and he's coming.'

* * *

Namibia is as different from Botswana as a kettle from a pan. My country of residence is laboriously flat, whereas Namibia has mountains and more mountains which form a spine down the entire western length of the country. To the coastal side of this range lies the oldest and very nearly the driest desert in the world, second only to the Atacama in Chile. Unlike the Kalahari sands (of which eastern Namibia

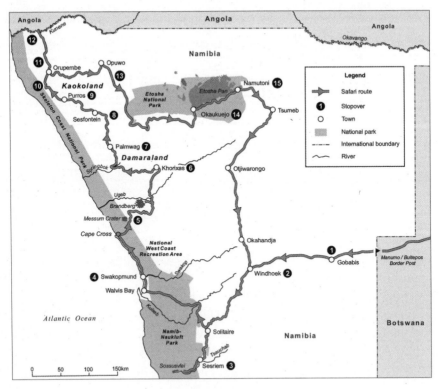

A SAFARI IN NAMIBIA

has plenty as well), the Namib fits the traditional image of a desert, where rainfall struggles to average half an inch in a year – an almost pointless statistic, when the evaporation rate is 100 times higher than that. The Namib is desperately arid.

Yet Namibia is a geologist's dream. Here the textbooks spring to life, offering real examples of just about every type of stratum that you can think of, and a whole lot more that have probably escaped your attention up to now. Mountains extracted from the earth below like reluctant teeth have been sliced, over countless millennia, by fierce desert winds to expose their innards. Layers of sedimentation have been uncovered so that geomorphologists can gaze with admiration at the wavy lines of their evolution like radio waves on a chart. Namibia is the home of gemstones – precious, semi-precious and just about everything else that could cross your imagination. I once camped on a knoll of tiger's eye, exposed by recent road works. It was so common that I did not bother to pick up a single memento and still berate myself daily for that neglect.

With a childlike eagerness I looked forward to revisiting this arid country – not simply because I love the vast emptiness of Namibia, which I already knew well, but because on this safari we would be going into Kaokoland, all the way north to the Angolan border. This was uncharted territory, not only for me, but for just about anybody. We needed large-scale contour maps to plot our way through that unoccupied land, and as these were only available in Windhoek we left four days early to give ourselves time to prepare.

We took two staff members with us – Sonny, a chef who used to work for a hunter and whose cooking experience revolved mostly around freshly shot animals and assorted tins, neither of which thrilled Salome. What did endear him to her, however, was an open smile that beamed out from a round, happy face. The other man, Isaacs, was an enormously tall, regal Bayei who had done only a few trips with us but who was strong, tireless and smart. He grasped a new concept quickly and would immediately point out the pros and cons of any suggestion that I made. Aside from this interaction, however, it was almost impossible to draw him into any meaningful conversation, so I drove with him in silence while Sonny yakked ceaselessly at Salome.

Unsurprisingly, the roads leading to the Namibian border at Mamuno were dreadful, and it took us two and a half gruelling days to cover the 1 200 kilometres to reach that far-flung post. Then, Gobabis, the first town that we came across, had one horse – which we chuckled at when we saw it leaving on the back of an open trailer. What remained was an unremarkable place with a clutch of churches and six tiny bottle stores, most of them with a selection of only two brands of beer, one of brandy and several brightly coloured soft drinks to disguise the taste of the cheap spirits. On the main road into town were three petrol stations, grouped in a tight defensive cluster as if they were forming a laager against the world, and a series of small shops. Someone had opened a toilet-paper manufacturing business, but since it was thousands of kilometres from the nearest sawmill and hundreds from a market with enough bottoms to wipe, it had inevitably closed. Only the faded signboards remained, recalling the empty dreams.

It took but an hour to walk from one side of town to the other, even if you visited all the shops that are open at any one time. The reason I know this: a broken radiator hose. My Land Cruiser's engine had been cooked as we followed the horse out of town. As a result I spent four days in Gobabis with Django for company, while Salome went ahead with the staff in the second vehicle to prepare for the safari. Four days may not seem to be a lot, but in Gobabis I was introduced to what a coma must feel like. People woke up, shuffled about their same dreary business, and sloped off at 5 pm, leaving behind a dorp that was almost as lively as the adjacent cemetery.

My Afrikaans is embarrassingly poor but as no one spoke English I struggled valiantly to communicate for the whole four days. On the third night I tired of the company of our jaded dog, who had taken to perpetual sighing and was blatantly even more bored with my company than I was with his, so we went to the bar. There I met the regulars – five of them, who looked as if they could be counted on to be on their same stools every lunchtime and every evening of the week, drinking the same drinks, telling the same tales and lamenting the same issues. This night, however, was different because one of them, a burly retired policeman, was celebrating his birthday. I ordered a beer for myself and a bowl of milk for Django, and that opened the door for the birthday boy to lurch over and engage me in heavily accented Afrikaans about a dog called Otto, a name which could be spelt backwards and still be the same. Somehow, after about 10 minutes of earnestly nodding my head at him while looking for a way to escape, I recalled that Otto was the name of the dog in a book called *The Sheltering Desert* written by two conflict-dodging Germans during the Second World War. My knowledge of this book elevated me, in his eyes, to a man of vast literary experience, quite unlike the rest of the illiterates in the bar whom he duly began to slate to the point that I thought that we would become involved in a brawl.

My new friend kept on buying more rounds of Jaegermeister and now included me. Confidentially he whispered that he had decided to tell me a story that he had never told any of the other regulars. During his time as a police officer he had served in a paramilitary outfit in the Rhodesian army, and then in Koevoet, a notorious counter-insurgency unit formed by the South African Police in South West Africa, as it was then. Both units were regarded as elite but ruthless. He was posted to Ovamboland in the north, from where most of the armed freedom fighters hailed. Clearly emotional, he told of mass graves he had witnessed, dug with earth-moving equipment and filled with dead bodies; men, women and children. He had apparently been ordered to shoot villagers, indiscriminately, in a mass murder of civilians reminiscent of the worst days of the Holocaust.

'It was bad,' he acknowledged, with tears in his eyes.

I could think of nothing else to say to this war criminal who was baring his soul to a stranger, so I asked him, 'Was it worthwhile from a military point of view?'

He did not hesitate. 'No. I was used by politicians. I wish I could turn back the clock but what is done is done.'

He looked truly remorseful, so I decided not to mention that his defence of acting under orders would not save him from punishment for war crimes in a court of law.

He ordered another birthday round and stood for a long time in contemplative silence.

'I have been to Solitaire,' he suddenly said. 'You and I have been to Solitaire.' (This was assumed, but correct.) 'These people have not been to Solitaire. They have no experience of life.'

It was odd for anyone, especially a man who had fought in elite units in two countries, to single out a visit to Solitaire, which is little more than a conveniently placed petrol station in the Namib, as a highlight of his life.

'I have climbed Kilimanjaro,' I replied.

This drew no reaction. I supposed that he had not heard of Kilimanjaro.

I continued: 'Then I found a coast full of history where David Livingstone's body was carried to a port.'

'Yes, there is a lot of history in graveyards,' he said solemnly.

He wandered back to his friends and insulted them a bit, which gave me the chance to watch them. Considering how adventurous and courageous their ancestors had been when they had trekked all over the continent in ox wagons, these folk led a deadly dull, routine existence, each day unvaried from the one before.

*   *   *

Ultimately I escaped from Gobabis and drove to Windhoek on a wonderfully smooth tar road, between endless fences decorated with regular signposts warning of kudu about to leap through my windscreen. I had beaten the clients' arrival by a handful of hours and had avoided the shopping.

Our clients for this trip were Belgians, and three of them had been on safari with us before. Michelle, an attractive blonde, was in an unhappy marriage to an aristocrat and lived a less than fairytale life in a castle. Her grown son, rather romantically, had wanted to be a safari guide and had spent three months with us in Kasane, where he learnt that it is much harder work than he was prepared to sign up for. He went on to market laundromats or condom machines and so could not join us on this occasion.

His grandparents, Jean-Pierre and Micheline, had retired in Spain. Before that his grandfather had spent a lifetime selling cigarettes in the Belgian Congo, during which time he had travelled the country on paved roads, something that is impossible today, because within five years of the former colony achieving independence as the Democratic Republic of Congo, an extraordinary 58 000 kilometres of tarred road disappeared into its own potholes. Countries with the word 'Democratic' in their name generally aren't, I find, and also are likely to fall apart.

Jean-Pierre was a tall, stooped man with silver hair who was in excellent condition for a person of his years. Micheline, a small woman who was as tough as the tyres that shared a similar name, was well in control of everybody around her. The fourth person, Maria, was a family friend who had apparently had her tongue sharpened on a grindstone especially for the trip. Django had no intention of becoming one of her victims and avoided her from the moment he first laid eyes on her.

We took the Khomas Hochland road to the sand dunes at Sossusvlei. This route starts without promise as it passes sheep farm after sheep farm, but then suddenly it stares down over a world of yellow sands and orange dunes that disappear into a distant horizon. Solitaire, that petrol station that bonds tipplers in Gobabis, lay far below us – a shelter for ants from our lofty perspective. As Namibia leads Botswana in providing facilities for tourists, we were able to unpack our cooler boxes and have lunch around one of those charmless concrete tables designed by road builders. We were seated on hard, immovable benches that were marginally too far away and frustratingly too high to allow any pretence of dignity. The view, however, made up for any discomfort.

I noticed Sonny lost in the landscape, mouth agape, shaking his head. He had never seen anything like this.

'What do you think?' I asked.

'Uh, uh uh,' was all I could get from him. He was suitably speechless.

Isaacs, meanwhile, had swiftly viewed the panorama, accepted it as a new experience and moved back to his lunchtime duties. Django leapt up onto a boulder and, with obvious awe, surveyed the world that lay beneath him. He had certainly never seen a comparable view while his paws remained on terra firma.

Lunch done, we dropped down to the plains below. The slippery gravel road twisted and turned alarmingly and I could see myself failing to make just one of those sharp turns and plummeting off the edge of the world. However, we made it safely to Solitaire. I was particularly proud that I had achieved this once more and fired off a quick 'wish-you-were-here' telegram to Gobabis then headed along the dusty road to Sesriem, where the Namib-Naukluft National Park headquarters for Sossusvlei were situated. We set up camp in a designated campsite – everything in Namibia is designated and strictly controlled in Teutonic fashion – and how else could it be, with a combined German and Afrikaans heritage? A group of idyllically spaced acacias, each with its own water tap and bounded by a low stone wall, made admirable sites, all efficiently arranged within easy reach of the communal ablution block.

Salome and I went off to organise some firewood and let the office know that Django was fully legal. The managers – a young couple – lived in a house adjacent to the office and as we walked past their gate their scruffy mongrel barked at us.

'Hi, just want to let you know that we have our dog with us and that he has permits for the parks,' Salome said brightly to the manager. I spotted that his pretty wife had looked up startled from her desk in the back office.

'What did you say?' the khaki-clad administrator barked in a threateningly aggressive tone.

Salome repeated herself in a distinctly more guarded manner.

'Let me see that permit.'

He grabbed the document and read it, all the time shaking his head so violently that I suspected it might fall off.

'This is not possible. I am going to take this permit to Windhoek now and get that bitch fired.' This, presumably, was the person who had so thoughtfully issued us the permit.

'No, you are not,' Salome said firmly. 'Make a copy if you like, but you return the original now.' She snatched it from him. 'How come you can keep a dog but we can't have ours here, even with a permit?'

'We live here – that's different.'

'Can we see your dog's permit?' she asked demurely.

He resolutely ignored her.

'If I see that dog I will shoot it,' he threatened.

At this point I took it upon myself to calmly and clearly explain to him just where I would insert his dog if he so much as dared to glance in the direction of mine. He did not shoot Django, and as far as I am aware did not glance at him, which was a good thing for his dog. However, we now had an indication of the reaction that we would get elsewhere, so we smuggled a fully permitted dog through the other parks.

A truckload of Italians with tiny blue tents moved in next to us and partied noisily late into the night, wrecking the silent desert ambience.

The Christmas bow tie.

On a canoe safari near Chief's Island.

Django's first helicopter flight.

Ready for take-off.

A mole-rat's hill ... irresistible!

In a mokoro with Salome and Skye.

With Salome at Makgadikgadi Pan.

Stroppy the elephant wreaked havoc at our
Chobe home.

Portrait on Makgadikgadi Pan.

Cooling off on a hot day in the Okavango.

Swimming with Peter.

On a game drive with Salome.

Off on safari ... Peter, Django and Salome.

Look — a scrub hare! Django and Peter on a game drive.

With Peter, admiring Zambia's Sioma Falls.

Django prevented Salome from blundering into Esmeralda the hippo at night.

Django took his responsibilities as Skye's guardian very seriously.

Somewhere in Namibia . . . a late-afternoon pit stop.

They ignored my repeated requests to tone it down, as we planned to be up at four next morning in order to see the sand dunes at sunrise. Groggily we set off for Sossusvlei before dawn, lustily singing 'Arrivederci Roma' to the sleeping Italians as we departed.

Namibians claim that their dunes are the highest on the planet; the Bedouins scoff at the suggestion. I have no idea who is right, but these are seriously impressive at over 300 metres above the surrounding land. The sand glowed an unnatural orange in the first rays of the sun, as if designed for surreal postcards – of which many thousands have been made, I can tell you – and the frisson of excitement in the back of the vehicle was palpable as we drew nearer.

We picked the largest sand dune and bounded up it. Well, Salome, Michelle and I bounded up the first 100 paces or so, by which time the older folk had slowed to an amble and Django had scooted so far ahead that we could barely see him. Every footstep then became a question of willpower. One foot placed a small step ahead of the last would slide halfway back again, and this was repeated pace after pace without the peak ever seeming to get closer.

We passed one of those dune lizards that seem not to know what to do with their feet. It would lift the front left foot and the back right foot and then swop around, as if it were performing an ancient dance. I despairingly felt that I was making much the same progress. Michelle gave up and sat down to admire the view, but we pressed on in the wake of our little dog. After a time we crested a brow.

'Just look at that!' Salome exclaimed.

Ahead of us on a dune that was absolutely devoid of vegetation was a gemsbok. It was powering its way to the summit and looked sleek and well fed, as though it had been quietly grazing in a meadow of waving grass, not struggling over barren sand. The glorious animal noticed us, stood and watched to see if we were a threat, quickly realised that we could never catch up with it and determinedly continued its journey. Django decided to play tag with one of his favourite antelopes and started to trot after it while we trudged sluggishly after them with leg muscles screaming at every pace. We finally caught up with our nimble dog as he waited patiently at the summit.

The scene beyond the peak was one of a never-ending series of sand dunes, broken only by the lone gemsbok already heading up the next one. Where it was going was hard to guess, as there was not a scrap of vegetation in sight. We took a long break and enjoyed the view before gravity helped us stumble back to base. The downhill lope is always exhilaratingly weightless, akin to what I imagine running on the moon would feel like. It is all too brief and almost makes you want to do it all again. Almost.

Instead, we had brunch under a shady camel thorn until a wind that was sweeping in off the cold Atlantic Ocean some 65 kilometres distant chased us into the vehicle. It strengthened as we neared the campsite, and on arrival we watched amused as the Italians frantically chased billowing tents that were lifting, like large balloons, into the air. Some flew tantalisingly just out of fingertip reach, leaving their desperate pursuers leaping futilely, while others floated inexorably out into the desert. Two settled on to the tops of giant camel thorns. Django decided that this was a game that he could enjoy and he spent a pleasurable half hour chasing tents across desert plains. He returned to stare at ours as if questioning why they hadn't lifted off too. They were of sturdy canvas and were weighted down with luggage – lots of it, in the case of our guests – and the worst that happened to them was that those with unzipped flaps had filled with sand. Once the wind had dropped we spent a smugly pleasurable afternoon watching denim-clad Italians climbing thorn trees, emitting frequent yelps of anguish, while attempting to retrieve their tattered accommodation.

* * *

Our next destination was Swakopmund on the Atlantic coast and as we set off after early breakfast the manager disappeared into his house at the sight of our approach, dragging his dog behind him to safety, while his wife wished us a tolerably cheery farewell. We passed through Solitaire again and followed the road north, with open plains to our left and the never-ending mountain range on our right. Django never lay down that day. He watched the enchanting world go by, his head out of the window and the breeze in his face.

We descended into a strange place dotted with rounded hillocks that resembled oat buns. This was the alien land of the Kuiseb Canyon, the site of *The Sheltering Desert*. It was little surprise that the two German fugitives could be wholly swallowed by this remote and desolate countryside for much of the six-year war. If they had not encountered health problems they would probably still be out there in their own paradise isolated from the madness of man and wondering if the war was still raging. We picnicked in the dry riverbed – at the designated picnic spot – under the romantic gaze of a pair of rosy-cheeked love-birds twittering in a towering ana tree.

Django and I needed relief from the chattering of the older women, and set off for a stroll over the rocky mounds. We had not gone far when the riverbed widened and we settled down on a rock to enjoy the tranquil view. A klipspringer bounced into view not ten metres from where we sat and Django started to shiver with excitement as we stared, transfixed, at this nimble, dainty antelope as it twitched its nose nervously and then, using the suction pads on the bottom of its feet, leapt gracefully from rock to rock to make its way down to the dry water course. The women, apart from my wife who was supervising the clearing of lunch dishes, were still chattering when we returned and they completely missed the gleam in our eyes. Django and I had just shared another magical moment.

A vast treeless plain lies between Kuiseb and the Atlantic Ocean at Walvis Bay, where we were headed.

Our sight of the ocean was the first ever for Sonny and Isaacs. We stopped at a spot with an extensive view over the blue expanse towards Walvis Bay, the only deep port along the west coast. It was a hazy day out at sea: the evening mists had started to build and the ocean was like a sheet of glass, with barely a ripple. Behind us towered the sand dunes that made this the biggest beach in the world. To the north, towards Swakopmund, was a large concrete platform, its feet perched on rocks in the cold Atlantic – a huge guano collector.

Salome, with Isaacs and Sonny for company, drew up behind us and everyone clambered out to appreciate the view. Django leapt from the vehicle, recognised the smell of an ocean, and charged around sniffing at distant smells – which no doubt included those from the platform.

Like the Native Americans when first confronted by approaching ships, Sonny and Isaacs had no conception of what they were seeing and their expressions remained unchanged.

'Can you see the boats?' Salome asked them. 'And look at the water. That water goes as far as you can see and then further again.'

Slowly comprehension started to dawn.

'It is a *lediba*, a lagoon, that goes for ever,' Isaacs said in hushed tones as he stared out at the water.

Sonny whispered in awe, casting his gaze back to the ships and pointing at one, 'It is a big mokoro.'

'Uh huuuuu,' agreed Isaacs. 'A very big mokoro. You can put your whole family in one.'

A long pause ensued.

'Uh huuuuu, and your hut,' suggested Sonny.

'Uh huuuu, and your whole village.'

'And it would take a week to pole it to the edge.'

This unfolding consciousness of a brand new concept was rewarding to watch, and, deeply thoughtful, we all climbed back into the vehicles.

That night was spent in Swakopmund and next morning we set off to the moon. Outside the town, away from the ocean, is an opportunity for an enchanting three- to four-hour drive in the Moon Landscape. This harsh and barren countryside has been sculptured over countless millennia by fierce winds and the Swakop River itself. Aside from the trees that line the riverbed there is very little vegetation, but what does occur verges on the implausible.

Perhaps the strangest of all the desert plants is a tree that lives buried up to three metres underground, apart from its two leaves that peek out above the surface and are ripped to shreds by the winds that howl up and down the coast. Friedrich Welwitsch fell to his knees when he saw his first specimen in southern Angola, at about the same time that the celebrated artist Thomas Baines said to himself, just outside

Swakopmund, where we now were, 'What a strange wee plant; I think I'll have a shot of the finest scotch and then set about painting it.'

Any work of art portraying a welwitschia looks like the artist has had a shot or two of whisky first, such is the nature of this straggly plant. The average tree seldom reaches much above knee height, yet can be 600 years old, while a mature specimen can live for 2 000 years or more with its foliage reaching the height of your front door. My tree book describes it as 'a dwarf but massive tree', an indication that botanists don't really know how to begin to describe it. They also don't know if it is an ancient conifer, because it has cones, or a more modern flowering tree, because it also flowers, which means that it fascinatingly straddles the evolutionary gap.

The confusion didn't end with its identity. There was also a dispute over who had first discovered it, because Baines and Welwitsch both sent samples back to Europe. In the end Baines's claim was dropped from the equation – probably at the behest of Livingstone, with whom he had previously fallen out – and so poor Thomas lost out on yet another small slice of fame. Django looked at one of these shredded, dishevelled-looking plants pityingly and peed on it.

Back in town Salome gave the staff a handful of money to use as their hearts most desired while we chose to sample Black Forest cake and good coffee. Sonny went off in search of exotic food and trinkets for his children. Isaacs spent his money wildly driving arcade machines in the adjoining laundromat.

*　　*　　*

Next morning we headed for the Skeleton Coast National Park. North of the Swakop River the land is as smooth as the ocean and on a misty day – which is the norm – it is difficult to tell the difference between land and sea. Pockets of warm and cold air occur all the way up the coast for no apparent reason. The terrain does not vary and there is no obvious change in the sea conditions, but one moment you are basking in warmth and the next you are reaching for your fleece. The vagaries of the weather in this area were of no concern to our dog however, as he was snuggled down warmly in Salome's handbag ready to enter yet another sanctuary with minimal official intervention.

Cape Cross is a protected and vital seal colony, but we had to settle for only a modest 80 000 Cape fur seals as company. There would have been many more had we come in October, but all the males were off at the pub or wherever it is that they go until it is time to return and fight over the women, establish their territories and then make pups. Once the excitement is over, they set off again into the wide ocean for a bit of peace and quiet. The continual bark and bustle of tens of thousands of these creatures kept Django spellbound, as did the sight of the black-backed jackals that moved between the seals looking for dead or unprotected pups. These scavengers, stuffed full on the rich fat that pads the seals against the freezing waters, were enormous in comparison to their brethren in Botswana. Django was less than impressed with the stench resulting from so many animals tightly packed together, however. It was offensive enough for my nostrils, and with his sharper sense of smell it must have been overpowering, because he finally retreated to the car and buried his nose in a blanket.

As we drove further north the sky closed in even more, and a strange feeling akin to heading into the surreal mists of a *Lord of the Rings* movie overtook me. Finally we veered away from the coast, and crossed the world's largest lichen fields, where the ground was a kaleidoscope of colours. Django watched in amazement as these ancient and unusual organisms, part algae, part fungus, unfurled and flowered when he peed on them – so he peed some more. This was more fun than anointing garden posts.

At Messum crater we camped together with a dassie rat, which is neither a dassie nor a rat but forms its own family of one, considered to be older, from an evolutionary perspective, than that of rodents. It showed no sign of fear and came so endearingly close to our tents that Django received a cautionary warning not to chase it.

Beyond the crater we were surprised to strike a large, graded highway in a place where our map showed no such thing. Perplexed, I stopped the vehicle at the T-junction and stared at the chart. Neither direction appeared correct.

I stared at the map and then the landscape. Left did not seem to lead anywhere, but then neither did the other way. My inclination was to continue straight on but, as there was no road, that was not an option.

Micheline leaned across and tried to take control. 'You must go left.'

She stabbed at the map. 'We are here so you must go this way.'

'Just a minute, let's make sure.' If we really were where Micheline was pointing, then we had somehow been transported in time to a part of the Namib that we had no intention or cause to ever visit.

'Look,' I said. 'Here's that mountain over there,' and I pointed at a flat-topped mountain adjacent to a cone-shaped smaller one that corresponded to the contours on our map.

'No. We are here. Go left now.' She was very patronising.

Salome drew up next to me. 'Trouble?'

I glanced at her without saying a word and she immediately suggested a stretch to pour water on lichens and enjoy a quick cup of coffee.

'But I know where we are! Doesn't Peter know how to read a map? I have done the navigating for Jean-Pierre right through the Sahara and we never once got lost,' she went on and on. Jean-Pierre is a placid person, not easily ruffled, but I would have liked to have seen how he coped with her in that huge desert.

'Will we be all right in the Kaokoveld?' she enquired shrewishly of Salome.

'Yes, I'm sure we will; one sugar or two?' my redhead replied soothingly.

My wife is a gem for defusing a fraught situation and we duly turned right when we got going again. God knows where (or if) we would have come out had we listened to Micheline because, according to our map, that direction seemed to lead nowhere, unless perhaps to a recently opened mine. As we headed off in the direction that I had chosen I could hear her deep sighs of resignation that I could be so bull-headed, but slowly this changed to tight lips of contrition as it dawned on her that we were going the right way.

The right-hand turn took us straight to our planned destination, Brandberg, famed for a Bushman painting known as the 'White Lady'. Described by Reinard Maarck, who discovered her in 1929, as 'a painting of a woman who has a white body', it caused heated debate about where a white woman could have come from, but the truth is that she was not even a woman. Maarck had clearly been out in the desert for far too long without female company, and had not noticed that the figure lacked breasts. It was not, however, the White Lady who caught my attention, as I had met her before, but the ugly iron bars that now prevented us from defacing her. A certain class of visitor had travelled to this remote mountain to see a famous painting and found that if they threw whatever liquid they had to hand (brandy and Coke seems the most popular) they could take shiny pictures. As a result the White Lady is now behind prison bars and the culprits roam free. Disgruntled, I stalked back to the car and threw some Coke on the sign that said 'Do not throw Coke'. Still quietly fuming, I wandered a few paces from the vehicle with Django, where we spotted my first Herero chat – a rare bird in most people's books – which cheered me up considerably. It really doesn't take much to lift my spirits.

Bergsig offers magnificent views from the top of this remote escarpment and while we were absorbing these, Salome and I were reminded of a trip we had done with our friends John and Jane from Swaziland, and their American friend, Jennet. She came from New York and had lived in cities in Africa for a few years, but she had never before experienced this kind of solitude. Fences, I find, create comfort zones for people and there are no fences in Damaraland, just wide-open arid spaces. No one lives here because it is well-nigh impossible to scratch out a living in an environment too parched even for goats to survive in.

With John, Jane and Jennet we had descended from Bergsig towards Springbokwasser, the northern entrance to the Skeleton Coast National Park, and set up camp near the dry bed of the Springbok River. The desert encircled us and was eerily still. A few birds chirped sporadically from riverine trees, but that aside, there was no sound. Not the slightest breeze blew and there were no vehicles, no houses, no lights and no airplanes droning overhead. For me it was such paradise that

I had light-heartedly suggested to Salome that we should come and settle here.

She'd laughingly agreed and strolled off with Django along the riverbed, where they came across some fresh signs of a black rhino having passed that way. She called us over and we all followed the tracks unsuccessfully until dusk. Jennet had been a very quiet and subdued companion – until we returned to camp. There she threw her toys out of the cot, all of them at the same time and as far she could. She ranted and raved and screamed, finally subsiding into a little sobbing bundle, desperate for the sounds of revving engines, screaming tyres and ambulance sirens. She had discovered an unexpected side of herself, unprepared for unlimited nothingness where man made no impression, nor did he pollute the environment with light, noise or chemicals. Because there was no chance of accessing civilisation before daylight, Jennet had to confront her demons, alone in her tent in that isolated place, for a long night of infinite silence. How our ancestors would have shaken their heads in amazement.

Now, with our Belgian party we pushed on to Sesfontein, a small village built around a derelict fort. We pulled up at the ruin and poked around its broken walls and sand-filled rooms, feeling a touch of nostalgia. It was built, initially, not as a military post but to help control cattle following the rinderpest outbreak of 1896, which decimated southern Africa's livestock. In 1905 it was converted into an army base, and housed as many as 40 soldiers with 25 horses (I wondered what the unfortunate unmounted 15 men might have done wrong to be made to march through this unforgiving terrain). Four years later the military rode out – except for those 15, it would seem, who had to walk again – and they were replaced by three lonely policemen who, in turn, were sent packing in 1914, presumably to go and fight a war in Europe.

The fort never saw military action and it was the effects of time that had ravaged it, hence my introspection. Django explored the ruins with scant regard for its history, anointed each room, and then came back to give the 'all clear' – we could move on.

Three powerful BMW motorbikes pulled up as we were about to

leave and a very large German clad in black leathers strolled stiffly towards us. Nothing could have been more incongruous.

'You like zis place, ja?' he asked.

'Interesting,' I replied politely.

'Good. I am going to make a hotel here.'

I looked about me at the few scattered huts and then at the broken walls. The man was clearly certifiable and might even be dangerous. We left promptly but he stayed and built what turned out to become a thriving hostelry.

*   *   *

The track north led to Purros, and beyond that into the Kaokoveld, where we would spend the next week. It was the most stunning wilderness I have ever seen, and there was scarcely a moment when you could not have taken a perfect postcard picture. The never-ending mountain chain to the east formed a relentless varying backdrop, and the country to the west alternated between hills, mountains and dunes which occasionally spilled over into vast plains of tall wavy grass. The colours danced off every surface in a display of speckled chocolate, eggshell and slate that left no heart unmoved. The trail often disappeared completely and we would have to rely on the topographical maps to make our way forward. Micheline, after her embarrassment outside Messum, kept her counsel tightly bottled.

This land was virtually unpopulated save for scattered settlements of the Himba tribe. They have largely resisted any encroachment of the first world; their dwellings are small, made from bent boughs and covered loosely with karosses and blankets. Outside the first one we encountered, an empty plastic basin and an equally empty 20-litre water container lay discarded and, apart from a torn grain sack, those appeared to be their only perceived concessions to civilisation.

A woman, so wrinkled and aged that she may well have been Vita's mother, was sitting on the ground, her legs stretched out before her. Vita was the Himba chief who had fled the Nama wars and transformed the tribe from landless beggars to rich and proud cattle owners in the late 1800s. The old lady seemed to be incapable of walking, as she never rose the whole time we were there. The three younger females with her, one of them pregnant, were all dressed in skirts made from hide and wore nothing else but a necklace. Hanging onto their mother's wraps were young children who stared in voiceless wonder at the strange people who had descended upon them. A young man with a lithe body that I noticed our women appreciated, judging by the furtive glances they cast in his direction, made up the group. All the women were bare-breasted, and rubbed in butterfat with an ochre dye that gave their bodies a shiny red sheen. From what I could tell, the butterfat acted as a sun lotion, while the ochre was purely decorative. Whatever the reason, it was certainly distinctive.

Salome gave our clients some meaningful advice on the etiquette required when meeting a new culture – don't impose yourself on these people; treat them with respect; request permission before taking photographs; do not offer them goods that might impinge on their culture, and so on. I know that they understood, yet they later did everything that they were asked not to do.

We introduced ourselves in all the eight languages that we could muster between us, to no avail. We had no common tongue, yet it did not take long before we had established a few rules of engagement. Firstly, we could take pictures; secondly, they were desperate for some drinking water, and thirdly – and most importantly – the pregnant woman had a stomach pain and could we help? The young man, almost professionally, cadged a cigarette off Isaacs.

Django slipped into one of the huts to investigate and when he came out he was smeared with red fat. How he got so much of it on himself is uncertain but he must have found the smell appealing and rolled in it. One of the young women noticed him and squealing with delight rubbed the fat evenly over his body, transforming him into something matching my wife's hair.

When we – rather reluctantly, it must be said – brought out a 20-litre drum and filled the thirsty family's container, their gratitude was immense. We did not have a whole lot of water to spare because we were a minimum of three days from the nearest supply ourselves and I had already made it clear to our party that there were to be no showers while we were in the Kaokoveld – we would give each person a bowl of water per day to wash in, though drinking water was unrestricted. We had none, however, to waste on Django and the best we could do for him was to rub him down with a dry towel which failed to get rid of the clingy fat, so everywhere he went for the next few days he left red smudges.

Salome did not want to do anything too drastic for the pregnant woman because she had no idea what was wrong – she may have eaten something disagreeable, which, given how they lived, was a distinct possibility, or she may have been in labour, so my wife gave her an Alka-Seltzer, which seemed to be the right placebo. Meanwhile our clients poked around uninvited inside the beehive huts, thrust their cameras intrusively into ochre faces and generally were a huge embarrassment to Salome, our staff and me. Django was too busy with his own exploration of some old bones to notice. When Salome reprimanded them, Jean-Pierre sheepishly apologised and said that they could not help themselves as it was such a special experience. Finally, when it came time to leave, the old woman put out her hand. Salome had some maize meal and sugar ready and handed these over, but the crone also wanted something from the clients, who then backed off in a manner that made everyone feel uncomfortable, so Isaacs and Sonny searched their pockets and one of them found a last five-dollar coin, which they proffered as a thank-you offering. The old woman took it, looked at it in a perplexed way, put it to her mouth and bit on it. It obviously did not taste good because she handed it straight back to the men. Suitably chastened, we left in awkward silence.

One of the young women had taken a shine to Sonny and had unashamedly given him the eye. Salome teased him when they were back in the car.

'Do I need to tell your wife about this woman? I saw her looking at you.'

'No, I am not going to marry her,' Sonny said bashfully, eyes averted.

'Well, if you do, you will spend all your salary to get her clean,' laughed Isaacs.

The town of Purros was the only habitation shown on the map between us and the Kunene River on the Angolan border. Our guidebook made no mention of it so we had no idea of what to expect, but as the map indicated an airstrip, I was hopeful of a supermarket, a petrol station, and maybe a pub with cold beer. The very least I hoped for was a well where we could recharge our empty water bottles. As it turned out all it had was a few more huts than we had come across before and absolutely no facilities. That it appeared on any map was an indication of just how few people lived in this part of the world.

Interestingly, we saw among the half-naked Himba people a scattering of Herero women clad in their full Victorian-style dresses, with layer upon layer of petticoats. They are historical cousins and while some seemed underdressed for the elements, the others were considerably overdressed. We drove past with a wave and they looked at us bleakly as if to say, 'Not more tourists. We had a bunch just the year before last.'

The next two and a half days blurred into a single impression of spectacular countryside that went on for 10 hours a day and which changed moment by moment, but in its constant changing remained the same. We drove on riverbeds and crossed gullies so steep that the undercarriages of our vehicles caught on the hard ground and sounded as if they were being torn apart; we drove until late afternoon, set up camp, cooked, ate and slept. The next morning we were up before dawn, had breakfast, packed, drove until late afternoon, set up camp, cooked, ate and slept.

What we enjoyed most of all was the experience of freedom from other people. The only sign of humanity in three long days was the welcome sight of a red drum that matched a landmark on our large-scale map. It confirmed that we were on course, which was a comfort, because we did not want to make a mistake out here. It was so isolated that any error could prove fatal. One evening, to add to the sense of solitude, mists from the ocean rolled in and hung motionless above the valley, like a blanket on a washing line. Jennet would have needed a large cot out here together with extra padding and a dummy.

Beyond the red drum, we turned up the Marienfluss valley and negotiated a gorge with towering mountains to either side of us, until we had to stop because we had reached the Kunene River and the Angolan border. The craggy peaks to the west of us were the Baynes Mountains, the home of a tribe of Stone Age hunter-gatherers who were the last people to be discovered on earth.

It was as recently as 1964 that a delegation of scientists met the Tjimba and proclaimed their existence to the outside world. They lived a similar hunter-gatherer lifestyle to the Bushmen, and still made fire with sticks and used knives of stone, though they were not of the same racial group, nor were they related to the Himba and Hereros. Short, stocky and with small hands and feet, they were much darker than the local tribes and had descended from a negroid group who had come to southern Africa centuries ahead of the Bantu peoples. By 1974, there were only 150 Tjimba left, and they mostly spoke the language of the Herero, the dominant tribe of the region and for whom they herded cattle, their own ancient way of life consigned to the history books for ever. It was humbling to gaze at these mountains in the 1990s and think that only a quarter century before we drove up a tribe had lived there, unknown to the outside world, and that they were still hunting with stone arrowheads while the Americans were preparing to walk on the moon. This was indeed a wild and inaccessible part of the earth.

We camped in a designated campsite – amazingly, some official had journeyed all the way up there to paint rocks white – beside the river and spent a full day recovering from the long trek. The Kunene is home to a large population of exceedingly aggressive crocodiles and we had to be careful – especially Django, who flopped into a small rocky pool and just lay there, heat evaporating off his half-submerged body. There was also the small matter of a civil war that was raging in the south of Angola, a country that had been at war with itself for 30 years, and disconcertingly lay about 40 paces away from where we were swimming on its border.

Apart from dodging crocodiles and bullets there was not much to do in this stifling gorge, although there were some interesting herdsmen running cattle a few kilometres away who were clearly not Himba.

I looked closely at them and noticed that they were small and dark, with petite feet and hands. I suspected, perhaps hoped, that they were Tjimba, so with much enthusiasm we went to greet the most elusive people on earth. They were reserved but not unfriendly and chatted animatedly amongst themselves when they spied Django. They called him over and made a fuss of him, tousling his hair while looking at us and making incomprehensible suggestions in a strange tongue. I was over-awed to meet these singular people but disappointed that we could not communicate, so we smiled and nodded at each other for a while, swapped unintelligible anecdotes about female perceptions of hand sizes, and then went back to cool off with the crocodiles.

*   *   *

Once we left Marienfluss our southbound journey started with a two-day drive to Okaukuejo in the Etosha National Park. En route, we had refuelled the vehicles at Opuwa, the only town in Kaokoland. Pert-breasted Himba women pressed up against my back while queuing in a crowded shop, leaving tell-tale red ochre stains on my shirt that I had to explain to my wife. Now I may be a bit off the mark, but if supermarkets around the world could persuade their female customers to dress in this manner this would, I am certain, encourage men to take a more lively interest in shopping.

As we approached the Park gate, we saw dog kennels designed to check in your pets. After the freedom of the open spaces where we had just come from, they looked like prison cells. Django climbed into Salome's handbag, ready to be lawfully smuggled into one of the world's great conservation areas.

At Okaukuejo that evening, in the pale light at the floodlit waterhole, the rare sight of black rhino, elephants and lions together down at the drinking hole enthralled us. The black rhino pair fought above their weight division and repeatedly charged the elephants, which would take a step or two back and then stand their ground. Frustrated, the aggressive rhinos would turn on the lions and scatter them. They spent more time in confrontation, short-sightedly peering into the gloom for a foe, than they did drinking, and they reminded me of acquaintances from the Duck Inn.

Here we did not use the campsite and appreciated climbing into crisp sheets in our chalet instead. That first evening was a joy, but by the second day I was ready to get out of Etosha. The camps are fenced and boast shops, restaurants, bars, swimming pools, petrol stations, a range of various standards of accommodation, a campsite and all the trappings of civilisation. You drive on tarred roads to reach these urban spreads and on smooth, graded roads to travel from one artificial waterhole to the next – preferably with the window up and the air conditioner on to avoid the natural elements. At night you sit on benches and watch the animals come down to drink – as they do night after night – just as if it were a TV soap opera. I was suddenly glad that we were near the end of the trip.

Namutoni, where we stayed in the old fort, was even larger than Okaukuejo and offered a similar range of facilities including a swimming pool with a sign prohibiting spitting. I spent much of my evening fantasising about how I could torch this place and return it to the wild. It just seemed so incongruous to be in a preserved wilderness and feel like a preserve yourself. We left Etosha as quickly as the speed humps on the tar road would allow. It was time for the safari to end and, after an uneventful drive to Windhoek, it did.

On the way home, Salome asked Sonny and Isaacs what was their lasting impression of the trip. It was not the mountains or the sand dunes; neither were they truly impressed by the ships or the ocean itself. Even the Himba and the city of Windhoek paled, they decided, when compared to the arcade machines of Swakopmund.

Django may have been rightfully miffed at being treated like a criminal in a land where he was licensed to travel but he would have had a head full of stories to relate to his friends in Kasane.

13

KING AND COUNTRY

There were whispers, unconfirmed but alluring, that Liuwa National Park in western Zambia was the last untamed paradise in Africa, secretly harbouring vast herds of wildlife that roamed unfrequented plains. I needed to find out for myself and told Salome that the next action-seeking clients were in for real adventure in this land not charted. Was it shoddy cartography that showed no roads or, more intriguingly, did no one visit the region?

As events unfolded, it was our regular Japanese clients, Yoko and Shoko, who signed up – possibly because their limited English let them down with the small print, which contained clauses such as *'we have no clue where we are going on this trip'* and *'no refunds if you are eaten by cannibals'*. These two women had been with us on safari to Botswana a number of times before, always accompanied by Yoko's husband. This time he was unable to take time off work, but I am sure they expected something similar to their earlier trips. As this did not happen, it was a good thing that they were deeply appreciative of any unforeseen experiences, in that wonderfully magnanimous Oriental way.

We searched in Kasane for someone who could tell us what we might find, where to shop, what to avoid and so on – but we could not find a soul who had travelled there other than Mike Slogrove, who

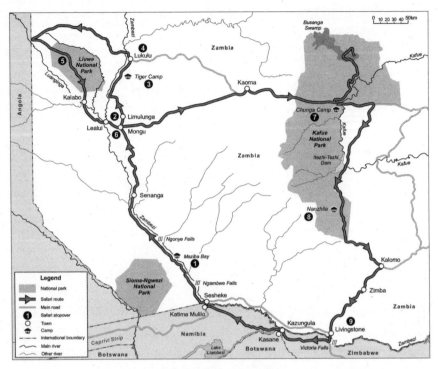

A SAFARI IN WESTERN ZAMBIA

had worked for the Zambian National Parks many years before. He could help us with a general idea of what to do and where the river crossings were, but, as he pointed out ominously, things had changed for the worse since he was last there. Usefully though, he had a friend who still worked in the National Parks office at Mongu, the only town of any significance in the area, and it was to this man that we turned. His first warning was for us to bring kwacha, and lots of them, because the bank at Mongu was unreliable and nothing but kwacha was accepted in western Zambia. Petrol in Mongu was expensive, and he guessed that we would require around a million kwacha just to fill the vehicles. Furthermore, this obscene amount could only be sourced in Livingstone.

Based on his advice, eight million kwacha was what I calculated we would need, so a week before our departure date we had to take an inconvenient trip via the ferry crossing at Kazungula followed by a pot-holed road journey to Livingstone, where the three of us located the few banks in town.

Having stared uncomprehendingly at selling rates that were notated in pins and Ks, we eventually settled on a bureau de change that was located up some dingy stairs and seemed to offer more pins (1,000 Kwacha notes, and named after the comma) to the US dollar. The street-level entrance was a locked iron gate, with an armed guard wielding an AK-47 on duty behind it. He cautiously opened the barrier, peered intently up and down the street, and allowed me to enter. I made my way upstairs, only to find that I was barred by a similar gateway, again protected by an armed guard. Once he had granted me passage, I came to a locked door that was very obviously fitted with an armour-plated glass window, and this was opened to the sound of a buzzer when it was deemed that I was not intent on mayhem.

I handed over a modest wad of US$100 notes to a man seated behind more armour plating and received in return three shopping packets stuffed with money. I took bundles of these notes from one and crammed them into my pockets until they bulged alarmingly, and then found that I had not yet emptied the first bag, so I picked up the remaining containers and headed for the exit.

'You can't go out like that!' The cashier called me back with panic in his voice. 'You will be killed for that kind of money.'

'What do you mean?' I queried, startled.

'Did you not see our security? There are armed gangs that have raided us three times recently. You will lose your money, maybe your life.'

I looked around helplessly. If I left the bags and did a shuttle to and from the car, I would be emptying my pockets in full view of any armed gangsters, which would leave my wife and dog unacceptably exposed. I shrugged, picked up the packets, said a final farewell to the concerned face behind the glass and headed for our vehicle, which was not far away, with Salome on guard inside it and Django on sentry duty outside.

Perhaps the robbers were on a tea break, or maybe they were executing a bank heist elsewhere, because I managed to throw the packets into the back of the vehicle and clamber into the driver's seat without being hijacked. Django leapt onto the seat beside the money and we sped off, checking at regular intervals to see if we were being followed. When I was certain that we weren't, I steered towards the lonely road to the border ferry, happy once more to return unharmed to the sanctuary of peaceful Botswana.

We had to smuggle that cash – which, ironically, no one would accept outside of Zambia or even on board their own national airline – into Kasane for the sole purpose of smuggling it out again when we left on safari, having risked lengthy jail sentences in the process.

We had tried to organise a permit for Django, but our application had apparently fallen off the desk in Zambia into the 'too hard' bin, so he came along, not as a refugee hiding from the authorities, because we would have an armed Parks Officer with us, but in his capacity as an honorary person – albeit one who was prepared to hide inside a handbag at the nod of a head. My mother-in-law had also been invited to join us and all I received in return for my suggestion that the old dear might also need a permit was a hostile glare from her daughter.

*　　*　　*

Shoko and Yoko flew into Kasane and our first stop in Zambia was at Maziba Bay Lodge on the Zambezi River, just south of the Ngonye Falls. The road on the western bank was a broad gravel highway that at one time had been kept in good repair by a dedicated driver and his trusty grader. The old man would start at the southern end of his 150-kilometre section and work his way northwards. Once he had completed his task, he would trundle southwards and resume the process. He was so well organised and dedicated that he managed to scrounge enough diesel to run his beloved grader as well as the spares to repair her, despite the critical shortages that plagued Zambia's economy at the time. Since his death the decaying grader has remained on the side of the road where he last parked it, like a grand memorial to his achievements. No one took over from him and the road had by now become so corrugated that it threatened to part the fillings from our teeth.

Comprehensively shaken, we arrived at the rustic lodge and met its owner, André van der Merwe. Apart from his managerial duties, he was enthusiastically planning to upgrade the site, improve its airstrip and establish a second camp within the nearby Sioma Ngwezi National Park. Less encouraging, but no less enthusiastic, were his intentions to log the hardwood forests.

That night Django and I had a whole new bush experience. After dinner we had all retired to bed when Salome asked for some drinking water. Grumbling a bit, I climbed out of the tent and made my way through the darkness to the lodge's kitchen, with Django following me. We were confronted by a cacophony of hisses and growls that appeared to be emanating from a massive toothpick holder reversing rapidly towards us, making a noise similar to the rattling of spears from a Zulu impi. Django growled and feinted to the left, deliberately attracting the attention of the shuddering mass. This gave me time to escape, while the dog easily dodged the cumbersome porcupine, which had the added disadvantage of not being able to see beyond its splayed quills while travelling in reverse and finally managed to impale itself on a sack of maize meal that had negligently been left on the floor. Startled by its abrupt halt, the confused creature then tried pulling itself forwards, and in doing so left most of its quill cover embedded in the sack, which took on the appearance of a large pincushion as the half-naked porcupine beat a hasty retreat.

All the water that moves on to pour over the Victoria Falls first cascades spectacularly over the 20-metre-high, horseshoe-shaped Ngonye Falls nearby. We went to view them by boat, which André parked on the far bank downstream from the falls, and we climbed out of the gorge and trekked through a forested area. Ngonye Falls is on a miniature scale to those that Livingstone made famous, as they are only one fifth of the height. Yet nothing prepares you for their sheer beauty. Should the Victoria Falls not have existed, these falls would surely have acquired their due fame.

Intriguingly, the rocks on either side vibrate, caused by a part of the river that gushes beneath them, and this left us feeling as though we were still on that corrugated road. To see the smooth slow-flowing water above the chasm crash into the cauldron below is to witness a change in geology – a transition point from Kalahari sands to the basalt dyke that eventually forms the mighty gorges of the Victoria Falls. This marks a critical point in the history of the Kalahari, for it is here that the Zambezi first met the fault lines that swung the river to the east, depriving the vast Lake Makgadikgadi (which lay in central Botswana and once formed the largest lake in Africa) of its water source. What was once a climate-altering lake has now become a dry saltpan the size of Wales.

André, a dynamic adventurer, made sure that we were active at Maziba Bay. He took us white-water rafting, which was fun without having quite the adrenalin rush of the water below Victoria Falls. There was no life jacket small enough to fit Django so we left a reluctant dog back at camp where he made a friend. André had acquired an orphaned elephant that he hand-fed countless litres of baby concentrate each day, and this feisty young bull, which could not have been more than six months old, lunged aggressively at everyone other than his foster father. When he spied Django he ran full tilt at our dog, who nimbly evaded him. This confrontation soon turned into a game, and if Django disappeared for any length of time we would be sure to find the two playing tag nearby.

A game drive into Sioma Ngwezi National Park – a forgotten 5 000 square kilometre reserve surrounded by a 35 000 square kilometre Game Management Area, was rewarding beyond expectations. As it was completely undeveloped, we could drive in at any access point that we liked and Django loved the novelty of not having to dive for a handbag.

One evening Django was lying at the entrance to the verandah enjoying the view of the setting sun when he suddenly jumped up and stood pressing against my legs while growling softly and staring towards the bush. He wanted no part of whatever was out there. Then a partly bald porcupine trotted up the steps, looked us over to see if he could impale anyone, and then sauntered back down and disappeared from whence he came.

Among the varied attractions that André offered was a flight over the falls in his microlight, and we enthusiastically accepted the opportunity. The flimsy airplane needed to be readied for action, so we helped André clip the wings in place before our daring ladies took it in turns to soar over the falls – the first time any of them had ventured skywards in such a frail craft. Because I was the only one who had flown in an ultra-light before, I had volunteered to sit this one out and was expecting to help fold away the aircraft as dusk approached and the last sortie ended. However, André came up to me with a twinkle in his eyes and said, 'There's something I want to try, if you're game? We must rush, though, if we want to beat the dark.'

Without asking what it was that he had in mind, I climbed aboard with my camera at the ready and off we went. His idea of something new was to skim so low over the river that my feet could feel the spray as it blew up from the rippling water beneath us. Then, twisting and turning through the gorge under the power lines, he flew to the very face of the waterfall. Suddenly petrified, I remember thinking with absolute certainty that I was going to die. It was unavoidable. I could almost reach out and touch the wall of water and I was also aware that we were powered by an engine that is more at home on a lawn mower than an aircraft. With the horseshoe gorge wrapped around us we were soaked by spray. André tugged on the controls and we started to lift, agonisingly slowly, towards the lip of the falls, and when we crested it in a cloud of swirling mist I instinctively lifted my feet to avoid the rocks that marked its rim. He smiled at me triumphantly. He had just fulfilled a personal challenge, and now that we had survived I realised that I too had enjoyed being there right on the edge with him.

While André was obviously proud of himself, my mind must have been in much the same turmoil as the billowing cloud that we had just flown through, because I astounded myself by indicating to him with hand signals that we should do it again. I had instantly become an adrenalin junkie. Perhaps it was just as well that we were out of daylight. I was so abuzz with nervous tension that I left my camera either on André's truck or at the airstrip and, sadly, never saw it again.

After the excitement that André had provided, our Japanese ladies were sad to leave Maziba Bay and when Django appeared reluctant to leave his new friend behind, I had to explain to him that we had no space for an elephant, thereby concealing the fact that I was quite keen to move on in case André had any more 'firsts' to try out on me.

*   *   *

As we made our way north along the western bank of the Zambezi towards Mongu, I knew we would have to cross over to its eastern side to avoid a treacherous sandy stretch of road that lay ahead. The fact that I was towing our heavily laden trailer did not ease my concerns as I contemplated the ferry trip that this would entail, as well as others to come. At Senanga we boarded a large well-equipped vessel, however, and forded the river with ease – marred only by the fact that it was at this stage that we discovered the loss of our camera, which caused anguish during what should have been an enjoyable, uneventful passage.

When Zambia gained independence the tiny kingdom of Barotseland, which had been ruled as a separate colony by Britain, had decided after many reassurances to join the new African state. Sadly, many of the early promises were not kept and the kingdom slid into abject poverty – a neglected province within a country that was itself facing total economic collapse.

Mongu was the capital of what was now Zambia's Western Province. It was here that regulations decreed that we should pick up an armed Parks ranger to guide us through the Liuwa section of the safari. We were assigned a young man named Nelson who, we were informed, had grown up in the region and knew the countryside like the back of his hand. We resupplied and refuelled, which, in the capital of any province, should have been a simple exercise. Mongu, however, provided a challenge when I realised that one of the vehicle's batteries should be replaced, and we searched the petrol station and scoured the spares shops to no avail. This once vibrant trading town was the only major commercial centre for four hundred kilometres in any direction, yet there were no car batteries available at any price.

As we drove out of town we dropped down to the Zambezi floodplain,

where we faced myriad un-signposted tracks. Nelson, however, directed us at every fork with a 'left here', or 'right here'. He lacked conviction, but we did find a pleasantly wooded camping spot for the night
that was isolated from nearby habitation.

The next morning we picked up a hitchhiker who said he would
show us the way to Tiger Camp, our immediate destination. He took
us on a narrowing track that became a footpath, and then faded into
nothingness at the edge of a ploughed field within sight of a collection of huts. I stalled the vehicle on the sandy humps and was unable
to restart the engine because of its faulty battery. As I irritably hauled
out my toolbox, our guide thanked us for the door-to-door service we
had provided and walked the short distance to his house, leaving us
stranded in his maize patch. I could not help but admire his gall.

Eventually, after much cursing, I solved the vehicle problem and
managed to find the way to a track that led us to our goal. It was there
that all our frustrations dissipated – Tiger Camp was perfect. Owned
and managed by Bernie Esterhuyse and his wife, Adrienne, it was an
angler's paradise and named suitably after the impressive tiger fish
(a close relative of the South American piranha) that patrols certain
African waters. Unpretentious tents, complete with covered showers
and flush toilets, were set along the river and the communal dining
area was spacious and welcoming.

They had chosen one of the most difficult places in Africa to run a
lodge. Supplies either came from Mongu (and we had seen how limited
an option that was) or had to be flown 450 kilometres from Lusaka.
Even the purchase of fuel for their boats, vehicles and generator en-
tailed a 400-kilometre road trip. As a result, much of what Adrienne
did by way of catering was homemade, including the world's best
home-baked cookies. The freshwater fishing in the vicinity of the camp
was some of the finest in the world too, and she prepared the catches
in tasty and original ways.

Bernie, however, looked flustered from dawn to dusk as he dashed
from broken boat engine to failed generator to leaky plumbing. It was
a difficult life, but they had chosen this spot because of its exceptional
angling opportunities, and Bernie could boast about numerous world

records caught from his camp. Django loved the freedom of the place, but was a bit scornful of the minced tiger fish given to him for supper.

Yoko and Shoko were not keen fisherpeople and so we suggested a boat drive along some quiet loops in the river which bypassed scattered villages. The people we saw were destitute and so removed from access to worldly things that the children ran along the riverbank shouting, 'Tinnie! Tinnie!' The value of an empty coke tin, which we discard without thought, is immeasurable to them as it provides a cup to drink from, a pot to brew their bush tea in or a container to collect and store small fruit and seeds. Coming from Botswana, where the roadsides are littered with cans, it was an eye-opener – and disturbing – to see how prized they were here and how impoverished these people were.

During the cruise I threw a line into the water, using whatever lure was attached, and trawled as we went along – mainly to reassure Bernie that I did fish, in case he refused to have me back. Then my line hooked on something large.

'Hold it!' I called to the boat driver. 'I've caught something.'

He looked dubiously at the tip of my rod, which was almost bent double. 'You have snagged a log,' he stated.

'If it is a log, it's the only log I know that fights back!' I retorted.

Ten minutes later I had proudly landed an enormous olive bream, or *nembwe*, as they are called locally, and it was by far the biggest specimen I had ever seen. I wanted to release it but our boatman condemned me, with one withering look, as an inconsiderate wastrel.

'That is a big fish. We can eat from that. Here we do not throw fish back when people are hungry.'

Abashed, I allowed him to keep it, though I did not cast my line again. When we reached the camp, Bernie immediately grabbed my catch and rushed off to weigh it.

'You were an ounce and a half off the world record for a *nembwe*,' he announced excitedly. 'What did you use as bait? What depth were you at?' Questions rolled off his tongue but I could not help him with technique. I simply hadn't used any.

*   *   *

When we bade Bernie and Adrienne goodbye, our immediate destination was the small missionary town of Lukulu, where we would cross the Zambezi on a ferry run by the mission station, after we had bought our permits to enter Liuwa. We had been told that the Parks office was at the petrol station on the main road and easy to find – but that fuel itself would not be available because the pumps had not worked for 30 years. The office was firmly locked and we spent two hours tracking down the official responsible for issuing the permits. We finally found him drinking tea at a friend's house and he seemed rather disconcerted to hear that we wanted to buy park entry permits from him, but came along with us. When we arrived at his office, a search for the Issues book commenced.

'I have only been here for three years, so I haven't actually sold a park permit yet,' he explained as he rummaged through drawer after drawer and then repeated the same procedure in an adjoining room.

He picked up an antiquated phone of the type that requires you to crank a handle in order to alert an exchange operator, who in turn puts your call through. It took an hour to connect to Mongu and ask what the book looked like. After a long and detailed conversation, he finally set down his lifeline and returned to the filing cabinet, from where he eventually emerged, triumphantly waving a ledger above his head. It had lost its front cover, despite having been utilised for only two entries, one from four years earlier and the other six years before that. Liuwa, I began to realise, was no tourist trap.

The harassed official was fearful of making a mistake in the almost pristine ledger, so he laboriously practised on scraps of paper until he was certain he could spell our names correctly and had our addresses and passport details pat. When I returned with the Dents, my most regular clients, two years later, we were still the latest entry in the ledger.

Armed with a permit, we went to the hospital, where that section of the mission station that ran the ferry was situated – we needed to find a doctor who would help us cross the river. The hospital was surprisingly large, clean and busy, but was not overcrowded – unlike so many others of its kind elsewhere in Africa. We finally found the surgeon who, between operations, controlled the ferry movements. Things were done strictly by the book, an unusual occurrence in Zambia, and the cashier at the front office even issued official receipts.

The Lukulu ferry was far smaller than the one at Senanga and could only accommodate one vehicle and its trailer at a time. As it had just one entry/exit ramp I had to reverse my outfit to the far end of the vessel, and this was no easy task with a large trailer, but it meant I could eventually take a straight run at the noticeably sandier bank that lay in wait for us across the river. This we managed without a hitch and we set off again on the other side, elated that it had all gone so well – until, less than 20 minutes later, I bogged the vehicle and trailer in a patch of treacherously soft sand.

Hours of hard toil failed to extricate the heavy trailer, so we camped right there on the road. This lightened the rig and I managed to dig it out on my own while Salome and our staff set up camp. As arbitrary sites go this was close to perfect as it was near a gurgling forest stream, but we were aware that we had made little progress that day.

After a light breakfast next morning we left early for Liuwa, which Nelson confidently predicted we would reach by lunchtime if we did not get stuck again.

A bend in the road brought us to a small village where a few children were playing happily in the road. Startlingly, a pre-adolescent boy glanced up at us and started screaming hysterically, then ran blindly away from the vehicle as if he had seen the devil himself. I noticed that the older boy with him had had a self-satisfied smirk on his face as this happened, but his expression became uncertain when I pulled up next to him.

'Nelson, please ask him why the youngster ran from us like that,' I requested.

After a brief chat with the teenager, our guide said with a grin, 'It is his 10-year-old brother who has not seen a white man before, and this one here had told him that white people cook and eat little black boys!'

As we drove away I struggled with the concept that, after 10 years of life in this glorious global village, that child had never yet encountered a white person. I felt much as I supposed David Livingstone would have before me.

Once more we followed Nelson's instructions, and after taking more right-hand turns than left-hand ones, we emerged from the thick forest and there, directly in front of us, stretched a broad river.

'What's that, Nelson?' I asked.

'It is a river,' he answered.

That was all I could get from him. My inadequate maps showed no broad river anywhere near where we should be, but we were certainly looking at a wide body of water. We continued travelling west, not knowing where we were and not caring much because it was a pleasant drive, when Nelson suddenly shouted, 'Stop!'

I pulled to an immediate halt. 'What's the matter?' I asked.

'That is Angola in front of us,' he replied nervously. 'We do not want to go there. They are fighting.'

'Yes,' I agreed, 'we do not want to go there.' Savimbi had his headquarters in this region. 'But how can you tell?'

'See that green sign behind the bush over there? That is Angola. Turn left here.'

'But there's no road.'

'Better no road, sir, than going to Angola. We will find a road.'

Back in the maize patch again, I thought, except that this was a huge one, with guns pointing at you if you took the wrong turn.

We bounced around over grass plains for about an hour before we came upon a track that we hoped was headed in the general direction of Liuwa. At least it was leading away from the war zone. This approach to our destination, although unconventional, was both fortuitous and outstanding because it took us along the entire length of the Liuwa plain and we witnessed the true extent of its wildebeest migration. This was one the finest wildlife spectacles left in Africa and it was humbling to find ourselves surrounded for hours on end by 360 degrees of endless wildebeest. Furthermore, there was the added bonus of selfish, solitary game viewing – unlike the Serengeti/Masai Mara experience, where you could be excused for thinking you were in a Singaporean traffic jam. It was not only wildebeest that inhabited this untrammelled area and we encountered other species of plains game. In particular, I had never before, or since, seen so many oribi and these bouncy, diminutive antelope leaped from the grass and dashed off in theatrical displays that Django wanted to join. I believe he thought they were giant springhares.

Thrilled to have made the long trek to this unexploited corner of Africa, we were treated to a grand finale when we approached some large acacias and stumbled upon a pride of lions comfortably perched in the upper branches of one of the trees. There was no sign of the biting flies that generally cause these cumbersome cats to climb high enough to escape their attentions, so I assumed that this pride, leopard-like, used this height advantage to spot their prey. As a result of hauling themselves about like primates they had developed massively powerful shoulders: the wildebeest would stand no chance against them.

Liuwa is not only a preserve for game, however. It also has a community of rural folk living within its borders, complete with its own government school, which is an unusual formula for conservation, but it seems to work. Our campsite was close to the only water source in the plains and this shaded pool attracted a few fishermen and their dogs. Django went to investigate, but soon returned, disappointed that the mongrels did not want to play with him.

That afternoon a roaring bushfire, fanned by a strong breeze, threatened our camp. It arrived unannounced and left us no time to pack up and move away, so we fought it with some desperation in the scorching afternoon heat. I did not point out to the clients, who were participating with enthusiasm, that fleeing animals, especially snakes, are driven before a blaze and often land up unannounced at a fire-fighter's feet.

We finally defeated the blaze as darkness fell, and collapsed, with a mild dose of heat stroke, in front of our campfire. Whilst in that state, I wondered if the bush had been deliberately lit to drive us off, but could not find a convincing reason for such action, unless it was to deter us from eating children.

Despite unsettling thoughts about the possible cause of the blaze, we left those magnificent plains with reluctance. To do this we had to cross the Luanginga River by ferry. The road out of the area crossed a number of dry riverbeds filled with deep sand, and I had to clamber out of the vehicle frequently to check for the best route. It was a slow trek and finally, when we reached a ridge overlooking the river, my heart sank. Before us lay a precipitous slope of knee-deep, churned-up sand that led to an expanse of water broad enough to be the Zambezi itself. To reach its muddy bank was going to be like abseiling down a sand dune, only to be trapped at the ocean's edge with no option of return – once our vehicle had wallowed its way to the bottom there would be no way it could pull the trailer back up that slope.

Worse was to follow: I spied the ferry. It was minuscule. About half the size of the one at Lukulu, it too had no 'roll on, roll off' facility that allows you to drive on at one end and disembark from the other. It appeared an impossible task to fit our rig on to its diminutive deck – and, to compound our concerns, it lacked an engine. To coax the craft across the river the helmsman had to haul on a rope stretched between two rickety gum poles on opposite banks, but first he had to swing the ferry around so that the bow pointed towards the opposite bank.

As we did not have enough fuel to consider going back to Lukulu, we had no alternative but to attempt the crossing. Before I committed myself to that irrevocable descent, I meticulously measured the distance from the front of my vehicle to the trailer's wheels, and then floundered calf-deep in sand down the precipitous incline to the ferry, where I calculated its length. If I drove forward onto the vessel and pressed my vehicle's bullbar against the stern railing, the trailer's rear wheels would balance precariously over the bow. This would at least mean that I could reverse off on the other side of the river, where the bank looked encouragingly flat and firm.

Salome drove her trailer-less vehicle on board for the first crossing together with Nelson and the staff to lighten my load. She had no problems disembarking on the other side, which encouraged me while I sailed rather than drove down the slope, as if I were floating on the moon, and squeezed on to the ferry.

My rig was so much heavier than the first one that the operator nearly fell overboard when he tugged on the rope to turn us about and again when he repeated the procedure as we reached the far side. I shouted for Salome to tie a chain from her vehicle to the back of the trailer, to help pull us off. When this was done, I started to reverse slowly. The instant the trailer touched the shore, however, my vehicle's wheels were no longer thrusting it backwards, but pushing the ferry away from the bank at an alarming rate instead. Somehow I managed to react quickly enough to prevent the vessel from shooting out from underneath us and dumping the vehicle, Django and myself into deep water. Gingerly, I climbed out of the cab to study our position.

The tyres of the trailer were stuck in the muddy edge, and the back wheels of my vehicle were precariously close to joining them, while the nose of the ferry had lifted under the weight at the rear, as though it were about to depart for the moon. I needed to communicate some kind of strategy to my wife, but within minutes it seemed as if the entire village had been alerted to witness me submerge the vehicle, its trailer and all our equipment. There were literally hundreds of people, all chattering with anticipation – and each one of them had his or her opinion on how to save the situation, which they vented to each other at full volume in a language that I could not understand. The noise was deafening. I shouted, but made no more impression than a fart at a football final.

After frantic gesticulating, I finally managed to quell the crowd sufficiently for Salome to hear me.

'Take the chain off the trailer – we had it wrong!' I yelled. 'Your car needs to hold the boat itself. Move closer to the stern and fix the chain to the ferry.' I took a deep breath. 'When I say so, engage low gear, and then I want you to try to pull the ferry ashore.'

Once she had completed those tasks, I directed her to get somebody to tie a rope from the ferry to the gum pole, which would help stop the vessel from shifting position. I also suggested that she organise about 10 men to push the trailer when it started moving, and a further 10 to attach another rope to the vessel and haul on that too. Lastly I placed Django on the back of my vehicle. If we went under the water I did not want him trapped. As a strong swimmer, he would easily make the shore and I hoped the din would drive any crocodiles away.

When Salome was ready, I signalled and started to inch backwards. Her vehicle was digging into the sand and I could smell its clutch burning under the strain of keeping the ferry in station. Suddenly the gum pole was uprooted from the ground and the boat lurched backwards causing the men tugging on the stern rope to fall head over heels like skittles. The boat then pitched backwards a second time, but with Salome's vehicle in tow. We simply weighed too much for her labouring Toyota to hold us.

We tried again. This time as many people as were able found handholds on Salome's vehicle, and hosts of other volunteers put their shoulders to the trailer. They collectively shoved and tugged like rugby players in a scrimmage, while other willing hands hauled on an extra rope that we tossed to them. Then, quite unexpectedly and much to my relief, the Cruiser's rear wheels touched firm ground, gripped, and we shot safely to shore. Yoko and Shoko, typically Japanese in their prolific taking of photos, had been so agitated that they had not even thought to pick up their cameras.

* * *

That afternoon, much later than anticipated, we left for Mongu, driving through groves of immense mango trees that early missionaries had planted and which offered year-round shade to man and beast alike. In season, you cannot buy or sell a mango in the region because they are so plentiful that they are free to anybody who asks. The road was deeply rutted and I had to concentrate fully to avoid becoming mired yet again, which only added to my tension as I knew we had one more crossing ahead of us that day to return to the eastern side of the Zambezi. My nervousness proved unfounded, however; the ferry was large, motorised and in good working condition – we rolled on and off effortlessly.

We drove through Lealui at dusk. This is where His Majesty, the Litunga, King of Barotseland holds sway. Nominally the monarch of all he surveyed, at the time of our visit he was in conflict with central government in Lusaka, who had accused his son of complicity in a bomb blast in that city when a device had blown up a wastebasket in a quiet road late at night, causing no injuries. The Barotses believed that agents of the State had planted the explosive in order to set up the

Litunga's son. Nelson, our compulsory guide, was an armed government officer in uniform, and merely by touring in Zambia with him
on board we were perceived to be siding with the regime in Lusaka.
The atmosphere was icy and our drive through the village was greeted
with stony stares.

The Litunga dictates when his people shall go to bed at night. On
command drums are played from his unassuming palace and everyone
must get off the streets and retire to their houses. No noise, especially
music, is tolerated after the drumming has ceased. Fortunately, we had
arrived before His Majesty was due to retire that evening, and were
allowed to proceed unhindered.

Beyond the village lay the Royal Barge, centrepiece of the colourful Kuomboka festival, when, as the annual flood threatens to cut off
his village from the rest of the world, the King with his entourage is
ceremonially rowed to higher ground. It was a regal-looking vessel
but appeared stranded, like a *nembwe* out of water, as it lay high and
dry on the banks of a great looping canal that had been dug to supply
Mongu with water when the river was low.

We followed the canal into the gloom and camped on an open floodplain next to a curve in the waterway, where polers were still gliding
back and forth in their mekoro in the cool night air. In the distance we
could see the fires of two homesteads, but it was dark all around us.
Exhausted, we had a simple meal and crawled into bed early. Salome,
Django and I instantly fell asleep in our rooftop tent, while the clients
and Salome's mother retired to their tents around the campfire next to
the vehicle. Our staff and Nelson, too bushed to put up theirs, elected
to sleep in the open.

Later that night my dreams were shattered suddenly by the sound of
rifle fire from the middle of our campsite. We were under attack! I sat
bolt upright and forced Salome's head down low. Peering out through
the gauze window into the hazy moonlight, I could see Nelson cautiously groping for his own weapon. Were we about to have a firefight
in the camp? I waited tensely for a sign of movement or a noise, wondering what I could do to defuse the situation. Nothing came to mind.
Django had initially cowered from the loud gunfire, but came to sit

next to me, ears pricked, sniffing the air. He growled so softly that I could barely hear him. Then in the silence I heard the familiar splash of a mokoro pole in water. Somebody was on the move. I sat dead still for what seemed like hours, armed with my only weapon – a maglite – until I was certain that the intruders had left, and it was safe to relax. Only then did my ally drop his ears and curl up on his blanket.

In the morning, Shoko asked, 'What was that noise that I heard last night?'

'Some hunters shot a duiker,' I lied.

She looked at me inquiringly and clearly did not buy the story, but was too well mannered to press the point. I reported it to the Parks people when we dropped Nelson off. They seemed to feel it was a warning to the government following the recent arrest of the Litunga's son.

After we had shed another million or so kwacha at the filling station in Mongu, we cast an eye over the king's dry land palace and were amazed to see how modest it was. What was not modest, however, was the rigid protocol that applied to any person who wished to obtain an audience with His Majesty, the King of Barotseland. I had endured one such meeting at Lealui before, when I and a friend of mine, Simon Lamont, were offered some land above Ngonye Falls and we needed to seek the approval of the Litunga to clinch the deal. The monarch, we were informed on arrival, would not see us on this visit, but we would meet with his Prime Minister and cabinet instead. It wasn't that we had blotted our copybook; apparently no one is granted an audience with the king on the first attempt.

We were then drilled on etiquette, the first instruction being that one must never have one's head above that of the Prime Minister.

'He is seated on a chair, so you will enter the building on your knees; you will clap your hands in the African way before you greet the Prime Minister and then his cabinet; you will not speak unless spoken to ...' The instructions were interminable.

I decided that I could not remember all this and gazed around me. People who were merely passing the building went down on their haunches and clapped in deference to the site. I wondered what the punishment for any transgressions would be.

Simon looked at me incredulously. He had been a soldier in the Rhodesian war and kissing anyone's ass, no matter what rank, held no appeal.

'Are we going to do this shit?'

'I guess we've come a long way, so we might as well go through with it,' I reasoned. 'I will, however, tell the boys at the pub about you bowing and scraping.'

Simon glowered, not seeing the humour.

I felt a complete fool. I had always privately maintained that I would never bow to the Queen of England, who was merely another person like me, yet here I was, sliding on the knees of my good trousers over a dirty floor before a man dressed in tattered clothing, who was but the titular Prime Minister of a kingdom that frankly was not even a kingdom. Then I saw Simon on his knees ahead of me, with Django nipping at his ankles, thoroughly enjoying this novel game. I giggled. I could not help it. I stood up, as there was little respect shown by crawling on your knees while shaking with suppressed laughter.

I think that the Prime Minister was equally embarrassed by the situation, as he waved aside the protocol and we got on with the meeting. In true African style, we achieved nothing and were told to come back again. Oh, and could we please bring the Prime Minister a paraffin-operated hurricane lamp of the type he had seen once on a visit to Kasane? Yet another person wanted something else, and soon we had a veritable shopping list – but no land of our own.

*   *   *

On our way out of Mongu en route to Kafue I tried to buy beer but found that it was sold only in refundable bottles and only in exchange for other empty bottles. How, I asked the shopkeeper, does one ever start to buy beer if you have not inherited a case of empties from your late father? There was no answer. Apparently if dad died without leaving you a crate of empty bottles, you could go to your grave a teetotaller. In Africa, it is customary to pay a 'bride price' – *lobola* – to the bride's family before a wedding can take place. The going rate varies from region to region and depends on the status of the daughter concerned. Customarily it is negotiated in numbers of cattle, and takes time to assemble, but people were so poor in this part of Zambia that Nelson's *lobola* (and bear in mind that he held a secure government job) included boxes of matches, packets of sugar, maize meal and, god help the poor man, a crate of beer. I still don't know if he ever married his sweetheart.

The tracks in the interior of South Kafue had fallen into total disrepair, compelling visitors to use the main road to Itezhi-Tezhi, which runs outside the park boundary. This is the kingdom of the tsetse fly and they had us jiving in the back-up vehicle, as they swarmed over the truck each time we slowed for one of the many potholes. Django asked, with a nudge of his nose to my arm, to ride in Salome's air-conditioned vehicle. The women in the car in front were comfortable, thank you, with the windows wound up and cooling air gushing over them. They could find the swarming flies amusing as they careered into the windscreen, desperate to gain entry, while we in the open vehicle stoically donated copious quantities of blood to the ravenous insects' breeding cycle.

My first impressions of an area called Nanzhila to the south will remain with me for a very long time. After traversing long sections of miombo forest and then scrubland, we emerged into a scene reminiscent of the Okavango, and the immediate impression was one of open floodplains filled with fauna and flora. Lily-covered pans dotted the plains. Inside of two hours, we had seen elephant, buffalo, lion, eland and a host of smaller game. It was a surprising discovery and I wanted to linger there, but our timetable demanded that we continue on our way as soon as possible. With regret we joined the tar road to Livingstone.

Salome went ahead with the clients, while I followed with our staff at a more leisurely pace – that night we were to stay at a lodge on the Zambezi near Livingstone, and for once would not need to set up camp. As we crested a hill, there was my wife standing next to her vehicle, dishevelled and full of grease and dirt, wheel spanner in hand. She'd had a blowout at speed on one of the front tyres, and had done exceptionally well to hold the vehicle on the road. More than that, she had changed the heavy tyre on her own. My, was I proud of her. The clients also praised her calmness, and declared that they would be prepared to go to war with her. I hoped that Japan was not planning expansion any time soon.

We arrived at the five-star lodge and found it unprepared for us. Made to wait in a tight little circle on a concrete bench, like boat refugees, we sipped sweet orange cordial from sugar-coated glasses as we waited in a churchly hush for some attention. When the hostess bustled in, she parroted a long list of information with the same lack of inflection as that of the woman who reads the stock exchange results.

She finally finished and Django nudged me awake.

'What is that?' she spluttered, noticing our dog for the first time.

'Don't you mean "who"?' Salome said sweetly. 'That is Django and I informed your reservations office that he was coming. If you don't have steak he will settle for roast chicken. Please prepare enough for him. He has had to work hard on this safari.'

'We also requested that our camp attendants could have a place at the back of the property to camp,' I threw in quickly, before she could recover. 'They are fully self-contained and won't get in your way.'

She looked as if she were about to swoon. The likes of us apparently did not appear on page five, or anywhere else, in her training manual.

'I'll have to check with the duty manager,' she said abruptly, and spun on her heel to find him.

She was gone for ages, so I went outside to see if my waiting staff had organised their lunch. What they had done was reduce the imposing entrance to something akin to a rubbish dump, with soiled equipment scattered about in untidy piles. I appraised them. They were dressed in overalls now filthy from the hard safari and, frankly, had no place anywhere near the portals of this pretentious lodge – not even as garbage collectors. I had to remind myself that my dusty bush clothes were not much of an improvement on their uniforms, and that Salome certainly did not display her normal pristine appearance after doing battle with that tyre. We and they needed to freshen up.

A supercilious little man sidled up to me. 'I am the duty manager,' he announced in that infuriatingly affected hotel school manner. 'I understand you wish to see me?' He glared with undisguised dismay at the scene before him and at the dog at my feet.

I explained our predicament and asked for a tiny corner of their massive property for my people to set up their camp. In reply, he wrinkled his pompous nose at me and said, 'I am afraid not. We have standards to maintain.'

I felt slighted on behalf of my loyal team who had slaved hard to see us through this safari. In addition, having pre-paid for five customers for three nights, the US dollars we had thrown the lodge's way, if converted to Zambian kwachas, would have filled the Victoria Falls gorge. I considered that we deserved a modicum of professional courtesy from this pallid, desk-bound twerp. Django saw my mood and looked away, as he did not condone wanton violence. I regret to this day that I did not hit the pasty-faced snob in the middle of his flabby chest and walk over him.

What I did instead was to choke on my ostentatious lunch of *pâté de foie gras* and other fiddly spinach and sawdust puff pastries which they had insisted on us eating before we could clean up as the kitchen was closing for lunch. I said farewell and stormed out, with my dog close on my heels. He did not like the place either. Salome stayed behind with the clients, while the duty manager flounced uncertainly in my wake bleating that he had reconsidered, and that our staff and Django were welcome to stay – and that there would be no refund if we chose to leave.

'Don't worry,' I reassured him. 'Keep your money, I will make it up by including you in my book.'

14

LONG ROAD TO FATHERHOOD

'I am pregnant,' Salome announced quite unexpectedly over a game of Boggle that took place inside our caravan one blustery day.

'Only one word at a time in this game,' I said and carried on playing.

'I don't think you heard me. I am pregnant; I am expecting a child in December.'

'What will Django think?' I rolled the dice.

That is how I heard that we were to be parents; a surprise really, considering that we were both in our early forties and had not planned an addition to the family. The enormity of the occasion never really penetrated until my wife started demanding frozen onions. Then I knew great changes were afoot.

We bought a new vehicle, not only for our safaris, but also to convey Salome in some comfort to Pretoria for the birth of our daughter. Our shiny new truck was still full of that scent that they dunk vehicles in to make them smell, well, new. She was a shiny white double-cab Toyota, with turquoise racing stripes down both flanks and rigged out with a thickly padded safari seat mounted on the back tray, which could fold down and tuck snugly under a weatherproof fibreglass canopy when we were not on game drives. We also had other essential extras in the form of a spare fuel tank, a 60-litre stainless steel water container, a

12-volt fridge, a rooftop tent and the crowning luxury of a radio/tape player. My, were we proud of her.

Django approved of the new vehicle. He circled it a few times and peed on all the tyres. Then he hopped into the front and sniffed the newness of the interior, and I wondered briefly if he would try to baptise the seats as well, but of course, being well mannered, he did not. Then he bounded over to the back and lay down with eyes half closed. He claimed the entire rear seat and, more importantly, both windows so that he could charge from one side of the vehicle to the other to snap at trees or gaze at animals.

* * *

Botswana is tediously flat and the main roads are mind-numbingly straight. I suspect that those who design its highways need use only a ruler and pencil, without venturing from their air-conditioned offices, to link up any of the country's towns. Our first step on the 1 200 kilometre journey to Pretoria was the 300 kilometres from Kasane to Nata. This route is dangerous in the dark because elephants and buffalo are fond of it. They habitually stand on it, cross it and even lie on it, and the problem is that they blend in with the surface.

We left early that morning, long before there was a glimmer of light on the horizon. As we rounded a bend my vehicle's headlights suddenly illuminated a herd of buffalo dozing in the middle of the road and, as I spent a few crazy seconds trying to avoid them, I was reminded of Isaacs's frenetic actions in front of his arcade machines. How we did not hit any of the animals I do not know, but my late friend Gary Westland had not been so fortunate when returning from a safari. He collided with an elephant and both died. Salome was suitably wide-eyed with fright but did not say a word. Django, who had been flung across the back seat from his perch on top of the cooler box, just glared at me balefully.

Pandamatenga, the only village along the entire 300 kilometres between Kasane and Nata, offered very little. The petrol station had been open for only a short period and now lay abandoned. A small under-stocked shop, a liquor rest (as Botswana's wayside pubs were called) and one very large grain silo made up the balance of the settlement.

Beyond Pandamatenga, forest reserves give way to inhospitable dense scrub and we were travelling along the dead straight road in a state of highway hypnosis, when a man in a washed-out mustard Mercedes-Benz came flying past us at a speed the car's manufacturers would have been proud of. Moments later it swerved violently in front of us and came to a sudden halt, cutting us off like a Hollywood police car. I hit the brakes as hard as I could, and we in turn skidded to a gravel-grinding stop, sending poor Django flying from the cooler box again, this time into the back of my head. The driver almost fell out of his car in his haste as he scurried towards us.

'I am nearly out of petrol. I tried to get fuel at Pandamatenga but the station is shut,' he said breathlessly in an accent that I could not place. 'Can you give me a lift to Nata and I will get some there?'

Reluctantly I agreed. Something was not right, but being notoriously slow to think I could not come up with a good reason to refuse and, anyway, it goes against the grain to leave a person stranded in the bush. He moved his vehicle so well off the road that it was virtually hidden by the bushes. I pointed out to him that he had left his emergency lights flashing and might find himself with a flat battery when he got back from Nata. I also noticed that it had a foreign registration plate.

'I don't worry,' he answered as he leapt into the back, thrusting items to one side to make space.

I tried to make small talk but he was evasive and Django, who had regained his position, was clearly uncomfortable with his presence, judging by his body language and low incessant growls. I became acutely aware of Salome's handbag lying vulnerably on the back seat and suggested in Afrikaans, which I hoped he did not understand, that she put it at her feet. Our passenger constantly spun around to scan the vacant road behind us, and he was perspiring copiously as if I had forced him to sprint in front of the vehicle – something I now wished I had done. Django continued his low growl and stared at the back

228

of my head, demanding that I do something. I wondered what. Could I take him to the police station in Nata? What would I say? My dog does not like this person? I was still thinking about how to deal with this when we arrived at Ngwasha gate, a veterinary checkpoint that doubles as a police roadblock. An officer came to check my driver's licence.

Of course I failed to think, 'Here is a policeman, sent from heaven to help me.' (I told you that I am slow.) Instead, I worried that he might find fault with papers or vehicle, but we passed his inspection and he waved us through. As I started to pull off, he hailed me with some urgency.

'What now?' I thought, as I stopped again.

'You have a flat tyre,' he announced pointing to the back wheel.

I looked out of the window and sure enough, the rear right tyre was hissing piercingly.

'Thanks,' I mumbled and got out to change it.

Our passenger leapt from the vehicle and, with shaking hands, grabbed the jack and wheel spanner from me and frantically started to loosen the wheel nuts. Because the spare wheel had been lowered to accommodate the spare fuel tank it was almost impossible to locate the winding mechanism without the aid of someone to shine a light for you. Experience had taught me that a torch held at the right angle, and a rubber neck to help peer through the tiny aperture in order to fiddle the lever exactly into the slot were what was needed. It took time, practice and three hands. He snatched the winder from me and started wildly jabbing it around – which meant he had as much chance of finding the slot as he would have had finding a welwitchia seedling in a pine forest.

When I tried to help, he irritably shrugged me off. 'I will do it. We want to go.'

Something was definitely not right, so I stood back and pondered, deliberately of course.

'This bloke is extremely nervous. Why? Maybe it is because of the police. The police ...? What a jolly good idea!'

So while he was still poking the lever back and forth in frenzied desperation, I strolled over to the police officer and told him the story.

'A Mercedes-Benz with a foreign registration?' he repeated immediately.

'Yes,' I replied.

'Keep him there. I'm coming back,' and off he trotted towards their corrugated iron shelter, which served as headquarters.

I found our unwanted travelling companion on the verge of total nervous collapse, still struggling to find the slot, but this time he was happy to let me assist him, and the job was almost done when I heard a voice behind us. We were both on our knees, and when I looked back there were seven policemen with AK-47 rifles raised and pointed at us. Our passenger glared at me with hatred when I rose, but he submitted to the handcuffs without resistance.

The Mercedes, it transpired, had been stolen, and when our man had tried to smuggle it across by ferry into Zambia, a sharp customs official had become suspicious. The vehicle smuggler, who was apparently from Mozambique, had leapt into the car, jumped a roadblock in Kazungula and sped off. Having found us obligingly dawdling along the way, only a flat tyre at the worst possible moment thwarted his impromptu escape plan.

A few minutes after this dramatic arrest, a pursuit vehicle arrived at the gate, tyres squealing as it came to a skidding halt. Plain-clothed detectives disgorged themselves in astonishing numbers from the back of a standard police pick-up, and the scene resembled something from a low-grade movie. The senior CID officer, not surprisingly, had modelled himself on Columbo, and wore a cream trench coat during a 40 degrees centigrade afternoon. Perhaps he was hoping for a promotion to the rhino anti-poaching squad. He strutted about issuing contradictory orders in an officious manner. His men dashed first in one direction and then a barked order saw them all set off in unison on another aimless course. I confess to a smug feeling of self-congratulation. I had played my part in the arrest of an international car thief. Praise would surely follow, which I would shrug off with, 'Oh, it was nothing. Glad to help.'

Instead, Columbo arrested me as an accomplice.

For a full ten minutes – a lifetime when prison looms – an argument raged between him and the clearly lower-ranked arresting officer. My new friend stood firm and Columbo reluctantly released me, his dreams of a national TV appearance thwarted. All the way to Nata I kept wondering what would have happened if he had found the car thief in my vehicle before we reached the Ngwasha gate.

*   *   *

Salome wanted to have a water birth and had found a hospital not far from her mother's home that catered for this. She excitedly showed me the maternity room which was equipped with a bed, lounge suite, carpets and paintings on the wall, plus a very large, raised jacuzzi bath that dominated the scene. What sealed it for us – apart from the fact that I would be able to attend the birth of our daughter – was that Django could also be present.

While we waited in Pretoria for Skye to make her move, my radiant spouse waddled around the block in the evenings with Django and me in tow, and our dog convinced us that he manufactured more pee in urban settings than he did in the bush. He would also make brief, friendly acquaintances with other canines throughout the suburb of Bailey-Muckleneuk.

I had to spend a day in Johannesburg on business and when I returned in the evening I found Salome lying in bed, covered in bruises and grazes. A pack of Doberman dogs had escaped from the house next to the American Embassy and had attacked Django with the clear intent to turn him into tiny, bite-sized portions. My overdue but fearless wife immediately wobbled into the fray and bravely fought her way to victory – not, I might add, without receiving some considerable damage to her arms from snapping jaws and to her knees and elbows from an unforgiving pavement. Django, hopelessly outnumbered and with a huge weight disadvantage until his ally had launched herself into the battle, was largely unscathed. He cast loving glances as Salome as he poked my shins relentlessly until he was assured that I would fetch a steak for her, medium rare with cheese sauce.

The next evening, while we were furtively taking a sluggish hobble past the embassy, watching Django pull faces at the snarling Dobermans, Salome suddenly exclaimed, 'It's time. We need to get to the hospital!'

I duly panicked and ran around in circles looking for the car keys (which I found, lost and rediscovered three times in succession) and, as directed by the 'Expectant Fathers' manual, drove calmly to the hospital. We were ushered into Salome's allocated suite and, after a quick examination, the midwife announced that my wife was indeed in labour – a statement of staggering superfluity, judging by the moans that had already started and which were destined to continue unabated until the early hours of the next morning.

With unusual foresight I had slipped some garlic biltong and beer into the vehicle, so in order to escape the groans of agony, Django and I partook of occasional sustenance sorties into the darkened streets of the capital. When we returned to the ward of torture we were growled at, between howls of suffering, for the unbearable stench of our breath.

Finally, at 5.18 am, Skye emerged into the world. My wonder at this marvel turned to utter panic as the midwife handed me a loaf-sized bundle of pure fragility and instructed, 'Take care of your child while I attend to Salome.' How, I ask, do you take care of such a tiny, infinitely precious and vulnerable thing?

I walked around the room and showed her the paintings on the wall and the indoor plants. I explained, with elaborate care, the techniques used in oil portraiture and the secret life of plants, and told her that I would expect her to relate all this back to me the following day.

She stared wide-eyed at me in much the same way that she has done ever since when she thinks I am being ridiculous. This, I must point out, she still does a lot. Django was far more fun in her eyes, and they lit up when she saw him. He licked her lovingly on the nose, welcoming her to the planet, and the midwife shouted at me about hygiene. Our dog took to Skye from that first instant and became proudly protective.

* * *

Salome and I had received our perfect Christmas present, and four days later we needed to spoil the older child. My wife had bought and wrapped presents for the family, which her mom had placed under a small plastic conifer in her crowded abode. Django woke us early, nudging me with his nose until I reacted. Then he did something rare: he leapt on to the bed to wish us Merry Xmas, and to plead with us to get a move on and open the gifts. With the coffee brewed and the mince pies served, we settled down to business.

Skye, of course, was handed the first one and at four days of age did not seem to attach quite the same significance to the event that Django did when he was allowed to open his carefully wrapped gifts. I was always in trouble with my mother-in-law if I damaged the wrapping paper because she would fold it carefully and recycle it the next year, but Django had no such restrictions. When his toy was passed to him, he grabbed it and shook it enthusiastically, shredding the paper in the process as he ran excitedly around the room peeling off the rest of the wrapping until the present was revealed. Anything that squeaked in a high-pitched way when he bit it was an instant favourite. Sadly, these gifts usually survived but a few mad minutes before they were punctured and fell silent – but what a joyous few moments of doggy heaven they provided.

* * *

Skye was too young to be exposed to malaria in Botswana so Salome took her to the coast after Christmas while I returned to Kasane to run the business. I was consequently set adrift from my family, which, for a new bachelor dad, was a life-threatening condition in itself. Being lonely at night, my feet would tread a familiar path to John's pub, a convenient stroll away from our caravan in the campsite.

Beer became my staple dinner, and one night after too much dinner I felt my way uncertainly back to the caravan in a ravenous state. In the freezer I found some beef to fry, but no cooking oil. Finally, in the bottom of somewhere, I unearthed a container, the label of which seemed to read 'Rat Oil'. This, I pondered fuzzily, was an unusual name and I wondered why they had come to make oil from rats, or was it to be used to fry rats? I fried my meat anyway and chewed on it hungrily, all the while thinking that it wasn't up to Salome's standard.

The next morning I dragged myself from bed and tripped over the mystery container, which I now re-examined with interest. On one of its sides the label stated 'Rat Olie' in Afrikaans, while on the reverse the English version clearly proclaimed 'Gear Oil'. Immediately I felt off-colour and went straight to our friends John and Jane Collington, who were camping for the weekend, and told them that they should keep an eye on me in case I started to change gears.

When I told Salome, she ordered me to head for the coast in top gear so that she could keep me under observation.

'And anyway, you have to marry me,' she said over the phone.

'But we are married!'

'No certificate.'

'Customary law is our legal right,' I pointed out.

'Maybe it is in Botswana but not yet in the New South Africa. If we don't have a valid marriage certificate, Skye will be registered as a bastard.' I could hear the indignation rising in her voice.

'Is that a proposal?' I asked sweetly.

A pause followed and then she said softly, almost seductively, 'I suppose it is.'

'I would have preferred the traditional on-your-knees stuff. Did you ask my father?'

'No, I did not. You will marry me.'

'OK, put that way, I accept.'

We satisfied the lawmakers by getting married on our favourite beach at Leisure Bay. The setting could not have been more idyllic. An expansive, sweeping, crescent-shaped beach of yellow sand fringed by wild strelitzias and dense coastal vegetation which, combined with a rocky outcrop at the southern limit, hid human development from sight and gave the impression that we were the only people on earth.

I was barefoot, dressed in khaki trousers with the legs rolled up and sporting a new shirt. Salome, also barefoot, wore an ivory dress.

The bridesmaid, at less than three months old, was younger than average, and was bedecked in a lovely new blue outfit. The best man proudly wore a navy bow tie and carried Salome's wedding ring – encircled with elephants – and my gold Tissot watch in a pouch around his neck.

15

ALL THE PRESIDENTS' MEN

Heidy Allmendinger, the owner of Kubu Lodge on the edge of the Chobe River, knows how to throw a party and Django was included in our invitation to a big birthday bash there. He was content to exchange his bandana for a bow tie if he could just spend time with her beautiful Alsatian. The two would gambol tirelessly on the extensive lodge lawns and their romance had burgeoned over the months.

We gathered that evening for Heidy's birthday drinks in the cosy Kubu pub and found the room filled with her friends from all around the country, many of whom we too knew, including Lady Ruth Khama and her son Ian, the newly appointed Vice President of Botswana, protected by several bodyguards already positioned in the surrounding gardens. Walking in their company towards the marquee where the dinner dance was to be held, I asked Ian if he was looking forward to taking over as President when the time came.

Lady Khama answered a little sharply, interrupting her son. 'We will never do that again. We learnt a hard lesson last time.'

Ian, I noticed, remained silent.

Ruth Khama and her husband had nearly tilted the balance of world power when they married, so she knew something about pressure.

She, an Englishwoman, had met Seretse Khama, the Paramount Chief of Bechuanaland's Bamangwato tribe, while he was studying law in England. They fell in love and decided to wed. This liaison displeased his fellow tribesmen, who had wanted their leader to marry one of their girls, so they removed him from his hereditary position. It also displeased the English, who were not ready to have one of their daughters marry a black man, and it outraged the newly elected, whites-only, South African government that had recently introduced apartheid into its constitution. So angered were they at the prospect of this interracial marriage on their doorstep, that they demanded the United States should intervene – and threatened to withhold supplies of uranium, a crucial ingredient of America's Cold War weaponry. That the United States would have little influence over a marriage between a Motswana and an English woman was lost on the South Africans; neither did it occur to them that the union had absolutely nothing to do with them.

Seretse and Ruth went ahead with their matrimonial plans and everyone around them backed down, leaving this far-sighted leader the task of steering his impoverished country through troubled times. Botswana was surrounded by three separate race wars, and Sir Seretse did a remarkable job – comparable with that of any of the great political leaders of the twentieth century – by maintaining its comparative neutrality. This came at a personal cost, however, because he died in office whilst still a relatively young man.

It was small wonder therefore that Lady Khama wanted to shield her son from the same responsibilities, but he was a man born to the job and was willing to be swept to the pinnacle of power in one of the strongest democracies in Africa, so painstakingly fought for by his late father.

The evening at Kubu Lodge was one of Kasane's finest. A string quartet played background melodies throughout a sumptuous dinner and then dance music followed. Champagne flowed, and soon I needed to find a bush. Unfortunately the one I chose was not unoccupied as I peed on one of our Vice President's fully camouflaged bodyguards, concealed as he was under the shrub. In midstream, the bush lurched up in front of me, pointed its rifle in my direction and cursed me roundly before it scurried off.

Ian was not the only high-ranking politician to visit the picturesque river that has attracted the rich and sometimes the famous. Richard Burton and Elizabeth Taylor consummated their re-marriage at Chobe Game Lodge on the banks of this river, close to Kasane, and the then most powerful man in the world, US President Bill Clinton, was seduced by its beauty when he dropped in for a couple of nights towards the end of his presidency.

Big Bill came to town, not exactly inconspicuously, you understand, but for a weekend break during his widely publicised African safari. When people take a safari they are usually on holiday, but for the President of the United States it was State business. He was rewarding his country's friends with a presidential pat on the back, and Botswana, as a staunch ally in Africa, received both a formal visit to Gaborone and a bonus presidential weekend break along the Chobe.

When we heard he was coming we realised that there might be some security in place. We expected that a secret service agent, or maybe two, would arrive a day or so before him, remove the lampshades in the hotel rooms to check for bugs, connect their own red telephone to the hotel jack and peer under the bed for bombs, as they do on TV. In addition, we supposed it unlikely that they would advertise his itinerary. Naively, we believed that was about all that they would find necessary to do in our peaceful backwater. What happened was on a different scale altogether. Marines engulfed us. A whole deployment of elite soldiers arrived a full month ahead to sweep and secure the area. The actual time spent on inspection seemed to take a mere 10 minutes or so, after which they spent the rest of their stay supporting John Tugwell's pub, while sharing what they knew of Bill's plans.

Weeks before his arrival, a large section of Mowana Lodge was turned into a computer warren that contained more science than Neil Armstrong had at his disposal to land on the moon. Satellite dishes provided secure 24-hour communications with Vice President Al Gore, the FBI, London, Moscow and Bill's favourite cigar supplier. Telephone intercepts, satellite trackers, photocopiers, radio contact with the Marines and, in all likelihood, a remote button to detonate the nuclear arsenal, were included in this formidable array of technical hardware.

One would have expected the location of this command centre to be top secret, but it was conspicuously housed in a glassed enclosure directly beneath the lodge dining room and abutting the path down to the excursion boats – which meant that everyone in town, except me, knew where and what it was. Presumably, though, the security would be so rigorous that access would need to be authorised and strictly controlled.

Well, it was not that closely monitored, because Django and I bumbled right into the middle of the command structure when I noticed that it was new, and being inquisitive by nature, wanted to poke around, having simply assumed that it was an environmental education centre for hotel guests. We wandered through unchallenged, admiring sleek-looking computers of the sort that one only sees in magazines, and I fiddled with a shiny red button that had an intriguing warning caption – 'For the President's Use Only'.

When it dawned on me what I was looking at, I slunk away before someone could say, 'Excuse me, sir, but would you like to press that little red button that you were toying with? We can then use this screen above the coffee machine here to watch Moscow disappear.'

The President's itinerary was, as we had expected, top secret. There was concern that Kasane was a difficult place to secure because of its close proximity to three neighbouring countries. Mowana Lodge is built on the bank of the Chobe overlooking Namibia, with Zambia visible in the middle distance and Zimbabwe a mere 12 kilometres down the road. Danger, if it came, could originate in any one of four countries, so it made sense for the itinerary to be classified.

In addition, the control centre deliberately circulated disinformation:

– The presidential family will spend the first night at Mowana Lodge and the second night at Chobe Game Lodge inside the National Park.
– They will spend both nights inside the Park where it is safer.
– The Park will be closed.
– The President will not visit the Park because it is not safe.
– Rooms are booked in both hotels for both nights.
– They forgot to make any bookings. Does anyone have a spare bed for Bill and Hillary?

– They have their own people to move their clothes and have them ready at the Game Lodge.

– The Park will not be closed.

It was enough to drive an assassin insane.

Then a hotel employee discovered documents marked TOP SECRET lying next to the hotel's photocopy machine. These described the itinerary in detail and so, as a community gesture, she posted them in the village square. No, of course, she did not. The point is that she could have. Amidst all that subterfuge, some dozy White House clerk had left crucial security-related documents lying about. I phoned my broker and hedged bets on which side would win a nuclear war.

Then the Americans decided to close the Park to ensure that the President had sole use of this facility – security would be compromised if all-comers were permitted entry. The response from the office of the President of Botswana in Gaborone was a resounding no. Aware that the closure of the Park would disrupt the plans of guests from around the world who had paid good money to visit the country, this was not considered an option and the gates remained open to all and sundry, Botswana's citizens included.

The aircraft that carried the sophisticated presidential limousine was unable to land at the short Kasane airstrip, which meant that it had to be diverted to Victoria Falls and the vehicle driven across the border from Zimbabwe. The President's transport, it seems, follows him around the world, even for a weekend break. The Clintons spent the first night at Mowana Lodge and we witnessed their departure next day for a quiet morning game drive. The entourage flashed past us in the village, the black limousine with its darkened bulletproof windows preceded by three personnel carriers that bristled with arms and trailed by half a dozen or more armoured trucks crammed with special agents, US marines and Botswana Defence Force soldiers. Once safely out of town, armoured security was sacrificed for an open safari vehicle, though I think the President would have been obliged to stay in his limousine if it had had any chance of negotiating the sandy tracks.

The leader of the free world missed out on good game viewing. Not only did he have to swallow dust kicked up by all the armoured vehicles that surrounded him, but clutches of guides had been despatched earlier in search of lions and other treats, so he was escorted from one animal to the next as if he were visiting captive animals in England's Longleat Safari Park.

In retrospect, this was probably a good thing because every second shrub harboured a soldier, which more or less emptied the area of the very animals the venerable leader had come to see. The record is quiet about whether the President needed to relieve himself behind a bush during his drive, but at least we know it did not shoot him.

*   *   *

Rumour dispersal was of such a high standard that Salome and I believed the Clintons would spend the night at the Game Lodge inside the Park, and we felt at liberty to take our little Skimmer out on the river and enjoy the sunset. All was perfect peace as we set off with baby Skye, Django, a bottle of dry white wine and our bird book and binoculars.

The Botswana Defence Force was on red alert. It was a high point of their careers. They did not want a world leader assassinated on their turf and they had been briefed that the enemy could be very devious, so were primed to expect the unusual. My, was my family unusual that day.

Some way beyond the BDF camp we pulled up in a quiet bay, opened the wine, ticked off our bird lists, changed nappies and revelled in the late afternoon warmth. It was a classic Chobe sunset; the puffy clouds picked up gold and orange, silver, pink and purple and spread these hues across the heavens in an orgy of colour. Lechwe and hippo were backlit on the grass plains of Sedudu Island. Life, with my family beside me and a glass of chilled wine in hand, was peerless.

Then I noticed some activity way in the distance on the river.

'We are going to have the Clinton armada sail past us soon,' I announced.

'How do you know it's Clinton?' Salome questioned, doubt in her voice.

'Take a look. Every large tourist boat on the river is coming our way, escorted by the entire Botswana navy.' I handed her the binoculars.

Salome peered at the congestion of craft and looked concerned. 'Shall we move? They'll come right near us and we don't want to be suspected of ambushing the President.'

'No, sit tight and enjoy your wine. We'll wait quietly for them to pass and then head for home. It'll create bragging rights for the kids.'

The flotilla powered by and Bill and Hillary, leaning on the rail as they admired the sunset, waved cheerily at us. The marines and the BDF men also waved. A relaxed-looking family and its dog, bobbing in their boat on a river on a Sunday afternoon, surely represented no threat? We might even have been placed there to give some local colour and the President someone to wave at.

Once they had safely passed, and there could be no likelihood of our launching a surprise attack, I decided it was time to go. Salome corked the half-empty bottle and packed away our snacks, while I pulled on the engine starter cord: once, twice ... 10 times. The outboard motor refused to fire.

The sun had set and it was hard to see inside the engine, even after I had removed its cover, but there was nothing obviously wrong that I could detect. Tension grew on our little boat. We were about to be on open water after dark, which was against national park regulations I might add, and we knew the BDF and the US marines had their fingers on their triggers. The tone of our conversation, unsurprisingly, became terser. Skye, the baby that she still was, sensed our anxiety and began to cry.

We had a small electric motor on the front of the boat, designed to approach angling spots with stealth and not give your position away to wary fish. It was not intended as a means to navigate major waters, but I tried to use it to steer a straight course on the wide river. Instead we went around in circles, spinning like a sardine bait ball when they try frantically to flee predators, only very much more sluggishly.

Darkness descended and we had not yet reached the BDF camp. If an overzealous soldier spotted us, we would be dead. I had to get Salome and Skye off the boat. I was paddling slowly, while Salome helped with a cooler box lid, until we reached a point just outside the military post.

'*Dumelang borra, re kopa nthusa,*' (Hello sirs, we request help) I called into the night, using Setswana only. I wanted whoever was there to know that I was from Botswana and not a foreign assassin. 'I have a problem with my boat. Could you please use one of yours to help me get my wife and child to shore?'

An uncertain voice reached us across the water in reply. 'Sorry sir, all our boats are out. Nothing I can do to help.'

'Have you got a radio?'

'Yes, sir.'

'Could you please get a message to your gun-boats to tell them not to shoot us.'

'Yes, sir.'

I had very little faith that he had radio contact with the fleet. He was, I suspected, a cook ordered to look after camp while the rest went off to do exciting men's work.

It was one of those extremely dark, moonless nights. As we paddled on agonisingly slowly, the most powerful spotlight that I have ever experienced lit up the river from the direction of Mowana Lodge, at least two kilometres distant. It bore down on us at terrifying speed. With that gun-boat steaming towards us we felt defenceless as a rabbit in a hunter's spotlight, our plight made worse by Skye's wails.

It was not as though the BDF opening fire and killing people on the Chobe was without precedent. A well-known Motswana had lost his life when a young soldier shot him in broad daylight, while he was lawfully fishing from a boat on this very river. These soldiers who were approaching us would have much more excuse to open fire. If we were shot on the river after dark, and with the President of the United States of America in town, there would be no awkward questions asked and, presumably, a few medals for valour dished out for good measure.

The gun-boat pulled up next to us.

'What is the matter?' The call came from the darkened wheelhouse.

'We have broken down and need assistance. Can you tow us to our campsite in Kasane?' I called back.

'We are not permitted to tow you, but we can take your wife and child to safety.'

'Thank you, sir,' I answered, deeply grateful. 'What about the dog?'

'No,' was the flat refusal.

This was the flagship of the landlocked nation's navy after all, not an animal pound. I did not argue as Salome and Skye boarded the gun-boat, which sped off and left Django and me drifting in silence in its wake. I resumed paddling, making little headway, but relieved of the anxiety that had been ever-present when my girls had been in danger.

Out of the inky blackness came the distant sound of a marine engine firing up. I instantly recognised it as belonging to the boat of our campsite neighbour, Phil, and my spirits rose – Salome must have reached home and prevailed upon him to help. Under tow from Phil, Django and I soon reached the security of the bank. To celebrate our safe return, Phil and I together polished off the remainder of the bottle of wine, while Django trotted off to check on my daughter and her mother, and to see if the marauding reptilian and banded friends had left him any supper.

As I paced the few steps homeward in his wake, I wondered if the Clintons, surrounded mostly by strangers, were also about to have their evening meal after a long day. Unaware of the subsequent events, they perhaps even reflected enviously on exchanging places with that happy family they'd seen in their boat at sunset, their dog proudly standing watch in the bow.

16

WILLIE'S BIRTHDAY PARTY

Willie Phillips phoned us in Kasane. He despised telephones so this call was about as rare as finding dinosaur tracks in your backyard.

'Why don't you come to Seronga next weekend?' he asked. 'It's my sixtieth birthday and we can have a few drinks and maybe go out on my boat. There are some interesting places I can show you.'

This was no ordinary invitation, you understand. For a start it involved an 800 kilometre round trip, and on top of that it was an invitation to a Willie Phillips birthday party – the stuff of legend. I couldn't resist.

Willie had married his girlfriend, Anne, and moved to Seronga in the northern Okavango. The newlyweds lived in an unpretentious but comfortable home that Willie had built on a prime plot of land overlooking a picturesque lagoon. Once established, they had set up a couple of sea containers in strategic spots in nearby villages, out of which they sold basic foodstuffs. Their chosen lifestyle was a hard one. It involved standing in a hot iron box for hours on end, as they served people who needed to turn over every coin to make their dwindling funds stretch until the next payday. When their stocks dwindled, Willie would have to wrestle a large truck to Maun over deep sand ruts and long wearisome roads.

For us, the shortest route to Seronga from Kasane was through Namibia's Caprivi Strip, which is a long thin finger of land that pokes out from the top of mainland Namibia, grabbing for the centre of Africa, and is one of the crazier aberrations of colonialism. It came about as a desperate attempt on the part of the late nineteenth century Germans to link their eastern and western African colonies, which today are known as Namibia and Tanzania. Overlooking the fact that the land between belonged to the British, they had swapped the spice-rich and strategic island of Zanzibar for a largely uninhabited narrow stretch of bush. It certainly proved no great asset for German South West Africa then, and before Namibia became independent, the Caprivi Strip became the battlefield in a confused war between the African National Congress, Rhodesians, South Africans and the Namibian rebel group known as Swapo. Two Angolan armies locked in a civil war on its northern border added grist to this grisly mill.

Things had been quiet in the Strip for a while, so we chose this shorter route instead of the alternative one via Maun, which would have added 400 kilometres each way. What had not filtered through to us, however, was the news that a few days earlier Angolan rebels had attacked a vehicle there and slaughtered its occupants. This may have been designed to dissuade Namibia from supporting the Angolan government, but had we been aware of it we would have made the longer detour.

Our progress through the Chobe National Park and over the bridge towards Katima Mulilo, an inauspicious river town which is the major centre in eastern Caprivi, could not have been more benign, apart from the rain that started to fall as we crossed the Chobe River from Botswana into Namibia. As we continued in the wet, we had an early reminder of previous bloody conflicts when we passed the turn-off to Mapacha, the military airbase from which the South Africans had operated during the bush wars.

Beyond Katima Mulilo the only distraction is at Kongola, where a bridge spans the reed-fringed Kwando River and offers a pleasant, if not spectacular, scene. It was not the view, however, that attracted our attention that day, so much as the army camp that had sprung up next to the road. There we discovered we were about to enter a war zone and found ourselves joining a compulsory military convoy. A captain, in full combat uniform, addressed us while we stood in pouring rain.

'I will now announce the procedure you will follow when we are attacked.'

I noted the 'when' and wondered if we should forgo the pleasures of Willie's company in favour of a longer life.

The captain outlined the course of action to follow during the inevitable ambush. Essentially, we would have to bail out of the vehicle, lie flat on our stomachs behind the wheels on the side furthest from the shooting, and leave the Namibian Defence Force to do their job.

'What do we do if they attack from both sides of the road?' I asked.

'They won't,' he said flatly.

'But what if they do?' I insisted.

He glared at me for a long time, and clearly labelled me as a trouble-maker.

'Then you lie under the vehicle.'

After the lectures came the practicals. Three times we had to climb into our vehicles and then rehearse diving for cover into the soggy verges before he was satisfied. Our family was by far the slowest. First we had to explain to the little ones what was expected. Django caught on quickly and enjoyed the new game, but Skye was a lot slower. Perhaps this was because she was strapped into her baby seat and had to be painstakingly freed each time, and then wrapped up to protect her from the storm. The officer was plainly dissatisfied with our reaction time, but then glowered at me again and seemingly dismissed us as expendable.

The Namibians were taking this seriously. They considered that Jonas Savimbi, the Angolan rebel leader, was likely to strike again. If he could disrupt this particular convoy of 15 civilian vehicles and several motley supply trucks, the eastern Caprivi would be isolated from the rest of the country and he would have less pressure from the south. Four military vehicles escorted us, two of them from the front, one in the middle (I made sure that we stayed close to that one) and another at the rear, each packed with heavily armed, grim-faced soldiers.

The lead vehicle travelled slowly to make sure that the convoy did not spread out, with the result that the journey took longer than we had planned. When we safely reached Bagani at the western end of the Caprivi, we were more than grateful that we hadn't needed to crawl beneath our car under a hail of bullets. Savimbi had apparently decided to strike on a drier day.

By that time we had already determined to take a different and even more adventurous, but less life-threatening, route when we returned home from Willie's Seronga residence.

*   *   *

The deluge stopped as soon as we reached the border at Mohembo. There was no sign of rainfall on the Botswana side, even though we had just driven for hours through torrential downpours.

'What kind of import duty do you charge the heavens?' I asked the little outpost's customs officer, who was pedantically demanding our vehicle papers.

'What?' he enquired, suitably puzzled.

'You must have a high tax on rain. That's why we don't get enough in Botswana,' I explained.

When I told him about the storms we had come through he shook his head in amazement. They had not had a drop in weeks.

Finding petrol in Shakawe took time so we decided to spend the night at Drotsky's Cabins on the banks of the Okavango River – an agreeable lodge and campsite, resplendent within its opulent fern gardens. It also afforded us the chance to see our old friends, Jan and Eileen Drotsky. While Salome attended to Skye in our A-frame chalet, Django and I found them on the wooden deck that overlooks the powerfully flowing Okavango River. They had both known Django for a long time and greeted him effusively before acknowledging my presence as well.

We had been out on the deck chatting for about half an hour when a house cleaner came running along the path from the rooms, screaming as though she had just seen Satan – and indeed, in a way, she had.

Cruising down the river was a monstrous crocodile and in its mouth, gruesomely, was a man's lower torso and legs. It was the single most macabre image of my life. Django stared at the approaching reptile and growled urgently, but it was too late to do anything helpful.

Jan was the first to recover from the shock and shouted, 'Come on, let's take a boat – we must try to recover the body.'

Now don't get me wrong; I see the civic duty in retrieving human remains for a family to bury, but I was not sure that I was personally ready to wrestle a mutilated, gory body from the jaws of a man-eater. However, there was no time to argue as Jan urged us to action, so Django and I raced to join him and his wife in their boat. Eileen had grown up in the bush, and would not flinch from a challenge like this. I also noted that on her way to the boat she had scooped up an extra paddle as a weapon, displaying more prescience than I did. Django jumped on to the bow and stood there fiercely, ready for battle, but as we approached the scene the monster sank beneath the water with its prey and did not resurface, even though we cruised back and forth for an hour or more.

When we returned to the Cabins I could not shake off the image of that bloody, ravaged torso, so it was with some disbelief that I heard Jan ask me if I would go out with him that night to catch a crocodile. He had a little party trick whereby he would take guests out for a night cruise after the evening meal, ostensibly in search of sitatunga, a shy, water-loving, splay-hoofed antelope, and then cap the event by catching a small crocodile and offering it for close-up inspection. Safari clients and I had done this a few times with him in the past, but never immediately after witnessing such a disturbing encounter with their bigger kin.

Before I could claim a headache, Salome agreed enthusiastically to join Jan and his party on this occasion. It would be great for Skye to see the river at night, she thought, and in any event Jan needed help, as he could not drive the boat and catch a croc on his own. I felt like a lamb being led to the slaughter. Django stood up in the bow with me, while Salome and Skye huddled under a blanket behind Jan's clients. He, while driving the boat, also handled a spotlight that was connected to a battery via small crocodile clips.

As darkness fell we were lucky enough to glimpse a lone sitatunga and Django whined softly at his first-ever sighting, but it soon slipped behind a bush and did not reappear. Our host next showed us a row of about 15 brightly coloured, comical little bee-eaters, all lined up on a branch as they faced in the same direction with perfect military precision – except for the first one who, akin to a sergeant-major on parade, looked the opposite way. Salome relished this photo opportunity for her postcard collection.

I sensed that it was soon going to be my turn to take centre stage, and I was aquiver at the thought as we cruised slowly along the reed banks where small crocodiles like to hang out. Jan spotted the reflection of two red eyes in the water.

'There's one,' he called, 'next to the waterberry tree.'

I followed his light, and sure enough there was a young croc floating motionless in the water. The rule of thumb is that if its eyes are further apart than the distance between your index and little fingers, then it is too big to catch by hand. This one looked far bigger.

'Eyes too far apart,' I responded.

'No they're not. Are you chicken tonight?' And Jan laughed, knowing that I would now be shamed into doing it.

He carefully pulled the boat up alongside my quarry, while I readied myself for the capture. I knew I needed to grab it firmly behind the head with one hand and then by the tail with the other – but the croc looked bigger than anything I had attempted before.

As I lunged towards the dark waters, Jan unexpectedly yelled, 'No! Leave it! It's too big! and at the same time inadvertently jerked the clips from the battery, which plunged us into darkness. I was already committed, however, and was by then grabbing blindly at the blackness where I judged the croc to be. Unsighted, I took hold and, to my horror, discovered that I had grasped it too far down its body, enabling it to swing its head backwards and clamp its jaws on to my forearm. Jan reconnected the light and there we were – me clasping the crocodile firmly, determined not to allow it to corkscrew and rip my arm to shreds, and the reptile clasping me considerably more firmly, and with equal determination.

Instead of rushing to my assistance, Jan started giggling like a schoolchild. He found the scene enormously amusing, which frankly I did not. A crocodile clamps its jaws shut with more force than any other creature, exerting a pressure of at least 210 kilograms per square centimetre, and up to 350 kilograms in the case of the larger ones. My assailant was young and its grip was on the lower end of the scale, which was fortunate, otherwise it might have bitten my arm off.

Surprisingly, crocodile jaws do not have much opening power. This didn't help me at the time, but it is useful knowledge for local farmers whose animals are being preyed upon by crocodiles. To catch and eliminate them, they wrap a fresh goatskin around a fibrous sausage tree fruit, and when the reptile clamps down on the bait it is unable quickly to reopen its jaws. For now, I was that sausage.

Django rose up on his hindquarters, his forelegs against my thighs, trying to help, but there was nothing he could do. There was not much that Jan could do either apparently, because the only way to remove the crocodile from my person was to snap off its teeth until it let go. This he assured me would do the croc no harm, as they naturally replace their teeth as they grow, but he had no tools handy.

'Right now I don't care about its teeth. Take my Swiss Army knife from its pouch and free me,' I demanded curtly, as there is a certain degree of agony associated with having a crocodile attached to your arm.

Still finding it hugely amusing, Jan started to prise me free of the offending jaws, and when he eventually separated us he held the creature up to demonstrate to his startled clients how cute and soft its little feet were.

Salome, for the first time, approached to check if I was OK.

'I couldn't leave Skye alone in the dark, and I didn't want her to see how stupid her father is,' she explained.

'You were the one who said that we had to come,' I blustered, trying to staunch the blood from my lacerations – but she was too busy listening to Jan, as he rabbited on about endearing little crocodiles, to take any notice of my defence.

Once we came ashore she cleaned my arm carefully, as crocodiles do not brush their teeth and their bites often turn septic. I retired to the bar for a shot of peach mampoer – distilled liquor that wavers on the borderline of legality – and went to sleep, fitfully dreaming of mutilated bodies, mine mostly, floating downstream in the jaws of crocodiles. We left the next morning for Seronga.

*   *   *

Django had not forgotten Willie, and as he ran straight to him in joyous welcome I noticed, not for the first time, that our dog winced as he leapt up to greet his friend. After years of playing games and jumping in and out of high vehicles, Django's hips had started to stiffen – at times he looked like the old dog that he was becoming. He had, after all, passed his three score and ten in dog years.

Willie's house was designed in an almost conventional, suburban style – but there, as with the man himself, the comparison ended. The lounge was dominated by a large bookshelf that he had hewed from a dead tree and crafted into an indescribably beautiful work of art, using nothing but a chainsaw. I attempted to wheedle this creation off him, but he would not part with it, saying that he had made it for Anne. I suspect, however, that part of the reason he declined my offer was that it hid the boxes that he had scattered liberally about his living room, where his beloved chickens roosted at night. After dark the room would come alive with the sounds of clucking fowls, and you had to be wary not to sit on eggs, or other less savoury deposits.

If Willie has a drink he snores loudly and is often banished to the couch amidst his chickens, dogs and, it must be said, his mosquitoes, all of which combine to render sleep unlikely should you be the one on the other couch, which was once my own experience.

Django approved of the dwelling and even more of the biltong that Willie threw about for his Staffies, with whom he quickly renewed his friendship. As for the chickens, he was never quite sure how they should be approached, so he avoided them in case we got the idea he might be molesting them. The fowls were unused to him too and squawked and fluttered into the air, which caused our dog to cringe in unnecessary guilt, willing them to calm down.

Willie had an 'all or nothing' attitude to drinking, and for much of his life he did not touch a drop except on his birthday. His Maun birthday parties had become legendary. They were a time for excesses in a town that thrived on extremes and occasionally became life-threatening when the pro hunters and wannabees would decide to test their target skills on a nearby tree. If his actual birth date fell on the day after the party, he would stay sober until midnight – but after an hour or so you could be forgiven for supposing that he had had a three-day head start.

This particular birthday was going to be much more intimate, as we were the only guests. After an exceptional meal that Anne had created from specially ordered treats from Maun, we shared memories amidst raucous laughter, over a couple of bottles of wine. The conversation turned to matters extra-terrestrial and I commented that I was sure that life must abound beyond planet Earth. I was thinking about the extreme conditions where many adaptable organisms are able to exist – such as the deep ocean sulphur jets, and the subterranean bacteria that survive on gold, plus the fact that simple life forms had been created in laboratories from lumps of clay, mixed with salty water and electricity. Given the capacity for life to develop so readily in just about any environment, and the almost infinite number of planets that the universe certainly boasts, it seemed to me that the mathematical odds favour the existence of life – even complex life forms – throughout the cosmos.

'Yes, life out there does exist,' agreed Willie emphatically, 'I've seen it.'

I looked at him incredulously. He is the least likely person I know who might be seduced by flights of fancy.

Willie explained. He was in the Okavango on a hunt with a colleague, Peter Hepburn. They'd showered and were relaxing before dinner after a hot day of stalking. Looking out over the Delta just after dark had settled, they saw a bright airborne light come hurtling towards them. Their first thought was that a jetliner was in trouble and about to crash, yet there was no corresponding noise. The light stopped above them and hovered for a short while, revealing a cigar shape to the two no-nonsense hunters, before it soared off soundlessly and at inconceivable speed.

I studied Willie to see if he was being serious, and as far as I could tell he was.

'And did it take a part of your brain with it?' I enquired politely.

It was his turn to stare, and he did so for such a long time that I started to wonder if he had taken offence at my ironic remark. Then he stood up abruptly – not, I hoped, to fetch his rifle – and moved to a drawer, from which he returned with a copy of a local newspaper. On the day that Willie and Peter had seen their cigar, other sightings of a fast-travelling brilliant light had been reported from cities as far apart as Francistown, Gaborone and Cape Town, with mere minutes separating the stated times of these events. Something distinctly strange had occurred over southern African skies that night.

It was only after the ladies had gone to bed that Willie opened the whisky that was our birthday gift to him. We celebrated his way, which meant throwing the cap over his shoulder, as he considered it bad luck to leave any liquid in a liquor bottle. Dutifully, we finished its fiery contents and the birthday boy, now feeling invincible, went to fetch another. Fortunately he could not do so, largely because he was performing a lively crab walk along the corridor walls. Eventually he decided that the whisky was probably not on the ceiling anyway, and wandered off to sleep with the chickens, fully content with the stylish ending to his celebration.

After a necessarily leisurely start, the next day was spent nursing muzzy heads while seated in Willie's aluminium boat on the waterways of the upper Delta. He showed us rivers and channels that we did not know existed, as he described his plans for developing lodges to expand the area's tourism potential in a manner that would benefit the community and its flora and fauna, rather than himself.

We returned before dusk and made our way to the house, past the large truck with which Willie supplied his shops. His regular trips to restock in Maun were well known in a village where no public transport was available, and as a result queues often formed at his gate when he was due to leave – denying him the opportunity to travel in peace and quiet. One day he caught an unusual-looking python that he could not identify, so on his next visit he decided to take it to Maun and show it to a herpetologist. He bagged the snake in a pillowslip, which he placed on the seat beside him, and when he stopped to pick up a schoolgirl who was thumbing a lift, he invited her to climb into the cab. He made room for her by handing her the bag and asking her to hold it on her lap, which she willingly did – until it wriggled. His passenger screamed, dropped the writhing piece of cloth, wrenched the door open and hurled herself from the moving truck. Fortunately, she landed uninjured in the soft sand of the track, but word went around and the number of hitchhikers at his gate tailed off dramatically thereafter. The snake, incidentally, was the first Angolan dwarf python to be positively identified in Botswana. This startling fact, I am certain, would have impressed the young girl.

While we were in the Seronga area I wanted to spend some time with an old friend, Saraquo, who had been my trusted mentor many years before, when I was first unravelling the secrets of the Okavango at the start of my career as a guide. Thoughts of Saraquo evoke fine memories of carefree days spent in the sun, filled with animals, walks, fishing, falling out of mekoro and cooling off in beautiful clear waters. He knew the Delta better than any man, before or since, and it was with childlike excitement that we greeted each other for Skye's first mokoro trip – and Django's last. Two dugouts were used, Saraquo poling the lead one with Salome and our little daughter safely aboard as too precious a cargo to be entrusted to me, while I punted the equipment with Django for company; he had implicit, if misguided, trust in my poling ability.

Three blissful days wafted by as we immersed ourselves in the spirit of the Okavango. We camped on remote islands and took leisurely nature rambles, with Skye perched on my shoulders and Django running about exploring the sounds and scents. Clear water coursing over golden sandbanks allowed us to wallow luxuriously, and we caught bream with a hand line. In keeping with African tradition Salome, as the sole woman, would wade into a lily pond to pull up some tubers so we could enjoy *tswii* for supper – a dish made up of lily tubers and fresh fish boiled and mashed together, then eaten from the pot using fingers only. We would sometimes wash this down with tea made from the purple water lily that also acts as a mild sedative and ensures peaceful sleep. Saraquo would regale us with tales from the Delta as we relaxed around the campfire.

By day, we poled along narrow channels through russet-tufted miscanthus, and the seated mother and child would be covered in spiders and the spear grass seeds that somehow worked their way into clothing, as if they had little jet engines propelling them. At dusk there was a changing of the guard as day transformed to night and the crepuscular and nocturnal creatures started to make their voices heard, while the baboons, who had been active all day, bade the world a noisy goodnight.

Skye complemented Django on our game walks. While he would sniff out interesting creatures at ground level, she would tug at my hair from her lofty position and point excitedly at game and birds alike. It was solely movement that attracted her, so she never distinguished between species and my attention was painfully drawn to every Cape turtle dove that flitted past. She would have pleased Barry no end.

As we moved from place to place, we noticed that the tsetse fly people had been actively planting their little blue and black flags, and although we ourselves were tsetse free, we had to ensure that little Skye did not toddle over and ingest the poison with which the cloth flags had been impregnated. Django took on the job of guarding her in the bush, never letting her out of his sight, and wherever she flopped down he lay protectively next to her.

One morning we took an early walk and found ourselves in thick *moselesele* scrub. Its flower looks like an intricate Chinese lantern, but its branches are armed with vicious thorns. Suddenly Saraquo, who was in the lead, stopped and silently pointed out the fresh tracks of a large lone buffalo bull. This was not a good place for us to encounter a *kwatali*, and I moved forward to stand directly behind the old guide, who had scars through his chest and sides attesting to just how dangerous this species can be.

We continued cautiously on the narrow trail, until Django growled a low warning and I instinctively placed my hand on Saraquo's shoulder. We halted and scanned the bush ahead, seeing nothing unusual until I spotted a single branch that appeared slightly out of place in the entanglement of thorns. That branch, which was the same pale grey as the rest, had the curved shape of a horn – and there, sure enough, waiting in motionless ambush, was the grumpy old dagga boy. If it were not for Django we would have worked our way right up to him with no room to escape if he had stormed us from such close quarters. As it was, we were able to retreat to safety and I could fulfil yet another cheesy steak promise when we arrived home.

On our way back, we glided along an attractive channel lined with razor-sharp hippo grass that was short enough to allow good visibility. I was enjoying the sunshine and the easy poling, when Saraquo's mokoro stopped suddenly in front of me. The channel had widened to form a small pool, and at its centre loomed the head of a large male hippo, like a sentinel on duty. Not wanting to have my thigh bitten through, or worse still, have something happen to my family, I prepared to reverse. This is not an easy operation for an amateur because the poler must first turn himself in the unsteady mokoro without falling out. I had just wobbled my way around when Saraquo started to beat the water energetically with his pole.

'That's right,' I thought. 'Piss it off so it charges.'

However, instead of killing us, it submerged and disappeared, while our guide shot across the narrow pool to safety, leaving me to attempt to turn around once again and set off in his wake, knowing that the huge animal could surface at any time and find my thighs at convenient incisor height.

Saraquo's urgent shouts for me to hurry did nothing to quell my nervousness. As I made my way across I realised just how little room there was for the hippo to hide, and hoped I would not prod him with my pole as I tried to speed through. I felt slower than a slug in Antarctica. To my intense relief I joined the others with femurs intact, just as he rose behind me, snorted and performed an imposing threat display. Feeling suitably cowed, Django and I were out of there as fast as I could flex my arm muscles.

After the idyllic sojourn with Saraquo, we went to say goodbye to Anne and Willie. We found Anne busy inside her container, dispensing groceries to a line of regular customers, some of whom handed over handfuls of coins while others had their purchases recorded in a book, to be settled later. Children came to buy individual sweets from a large colourful bag, and eagerly skipped off to savour their chosen treat before an elder sibling came to relieve them of it. There is an innate sense of honesty in small African villages. Whenever Willie forgot to lock the container, an old man would take it upon himself to watch over it until he returned, just to ensure that nothing went missing. In a town he would have been cleaned out.

The old Tsetse Fly Control road, infrequently used and largely overgrown, was our chosen route home. Every few kilometres we would have to stop the vehicle to swing a fallen tree trunk out of the way or, if it was too large to manhandle, cut a path around it. It was tiring work and our progress was so unhurried that we spent two more nights along the way, camping in the middle of that undisturbed track with no fear that anyone else might turn up. Our reward for this labour was the pure wilderness that was ours for those three days. No amount of money can buy that solitude; but it can – and frequently does – wreck it. It was thus with some regret we eventually popped out onto a familiar road near Moremi. En route to Kasane we passed three vehicles that day and it felt like rush hour in the capital.

17

DJANGO'S LAST SAFARI

J ohn and Jane, friends of long standing from Swaziland, were determined to share a safari with Skye and so it happened that our extended family had idled its way through two weeks of unspoilt Africa
in a remote part of the Okavango. In the course of our ramblings we
had delighted in seeing our daughter develop into a little person, and
her relationship with Django strengthening as he endearingly took his
role as her protector and mentor ever more seriously.

What did not delight us was the fact that a few months after the
safari Django started to act strangely. He did not seem to be in any
distress, yet he would walk around in uncertain circles, not chasing
his tail, but rather as if struggling to find his balance. Salome dived
for her medical books – first the one on dogs, then another on pets in
general and finally a tome on 'Family Health' – but could find nothing
to enlighten her, so she took him to the vet. Blood samples were taken
and sent to Gaborone for analysis, and when the results were phoned
through I answered the call.

'Bad news, I'm afraid. Django has trypanosomiasis,' the vet announced.

'He has what?' I asked, baffled.

'Tryps, or nagana – sleeping sickness in people – from a tsetse fly.'

'But he hasn't been near a tsetse fly,' I argued. I had quite forgotten that we had briefly driven through a cloud of these harbingers of death while on the safari with John and Jane. 'Are you sure?'

'The tests are positive. I'm afraid there is no doubt.'

'Can it be cured?'

'Yes. If he is treated immediately he should be in the clear after a few days. I've ordered some tablets from Gaborone and I sincerely hope they arrive soon.'

Salome and the vet then puzzled over the dosage, because it had to be administered according to body weight. The amount needed for cattle and horses was well established but there was no record for a small dog's requirements, so they weighed Django and, after some complicated arithmetic, administered a dose.

The condition of our trusting companion improved dramatically, and we celebrated joyously with long walks up the hill and a variety of jumping games, though his hips continued to show increasing signs of wear, as befitted a dog in his eleventh year.

Then, two weeks later, he started to walk in circles again and was treated once more, this time with a higher dosage.

Instead of getting better, he deteriorated alarmingly.

'Call Onderstepoort while I pack,' I instructed. 'We'll leave tomorrow at 3 am and will be there before 5 pm.'

Salome took one look at my expression and without a word headed for the phone.

I drove south without a break. Onderstepoort, the leading veterinary training hospital in Africa, is based in Pretoria, which meant that we could stay with Salome's mother while Django was treated. When we pulled into this establishment at one minute before 4 pm, I went straight to reception and asked to see Russel Ryan, the doctor Salome had spoken to the day before – a respected veterinarian and an authority on African tropical diseases.

He saw us immediately and as he calmly conducted his examination I sensed that Django was in good hands. I was not calm, however, and paced up and down, past rows of sick animals in cages that were stacked as high as the ceiling.

'The tryps is well advanced,' Dr Ryan stated, 'and he has been poisoned by the two doses that he received so close to each other. There should have been a minimum of three weeks between treatments.'

Salome looked stricken as he said this. She, who had tried so hard to save our dog, now assumed the burden of blame for two well-intentioned but potentially life-threatening actions.

'We do have a good chance of saving him, though some of the damage to the brain may be irreversible,' continued the doctor. 'You will have to leave him here with me for a while. I'm going to tranquillise him now. Please hold him still for me.'

I felt like I was holding Marmalade all over again.

I placed Django – now even more confused – in an empty, head-high cage and watched in anguish his distraught, forlorn expression as he realised that we were leaving him. He made me feel as though I were abandoning him to a gang of ruthless torturers.

'Come around tomorrow. I'll inject him again tonight and we should have a fair idea by then whether he will pull through or not,' Dr Ryan advised as he showed us out.

We had a great deal of faith in this serene and compassionate man, yet both of us spent a fretful night and rose early the next morning, impatient to check on Django's progress.

The white-coated vet was rummaging in a cabinet as we arrived, but came over as soon as he saw us.

'Bad news all round, I'm afraid,' he told us. 'Your dog has not responded to the treatment as well as I had hoped, and he would need to stay here a lot longer if he is to have any chance of survival ...'

'We don't mind how long it takes,' Salome interjected. 'Please just fix him.'

'I'm afraid it's not so simple. The Administrator wants to see you now. He is across the quad in the main office.'

We found the Administrator seated behind an oversized yellowwood desk. I did a double take when I saw him. Slight of build, he had a 'short back and sides' haircut with a long fringe flicked over his forehead and a small, dark moustache trimmed to snuggle under his nostrils. My heart sank. This was a dinosaur from the dark days of apartheid.

'I am going to charge you with bringing a diseased animal into South Africa without prior permission, under clause 8 subsection (ii) of the Introduction of Diseased Animals into the Republic of South Africa Act of 1842' (or some such garbage), he announced with a self-satisfied smirk.

'He came through the border with all his documents in order,' countered Salome, as she scrabbled frantically in her handbag for the papers. 'We also informed Onderstepoort of his condition and were told to bring him here,' she added.

'Ja, but did you get Form 542 (a) 5 stamped by a current South African qualified veterinarian and did you inform the Ministry of Insensitivity that you possibly had an animal with a notifiable disease?'

He went on and on quoting just how many obscure laws we had transgressed, until I feared that my jail sentence would equal that of a serial killer.

'Listen,' I said to him, leaning over his desk to make deliberate eye contact, 'we informed your qualified vets that our dog had been diagnosed with nagana, which is not a contagious disease, and no one told us about any stupid forms. Our dog is dying and this is our last chance to save him. Adopt a heart if you can't find yours.'

He fixed me with a cold stare of the type that I imagine Hitler used when he ordered the construction of the gas chambers.

'He will have to fly back to Botswana today. Here is the signed order for his deportation. See, I have initialled it in all the appropriate places. You sign it here and here and make arrangements to have your dog transported to the airport, or I will have it put down.'

'In the gas chambers no doubt,' I murmured.

'What did you say?'

'Nothing, Adolf.'

'Don't you get clever with me,' he warned.

I went in search of Dr Ryan to tell him of our meeting.

'There's nothing I can do,' he said. 'I dare not treat your dog here, I'm afraid. He will order the animal destroyed. What I can do is keep him here until that man knocks off at 5 pm. Nothing will induce him to stay on later, and then you can spirit Django away. I can also give you the rest of the injections and show you how to administer them.'

We left the hospital deeply grateful to this dedicated vet and unsolicited ally, but Salome had to restrain me from storming into Hitler's office and thumping him in the middle of his chest. When we returned at the appointed time to fetch Django, I feared a confrontation with the vindictive tyrant, but he had shown himself to be the clock watcher that Russel had predicted. He had checked on Django, however and, finding him still in his cage, had instructed the vet to destroy him.

The understanding doctor then invited us to take our dog outside for a walk, and closed the door firmly behind us. I duly tucked our little companion under my arm and we strode past the security guards unchallenged.

*   *   *

We knew of a reputable vet based on the Natal South Coast, so we decided to put as much distance between the soulless bureaucrat and ourselves as possible, and with heavy hearts we drove away from Django's best chance of survival. Next day we dropped him off at the coastal surgery. Its very location caused me to wonder whether a practitioner, based more than 800 kilometres from the nearest tsetse fly, would be the right man for the job. I also wondered if anyone was the right man for our rapidly deteriorating pet.

Salome and I took Skye down to the beach to watch the sun set. It held no charm on this evening. We talked of the number of lives – ours mostly – that our dog had saved, and of how helpless we felt to save his in return. As the sky darkened and the breakers roared their protest, we made our way back to our apartment to spend an anxious, sleepless night.

I phoned the surgery first thing in the morning. 'How is he?'

A bored, uncaring voice replied, 'Oh, the doctor decided that he would not recover and put him down.'

'Put him down?'

'Yes. You can come and claim him and settle the bill.'

'Claim him?' I repeated numbly, and replaced the handset.

Salome did not need to ask. It was written all over my face. She hugged me silently.

I sat down and stared at the carpet.

'I think it is better if you go alone to pick him up and bury him. Skye is too young to understand,' my caring wife said softly.

'I am also too young to understand.'

'I know.'

'Where shall I bury him?'

'Bury him at our beach, overlooking the sea. He will like that.'

'Will he?'

'Don't forget a spade and a blanket.'

I left for the surgery in a daze.

The receptionist was alone at the counter. 'Here's your bill.'

I numbly handed over an obscene amount of money – extortion for blatantly callous behaviour. Then I followed her onto the porch where there were some folding chairs, a table and a large deep freeze. The receptionist surprised me when she headed for the freezer and, opening it, reached inside and tugged out a black garbage bag.

I peered in and there was Django – or rather, a frozen, stiff-legged lifeless form of him. He could have been a leg of lamb, such was the insensitivity with which she returned him to me. Didn't she realise who this was in this garbage bag? Didn't she care?

'Why didn't you phone us so we could say goodbye to our dog?'

'We haven't the time to waste calling everyone with a dying animal.'

'Oh, you have so many, do you? Perhaps you should look for different work.'

* * *

I looked at Django's body again. He seemed familiar on one level – the same scruffy hair and the handsome features – yet there was a contorted grimace and an unfamiliar coldness about him, an absence of spirit that rendered his remains nothing more than a carcass, a mere joint of meat. How I wished I could have been there, as I had with

Marmalade, to still and comfort him on his final safari, as he had so often comforted me.

I set him down gently on the passenger seat and drove down the highway. I remember little of that journey. In numbed autopilot mode, I made for Leisure Bay, where I found a secluded spot on the cliff that had a sweeping view of the ocean, and overlooked the beach where he had been our Best Man. It was a burial ground that befitted the last resting place for Django of the Okavango. I dug deep, removed the bin bag, wrapped him in his blanket, kissed his tousled forehead and lowered him into the hole. The final act of betrayal was to shovel in the earth to cover his small body.

I sat at his grave for hours, coming to terms with the fact that I would never see him again. How I wished that he had possessed the physical properties of a sea cucumber, so that I could have put Django through a blender and watched as he reformed into the lively intelligent being that he'd been. Then I thought about his exceptional life and recalled the places that he had visited and the variety of transport that he had used on his odyssey: vehicle, train, bicycle, helicopter, aeroplane, mokoro, canoe, boat and truck. I wondered whether any other dog had achieved all that, in so many different countries and national parks along the way.

Would any part of these memories survive his death or had they all died when his body went cold? My mind wandered down twisted corridors, where I battled with the duality of life and illusions of reality. What is memory, I wondered? Can we recall what we were thinking two hours ago – never mind two years ago? Can we remember where we were six months ago, and do we remember our dreams of last night? Might that which had seemed so real and urgent in the recent past, have no relevance now?

Yet there was an awareness that lay behind the functioning of that little body – the unseen power that inexplicably saw billions of cells work together for a common good, even sacrificing themselves for a greater cause that they had no obvious way of understanding. When his body died, did that awareness disappear altogether, or is it the one constant in this changing world? Is that awareness the stuff of God – the heaven of religions?

After an eternity of struggling with such imponderables, I stood up exhausted and looked for some flowers to place on his grave. I found a stand of feral plants that had escaped from a nearby garden, picked a bunch of the yellow blossoms and laid them down on the fresh soil.

Looking out to sea I spotted two southern right whales as they breached in joyful abandon and near them a school of dolphins dived over the waves in jubilant celebration of life. My mood lifted. Life in its varied forms would continue. Django had lived up to the motto 'here for a good time, not a long time' and had experienced life to the fullest. He died because he had been out in the bush, doing what he loved – and that is just what he would have chosen.

I drove back to my family, drained by the enormous release of emotion – a liberation that I had never before experienced. It was time to take little Skye to say goodbye to her friend, and for Salome to bid farewell to that 'which would never replace Marmalade'.

Our daughter wore a yellow dress and waddled off to pick some more yellow flowers. When it was Salome's turn to mourn, Skye turned to her and asked with the painful innocence of youth, 'Are you sad because Django is gone, Mommy?'

'Yes, my darling, I am going to miss him very much.'

I held my wife close. We would both miss the little fellow desperately, and again I wondered if somehow his spirit had survived the garbage bag, as the Dalai Lamas would have us believe. Would he reincarnate? Would I ever know him again?

Then Skye pointed to the heavens, 'Mommy you don't have to miss him anymore. Look, there he is, high up there!'

We turned our gaze to where she indicated, and there, in the otherwise clear sky, was a single cloud that looked uncannily like the ruffled inquisitive head of our dog, fixing us with his earnest stare. Although I am aware that this seems contrived, I hold that image clearly in my mind to this very day.

I slipped off to a nearby restaurant and returned with an extra-large T-bone steak, medium rare, soaked in a rich cheesy sauce. I laid this, with gratitude, upon his grave and smiled as I thought of him peeing his approval on the Pearly Gates.

ACKNOWLEDGEMENTS

My friend Roy Ashby is to blame for this book. Without his constant cajoling, encouragement and tireless input on the raw manuscript this work would not have been finished. His wife, Alison, patiently transformed our efforts into flowing language through her excellent proof reading and I owe them both a deep sense of gratitude. Mike Sears, wonderful friend and successful author, shared his experience and contacts freely. John Brancato, of Hollywood fame, inspired me through his professional critique and granted me the confidence to complete this task. I am deeply grateful to Salome, who helped recall many early memories and to our exceptional daughter Skye who patiently sacrificed playtime with her dad while I whittled with words. Finally I wish to thank my beautiful fiancée, Jen Cowie, who not only had unwavering confidence in me but who also showed me that the stars still twinkle.